Speech to Print

Speech to Print

Language Essentials for Teachers

by

Louisa Cook Moats, Ed.D.

Project Director
District of Columbia Public Schools site of the
National Institute of Child Health and Human Development
Early Interventions Project
National Institutes of Health

·P A U L·H·
BROOKES
PUBLISHING Cº

Baltimore · London · Toronto · Sydney

Paul H. Brookes Publishing Co.
Post Office Box 10624
Baltimore, Maryland 21285-0624

www.brookespublishing.com

Typeset by A.W. Bennett, Inc., Hartland, Vermont.
Manufactured in the United States of America by Bang Printing, Brainerd, Minnesota.

The case studies in this book are based on the author's actual experiences. In all instances, names have been changed; in some instances, identifying details have been changed to protect confidentiality.

Figures 2.1 and 3.1 from AN INTRODUCTION TO LANGUAGE, Sixth Edition, by Victoria A. Fromkin and Robert Rodman copyright © 1998 by Holt, Rinehart & Winston, reproduced by permission of the publisher.

Second printing, May 2001.

Library of Congress Cataloging-in-Publication Data

Moats, Louisa Cook.
   Speech to print : language essentials for teachers / by Louisa C. Moats.
     p. cm.
   Includes bibliographical references (p.) and index.
   ISBN 1-55766-387-4
   1. Language arts (Elementary)   2. Language arts teachers—Training of. I. Title.
   LB1576.M55   2000
   372.6—dc21

                                              99-086019

British Library Cataloguing in Publication data are available from the British Library.

Contents

About the Author

Louisa Cook Moats, Ed.D., Project Director, District of Columbia Public Schools site of the National Institute of Child Health and Human Development Early Interventions Project, National Institutes of Health, 825 North Capitol Street NE, Eighth Floor, Washington, D.C. 20002

Louisa Cook Moats is currently the District of Columbia site director for a 5-year study of early reading instruction conducted in Houston, Texas, and Washington, D.C., public schools. The project's principal investigator is Dr. Barbara Foorman of the University of Texas Health Science Center, who was awarded a National Institute of Child Health and Human Development grant (Grant No. HD 30995) to study elementary reading instruction in inner-city schools. Dr. Moats's primary responsibility in Washington is to design and implement professional development for teachers under a special appropriation from the U.S. Congress.

Dr. Moats spent the 1996–1997 school year as a visiting scholar at the Sacramento County Office of Education, where she authored and presented leadership training materials on early reading for the California State Board of Education. These materials are now required content in all of the professional development programs conducted under Assembly Bill 1086 in California.

Dr. Moats received her bachelor of arts degree at Wellesley College, her master of arts degree from Peabody College of Vanderbilt University, and her doctorate of education in reading and human development from Harvard University's Graduate School of Education. She worked as a teacher, neuropsychology technician, and specialist in learning disorders prior to her doctoral training. She was a licensed psychologist in private practice for 15 years in Vermont and a graduate instructor both at Harvard and at St. Michael's College in Winooski, Vermont, where she developed innovative courses for teachers linking the disciplines of linguistics and reading education. Specializing in reading development, reading disorders, spelling, and written language, she has written and lectured widely throughout the United States and abroad. Currently she teaches her own courses at the Greenwood Institute in Putney, Vermont, and at Simmons College in Boston. Her publications include journal articles; book chapters; a classroom basal spelling program; a book entitled *Spelling: Development, Disability, and Instruction* (York Press, 1995); and a book for parents, co-authored with Susan L. Hall, entitled *Straight Talk About Reading: How Parents Can Make a Difference in the Early Years* (Contemporary Books, 1999).

Acknowledgments

This book was many years in the making. I am indebted to all of my former students from the St. Michael's and Greenwood Institute courses for which I developed this material. Thank you for coming to "language boot camp" and affirming the importance of this content for teachers and clinicians. I am grateful to many colleagues who commented on draft material and helped me improve the book, including John Alexander, Marilyn Astore, Linda Bailey, Shirley Bate, Susan Brady, Sheila Mandel, Mike Minsky, Bruce Rosow, and Marilyn Varricchio. I have been encouraged as well by all those who have been advocates for better language instruction for teachers, including Liz McPike and Joan Snowden at the American Federation of Teachers, Tom Schiedler of the Greenwood School, the members of the International Multisensory Structured Language Education Council, and the International Dyslexia Association.

Without the expert instruction of Jeanne Chall, Carol Chomsky, Helen Popp, and Catherine Snow at the Harvard Graduate School of Education, I myself would not have known what there was to discover about language, reading, and spelling.

I appreciate the patience and expert assistance of Elaine Niefeld, Mika Sam, and the other editors at Paul H. Brookes Publishing Company.

Finally, I am grateful to Reid Lyon for piloting our field with extraordinary vision, perseverance, brilliance, and courage so that the need for this book could be realized.

To the memory of my father, Thomas P. Cook,
who could spin gold with words and thereby taught me to love language

Speech to Print

CHAPTER 1

Why Study Language?

In most colleges and graduate programs, language is studied by future linguists, speech teachers, actors, singers, and anthropologists. Seldom has language study been required of teachers, except in a general format designed not to overload the novice with too much detail. In such general courses on language development, teachers are often left on their own to find the connection between textbook information and instruction of children. The practical impact of understanding linguistics is seldom stated or illustrated. This book was written to alter that tradition and to show that language study is indispensable for teachers of reading, writing, speaking, and listening—the "language arts."

The aim of this book is to make language structure accessible for teachers of reading and writing so that they can use instructional programs with confidence and flexibility. The teacher who understands language and how children are using it can give clear, accurate, and organized information about sounds, words, and sentences. The teacher who knows language will understand why students say and write the puzzling things that they do and will be able to judge what a particular student knows and needs to know about the printed word. Literacy is an achievement that rests on all levels of linguistic processing, from the elemental sounds to the most overarching structures of text. To help the teacher deliver successful instruction, this book of necessity contains a great deal of information about the lower levels of language (units smaller than the word, such as sounds, sylla-

Table 1.1. Levels of language organization (from below word level to above word level)

Level of language	Parts of language studied
Phonology	Speech sounds (phonemes)
Orthography	Spelling patterns
Morphology	Units of meaning (morphemes) within words
Syntax	Phrase and sentence structure
Semantics	Phrase and sentence meaning
Pragmatics	Word choice and use in context
Discourse structure	Organization of connected sentences

bles, letters, and some morphemes) from which the higher levels (units larger than the word, such as phrases, sentences, and paragraphs) are constructed. (Table 1.1 shows the different levels of language.)

Reading and writing are forms of language processing. The print on any page is a visual representation of language form and structure that must be translated by the reader or transcribed by the writer. When we teach reading and writing, we are teaching language at one or all of its many layers. Reading, after all, is not a rote exercise in recitation of words but a translation of print to speech to meaning that is mediated by the language centers of the brain. Language itself is the substance of instruction.

What children bring to the printed page, or to the tasks of reading and writing, is knowledge of spoken language. What must be learned is knowledge of the written symbols that represent speech and the ability to use those productively. Knowing the difference between *sacks* and *sax, past* and *passed,* or *their* and *there* or knowing that *antique* says "anteek" requires language awareness at several levels. Students without awareness of language systems will be less able to sound out a new word when they encounter it, less able to spell, less able to interpret punctuation and sentence meaning, and less able to learn new vocabulary words from reading them in context. One of the most important jobs of any teacher of reading and writing is to give students sufficient understanding of the language they speak, read, and write so that they can use it to communicate well.

WHAT IS LANGUAGE?

Generative language is an achievement unique to human beings. Human language is generative because its systems allow us to invent new messages without limit. Unlike the signing systems of some highly evolved animals, such as wolves or whales, human language enables us to produce many messages that have never been spoken before. Speakers of a language share an understanding of the rule systems that govern the production of sounds, words, and sentences and when to use them. Speakers of English, for example, know that the sequence *Understanding basic is to language teaching reading* is not an allowable sentence but that *Understanding language is basic to teaching reading* is permitted. Speakers of English know that the names *Nkruma* and *Zhezhnik* are not English because sound sequences in those words do not occur in the English language sound system.

On every part of the earth, people have invented languages for talking to one another. More than 4,000 languages exist on the earth today,[1] but many are disappearing quickly as Western civilization encroaches on developing societies. All of these human languages share properties known as **universals.** From a finite set of speech sounds (**phonemes**), speakers of an oral language say and understand many thousands of words. Words are composed of meaningful units (**morphemes**) that often can be recombined to make new words. Words themselves have meaning; the study of word, phrase, and sentence meanings is called **semantics.** Words belong to grammatical categories and are spoken in an order determined by underlying rules of **syntax** or sentence structure. Every speaker of a human language shares with every other speaker of that language the capacity to produce and comprehend an infinite number of sentences whose structures share basic properties. **Pragmatics** is the rule system that tells speakers how to use language for social communication. Humans have also devised systems of written symbols (**orthographies**) to represent the sounds, syllables, and morphemes of spoken language.

This last achievement, the invention of tools for reading and writing, sets humans apart from all other creatures. In evolutionary terms, reading and writing are very recent accomplishments. Humans did not invent writing until the Chinese and Mediterranean peoples used meaningful written signs for concepts and words between 5,000 and 10,000 years ago. Alphabets, systems that use symbols for individual speech sounds, were invented little more than 3,000 years ago. It is understandable, then, that learning to read is not as natural or biologically "wired in" as are speaking and listening and that reading must be taught directly to most children over several years through formal education. Our brains are not as fully evolved for the processing of written language as they are for the processing of spoken language, and, therefore, learning to read and write are much more challenging for most of us than learning to speak.

Languages are constantly changing as the need for new expressions arises and as old expressions become obsolete. Every year the speakers of a language such as English generate several thousand new words and word uses to add to their language systems. The age of electronics, for example, has spawned terms such as *fax, e-mail, surfing the web, geek,* and *rad.* Committees that are created by some governments to preserve language purity, prevent change, or establish a standard are bucking a natural human tendency—to generate new language forms and uses within an established system.

No language is superior to any other in terms of the complexity of the rule systems that it embodies. English, however, has one of the most complex alphabetic orthographies, is spoken and written as a first or second language throughout the world, and has the largest vocabulary. It has become the language of international commerce. Nevertheless, English has many variants, including some "dialects" that are really different language systems and that present a significant challenge for teachers of reading and writing.

LITERACY IS THE MOST IMPORTANT GOAL OF SCHOOLING

Few would deny that teaching children to read, write, spell, listen, and speak is among the foremost responsibilities of educators. Without well-developed reading skills, children cannot participate fully in classroom learning. They are at much greater risk for school failure and lifelong problems with employment, social adjustment, and personal autonomy. Literate cultures expect literacy of everyone, even so-called low-skilled workers, who must read labels, directions, lists, forms, and records. Although a fairly large number of individuals in our society have always had difficulty learning to read, it is no longer acceptable to ignore them, give them failing grades, or banish them to the ranks of lower-status jobs.[2] The cost to society is too great. In addition, there are many children who would learn to read and write much better if their instruction were to teach them to understand the systems of their own language (sounds, spellings, meaningful networks, sentences, text organization) as well as the strategies to comprehend narrative and expository text.

When children are taught well and, consequently, begin to read in kindergarten or first grade, they are likely to reap benefits throughout their schooling. Those who read successfully from the start are more likely to enjoy reading, develop their knowledge of words and language patterns, and attain knowledge of the world by reading.[3] Failure to read well, in contrast, undermines vocabulary growth, knowledge acquisition, verbal facility, and writing skill. Once behind in reading, few children catch up to grade level[4] unless they receive intensive, individual, expensive, and expert instruction,[5] a scarce commodity in most schools. Teaching everyone to read well, however, is a goal that has eluded us in the past.

About 20% of elementary students are very poor readers; at least another 20% do not read fluently enough to enjoy or to engage in independent reading.[6] Thus, it should not be surprising that on the 1994 National Assessment of Educational Progress (NAEP), 44% of all fourth graders in the United States scored at a level "below basic."[7] According to the U.S. Office of Technology, 25% of American adults cannot perform the essential literacy requirements of a typical job.[8] The rate of functional illiteracy in our capital city, Washington, D.C., is the highest in the nation at 37%.[9] Individuals who are poor readers are much more likely than literate people to drop out of school; find their way to jail; or struggle to find and keep meaningful, satisfying work.[10]

For children who live in poverty or are from ethnic minorities and attend urban schools, the incidence of reading failure is astronomical and completely unacceptable for a literate society. African American students, Hispanic students, students whose native language is not English, and those from impoverished homes fall behind and stay behind in far greater proportion than their Caucasian, middle-class counterparts. The rate of reading failure in these groups is 60%–70% according to the 1994 NAEP.[11] This figure alone explains much about the poor academic achievement of some minority students and why they are underrepresented in professions that depend on higher education.

One's family background and cultural context, however, do not guarantee literacy. Students of all backgrounds and intellectual talents may experience difficulty with language and reading that erodes their overall academic achievement.[12] In 1996, California initiated a series of laws to reform reading education after 49% of children of college-educated parents in that state scored "below basic" on the NAEP.[13] One third of fourth graders who are poor readers nationwide are from college-educated families who presumably encourage literacy in the home.[14]

Exposure to books is vital to becoming a good reader, but it is not enough for most students to learn to read. Even if their parents read to them at home or they are surrounded with good literature, the majority of our students need to be taught how to read.[15] Many students need to be taught how spoken and written language work so that they have the tools to decipher and generate the written word. The good news is that when teaching is skillful and informed, most students can learn to read at acceptable levels.

SKILLFUL TEACHING PREVENTS MOST READING PROBLEMS

Most reading problems can be greatly ameliorated through appropriate instruction. According to the convergent findings of numerous studies from the 1990s, classroom teaching is the best antidote for reading difficulty.[16] Although parents, communities, and volunteer tutorial programs do influence how well and how soon students read, informed classroom instruction that begins to teach critical language and reading skills in kindergarten and that is sustained throughout school ensures success for all but a few students with moderate or severe learning disabilities. Reading scientists now estimate that 95% of all children can be taught to read at a level constrained only by their reasoning and listening comprehension abilities.[17] It is clear as well that students in high-risk populations need not fail at the rate they do.[18] Students who are African American or Hispanic or who live in poverty can achieve as well as their more advantaged age-mates when placed in schools with strong leaders, valid programs, and well-prepared and well-supported teachers. Teachers who incorporate critical language skills into direct, systematic, sequenced lessons can reach most children.[19] Reading programs that are well designed and well implemented are the best guard against reading failure.

TEACHING READING IS COMPLEX AND CHALLENGING

Teaching reading and writing requires considerable expertise. The degree of expertise has not been fully appreciated until now, as many teachers have been given only one survey course on reading methods and little background in reading psychology or language structure. Teachers who are successful with most students know their content and have learned effective teaching strategies through several years of study, experience, and mentoring. Many more children succeed in learning to read when teaching is skillful and organized around well-defined content. Learning to read is a complex linguistic achievement dependent for many students on effortful and incremental skill development, and the teacher whose work is guided by an understanding of reading psychology, language structure, and proven methods is most likely to enable that achievement.

What, exactly, must an effective teacher be able to do? Often it is said that there are many ways to teach reading, or that each approach is going to be helpful with some students. The consensus of research,[20] however, is that some approaches are more effective than others and that what works best can be explained on the basis of the developmental level of the student, the cognitive and linguistic characteristics of the student, and the language content itself. Thus, the choice of instruction should be based on awareness of the student and the content at hand. At a minimum, teachers must know how students learn to read (reading psychology), the content of reading (the form and meaning of language), and pedagogy (how it is taught). Then they must spend time implementing what they know until their skills are well honed.

What does a teacher actually do? In the course of any day, the teacher must continually pique children's interest in reading through incentive programs and discussions in which students respond to many kinds of texts, including stories, informational pieces, and poetry. The teacher must also organize the class so that she or he can instruct groups of students according to their levels. The teaching of component skills must be direct, systematic, and explicit to get the best results. To accommodate children's variability, the teacher must assess children and know how they are progressing. She or he must interpret errors, give corrective feedback, select examples for concepts, explain new ideas several ways, and connect many component skills with meaningful reading and writing experiences.

In years past, our courses on reading instruction presented menus of possible approaches from which teachers were to choose, based on convenience, whim, surface appeal, prior exposure, or any number of nonscientific reasons. As research evidence accrues to explain how children learn to read and what components of programs are necessary, we aim to guide the choices by accumulating solid scientific information documenting which methods work best with which children at which stage of reading development under what conditions.

NEW RESEARCH ABOUT LANGUAGE AND READING

The findings of scientific research in the field of reading have had a major impact on federal, state, and local policies pertaining to teacher preparation and reading instruction. Prior to the publication of the National Academy of Sciences' *Preventing Reading Difficulties in Young Children*,[21] teacher preparation and teaching itself was driven more by fads and philosophies than by facts.[22] This should not be surprising, because the methods of psychological experimentation necessary to unravel the mystery of reading were not developed until the mid-1970s, and there is always a long delay between developments in academic research disciplines and their incorporation into teaching practice. The tools and concepts of modern cognitive and linguistic science have been applied to understanding reading only since the mid-1970s.[23] As with other fields of scientific investigation, many studies in related disciplines were needed before consensus findings could be accepted and disseminated. It is not surprising, then, that new insights into language, reading, and writing are beginning to inform teacher preparation and that a course in language study[24] might be a new requirement for teachers in training. There are several reasons that we have been slow to understand how reading is accomplished and how best to teach it.

Language Processing Is Largely Unconscious

Our processing of language, especially at the level of sounds, syllables, and words, is automatic—that is, fast and unconscious. Our processing of print, if we are good readers, has also become automatic. We are not aware of how we are actually reading as we are doing it, and we are not aware of the mental events that allow reading to happen. **Automaticity** is the word for the ability to execute tasks without conscious attention. It is a characteristic of skilled performance of any kind, such as playing an instrument, playing an athletic game, or operating a machine. The mental processes of good and poor readers are neither self-evident nor easy to grasp because they occur below the level of consciousness by design. Introspection—that is, viewing one's own mental activity—is misleading for understanding the mind of the skilled reader, because the print–speech associations that occur during reading are too rapid and automatic to be perceived.

For example, do you think that you skip over words when you read and somehow extract the meaning of the print without seeing what is really there? That idea was prevalent in the early 1970s,[25] when instructional methods that promote guessing at words on the basis of context were promoted.[26] In fact, laboratory experiments that track eye movements during reading, using many different stimuli and many kinds of subjects, have shown that skilled reading is print driven.[27] That is, we process almost every letter of every word when we scan print, even though we fixate or focus our eyes primarily on the content (meaning-bearing) words as we scan a line. Those who read well process the details in the printed words accurately; those who read poorly do not process the details of the print and tend to skip over words they are unsure of because they cannot **decode** them. As many studies have shown, that tendency to skip over words is not a result of any vision problem in most cases but a result of a problem matching the print to sound, completely, accurately, and efficiently. Those who accomplish letter-wise text scanning with relative ease and fluency have a better chance of comprehending well. Those who comprehend poorly often lose meaning because they cannot read the words accurately.

Primary processes that drive reading include our ability to associate print units (letters, letter combinations, letter sequences, words, and punctuation marks) with linguistic units (phonemes, **onsets, rimes, syllables,** morphemes, words, and phrases). Linguistic units are neither auditory nor visual; they are abstract, mental phenomena and can be understood even by people who are hard of hearing. Because our attention is on meaning, we are not aware of the code translation process by which meaning is conveyed. Nor should we be—unless we must teach someone the same process deliberately, step by step. Until we are faced with a class of children who are learning how to read symbols that represent speech sounds and word parts, we may never have analyzed language at the level required for explaining and teaching it. Similarly, we may not know how a paragraph is organized or how a story is put together until we teach writing to students who do not know how to organize their thoughts. Thus, to understand printed language well enough to teach it explicitly requires conscious study of its systems and forms, both spoken and written.

Language Structure Is Not Self-Evident

Even well-educated adults often do not know exactly what goes into speaking, understanding words, using **phonics,** spelling, interpreting sentences, or organizing a composition even though they use these language structures every day. On direct measures of language knowledge at the "lower" levels (sounds, word parts, spelling), most adults show cursory or incomplete mastery at best.[28] For example, the concept that a letter combination (*ch, wh, sh, th, ng*) can represent one unique speech sound is unclear to a surprising number of experienced teachers according to a teacher survey given by this author[29] (blank surveys appear at the end of this chapter). Many identify these units by rote but are unable to differentiate conceptually between these spelling units (digraphs) and two letters that stand for two distinct sounds (consonant **blends** such as *cl, st, pr*) or silent letter spellings that retain the sound of one spelled consonant (*kn-, wr-, -mb*). Very few adults, unless they are studying and teaching the material, can explain why we double the consonant letters in words like *misspell, dinner,* and *accommodate* or why there is a "silent *e*" on the end of the word *love*. A deeper, explicit level of knowledge may not be necessary to read the words, but it will be necessary to explain pronunciation and spelling, where the words came from, and how spelling is related to meaning.

In addition, the relationships among the basic skills of reading and reading comprehension are not obvious or self-evident. When children read poorly in the middle and upper grades, we may assume that the problem is one of comprehension. We may not realize that difficulties with word recognition, accuracy, speed, **reading fluency**, and comprehension strategies all contribute to poor reading in older students but that word recognition and fluency problems are characteristic of most. Students who cannot read words well usually demonstrate weaknesses in **phonological processing**—the ability to identify, manipulate, produce, and remember speech sounds—but one might not perceive this weakness without the special training that begins with language study.

Good Readers Are Aware of Language Structure

Some children learn language concepts and their application very easily in spite of incidental teaching and very few examples. Just as some children seem to be born with insight into how the number system works, others just figure out how the system of print represents speech. Figure 1.1 shows the writing of a child on her fourth birthday who had already intuited a great deal about how sounds are spelled.

Hannah's understanding of sound–symbol correspondence was precocious; for example, she knew that letter combinations *th* and *ng* were used to represent sounds. She clearly had a good sense of the sounds that make up words because she was able to use letters that spell them. Awareness of speech sounds, or **phoneme awareness,** in turn, is an aspect of a more fundamental linguistic competence known as *phonological processing*. Children who learn to read well are sensitive to linguistic structure at the level of speech sounds, parts of words, meaningful parts of words, sentences, and text. They can recognize repetitive patterns in print and connect letter patterns with sounds, syllables, and meaningful word parts quickly, accurately, and unconsciously. Effective teaching of reading presents these concepts in an order in which children can learn them and reinforces appreciation of the whole **system** in which these elements are arranged.

Poor Readers' Problems Begin with Phonology

The language skills that most reliably distinguish groups of good and poor readers are specific to the phonological, or speech sound, processing system. These

Figure 1.1.   Hannah's birthday note.

skills include awareness of linguistic units that lie within a word (**consonants, vowels,** onsets, rimes, syllables, grammatical endings, meaningful parts, and the spelling units that represent them) and fluency in recognition and recall of letters and spelling patterns that make up words. Those who have the most trouble comprehending written language may be good at listening comprehension but have trouble at more basic levels of language, beginning with **phonology.** For example, children who comprehend well when they read also do better at tasks such as reading words taken out of context, sounding out nonsense words, and spelling nonsense words than do those who comprehend poorly.[30] Thus, skilled reading presents a paradox: Students who can most easily make sense of text are also those who can most easily read nonsense.[31]

Intelligence and verbal reasoning ability do not predict reading success in the beginning stages as well as decoding skills do. In fact, new data show that 80% of the variance in reading comprehension at the first-grade level is accounted for by how well students sound out words and recognize words out of context.[32] The relationship between decoding and comprehension changes as students move into the middle grades, after they have learned how to read words. Comprehension strategies and knowledge of word meanings become more of a factor in reading success as students move into more advanced stages. When appropriate, the emphasis of instruction will be on motivating children to read every day and to use interpretive strategies central to comprehension: summarizing, questioning, and monitoring one's own understanding.

HOW READING AND SPELLING DEVELOP

Again, longitudinal research indicates that students who read well in high school learned early to sound out words and read new words with ease. That is, they gained the insight that letters in our writing system more or less represent phonemes and used this knowledge to map written to spoken language. Early reading follows a predictable course regardless of the reader's speed of reading acquisition.[33] The learner progresses from global to analytic processing, from approximate to specific linking of sound with symbols, and from context-driven to print-driven reading as proficiency is acquired. Learning to spell and read words is not a rote process of memorizing letter strings of increasing length. Figure 1.2 shows the progression in reading and spelling development.

Prealphabetic Reading and Writing

In the first stage of reading and spelling development, the **prereading** or **prealphabetic** stage, children do not understand that letters represent the sounds in words, although they do know that print represents spoken messages. They remember words such as family names and signs by configuration or general visual appearance and are highly reliant on the context in which words occur to recognize them. They have no strategy other than rote memory of visual patterns or recognition of a word in its physical or meaning context to read it. Their spelling of words is often a string of familiar letters in random order, perhaps with a few idiosyncratic symbols or numerals thrown in the mix. They do not yet know the **alphabetic principle,** that is, the basic concept that letters represent segments of their own speech. An example of prealphabetic writing appears in Figure 1.3.

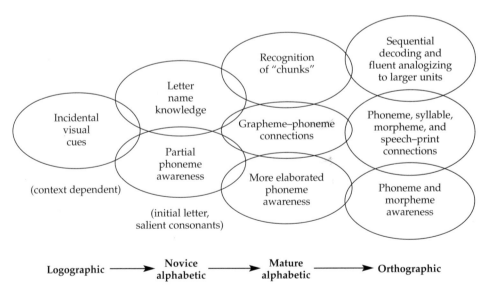

Figure 1.2.   Schematic representation of reading and spelling development. (Based on Ehri, 1994.)

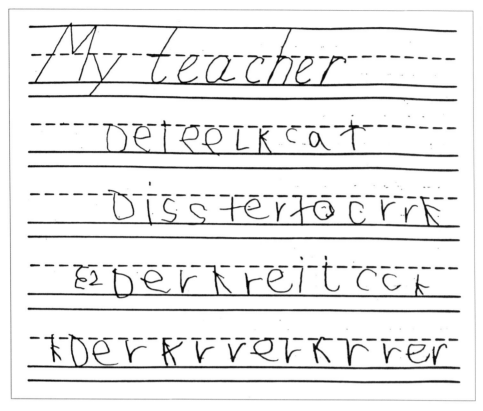

Figure 1.3.   Example of prealphabetic writing.

Early Alphabetic Reading and Writing

Next, there is a qualitative shift of approach in both reading and spelling when children discover a critical fact: Letters correspond to the sounds that make up spoken words (the alphabetic principle). From their growing awareness of speech sounds and knowledge of letter forms, children begin to spell and read by sounding out parts of words, often a few consonants that are salient in speech (as in KR for *car* and HP for *happy*). At this point, they may attempt to "read" words by guessing from the initial consonant and the context, and they may spell by writing a few consonants but leaving out the vowel or the internal, less distinct speech sounds. They are beginning to demonstrate awareness of phonemes and the use of the alphabet to represent them. Figure 1.4 shows one child's early alphabetic writing.

Later Alphabetic Reading and Writing

Skill at sounding out words and spelling them phonetically unfolds gradually as children become able to identify all of the speech sounds in a word to which letters need to be matched. As more elaborated phoneme awareness is acquired, children learn quickly how print patterns represent speech. At this stage, children render

Figure 1.4. Early alphabetic writing. Child's rereading of own writing: "I like elephants, I like birds, I like cats, I like kittens . . . "

detailed phonetic spellings of unknown words and try to sound out words if the strategy is encouraged. They are usually rather slow and disfluent as they start to sound out words because so much conscious attention is needed to match symbols to sounds in sequence. Sight words, however, are learned quickly if they are encountered often enough or if they are visually distinctive enough.

Exposure to text and reading practice are critical in moving the process of spelling development along quickly. If children at this stage are asked to identify nonsense words that look the most like real words, they often show surprising awareness of the letter sequences and orthographic patterns that characterize English spelling, even though they may not associate all of those sequences with speech sounds. For example, they may know that -ck is used at the ends of words but not at the beginnings, that letters can be doubled at the ends of words or within words but not at the beginnings, that only certain letters are doubled, and that syllables typically contain a vowel letter. Orthographic knowledge, knowledge of the spelling system itself, develops when the student has internalized awareness of the sounds to which the letters in words correspond. A sample of later alphabetic writing appears in Figure 1.5.

Learning the Spelling System—the Orthographic Stage

Children must learn a whole system of correspondence between sounds and their symbols to spell one-syllable words. Long vowel spellings, the use of silent *e*, vowels followed by *r*, and the conditions for spelling certain consonants certain ways at the ends of words, such as *-dge/-ge* and *-tch/-ch*, are learned as patterns, wherein many sounds are spelled with more than one letter. Children who are progressing typically then build up associations to syllables, word parts, and meaningful parts of words such as the ending *-ing*, which in turn allows rapid recognition of whole words after a few exposures to them. They learn about the relationship among sound, spelling, and meaning in phases; for example, they learn gradually that *-ed* means the past tense but is pronounced three different ways: /t/ as in *raked*, /d/ as in *played* and /ed/ as in *painted*. Children use an analogy strategy to recognize unfamiliar words as soon as their lexical knowledge permits. That is, they will identify an unfamiliar word by mentally comparing it with a known word that has the same pattern or configuration, such as comparing the /g/ pronunciation of *gh* in *ghetto*, *ghoul*, and *Ghana* with the more familiar *ghost*. Instruction that calls attention to sound–symbol correspondence and patterns in print hastens the learning process considerably.

Effective teaching, which is responsive to students' developmental levels, requires the explanation of both spoken and written language. The content of any lesson should depend on what students already know and should move them through the system of language organization. Teaching children about sounds is appropriate at the very early stages; an emphasis on meaningful parts, or **morphology,** is appropriate when the foundation is secure. Expert teachers will have

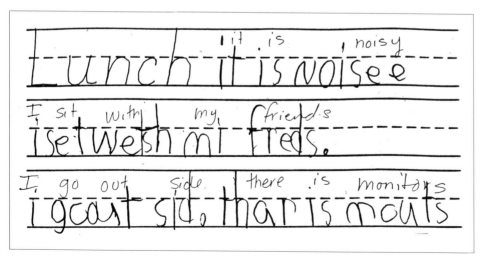

Figure 1.5. Later alphabetic writing with teacher's notes from student's rereading.

the knowledge, strategies, and materials to decide what to do with particular children not on the basis of ideology but on the basis of observation, assessment, judgment, knowledge of child development, and knowledge of language.

PRINCIPLES OF EFFECTIVE TEACHING OF READING, SPELLING, AND WRITING

Effective teachers of reading and writing raise students' ability to interpret and generate sound-spellings, syllables, morphemes, phrases, sentences, paragraphs, and various genres of text. They also balance skill instruction with daily writing and reading that is purposeful and engaging, no matter what the skill level of the learner. Middle and upper grade children with poor reading can be brought up to grade level with appropriate instruction, although the time and effort involved are considerably greater than that required to teach younger children.[34] Well-designed, controlled comparisons of instruction have consistently supported these findings:[35]

- Direct teaching of sound–symbol correspondence (phonics), word recognition, comprehension, and literature appreciation is necessary from when children begin school until they become proficient readers and writers.

- Phoneme awareness instruction, when linked to systematic decoding and spelling instruction, is a key to preventing reading failure in children who come to school without these prerequisite skills.

- It is better to teach the code system of written English systematically and explicitly than it is to teach it randomly, indirectly, or incidentally. The units for instruction (sound, syllable, morpheme, word) should vary according to students' reading and spelling skill.

- The most effective programs include daily exposure to a variety of texts and incentives for children to read independently and with others. Practices that build reading fluency include repeated readings of text, alternate reading with a partner, and simultaneous oral reading of easy material.

- Vocabulary is best taught with a variety of complementary methods designed to explore the relationships among words and the relationships among word structure, origin, and meaning.

- Key comprehension strategies to teach include summarizing, clarifying, questioning, and visualizing; these should be modeled explicitly by the teacher and practiced overtly if students are not comprehending well or if they approach reading comprehension passively.

- Effective teachers encourage frequent prose writing to enable deeper understanding of what is read.

To master all of these principles and apply them well takes most of us a lifetime. At least we can proceed with the confidence that reading and writing instruction can be grounded in a solid body of evidence about what works, for whom, and why. Although there are many questions left for researchers to explore,[36] it is no longer justified to cling to some of the myths that have affected reading education for several decades. It is beneficial to teach children about language structure. Teaching about language can be engaging, active, and well informed. Knowing about phonemes, syllables, morphemes, and the spelling system enables children to read words accurately and quickly. Knowing how the spelling system works enables children to learn more words and to write more fluently. But if we teach children this content, it means that we, the educators, must know it well. Just as a physician must study anatomy to understand physical functioning, so must we know the linguistic structure that supports communication. The major systems of language, except for pragmatics and **discourse** structure, are emphasized in this book. Within- and end-of-chapter exercises are included in this book to help the reader understand and apply new concepts immediately. Among the appendixes is information about orthographic structure, lesson planning, and case study analysis, in addition to an answer key and a glossary of terms highlighted in the text. In-depth discussion of pragmatics, discourse structure, and their relationship to comprehension and composition will be left for another volume.

ENDNOTES

1. Yule, 1996.
2. Shaywitz, Escobar, Shaywitz, Fletcher, & Makuch, 1992.
3. Cunningham & Stanovich, 1998.
4. Juel, 1988; Shaywitz et al., 1992.
5. Torgesen, Wagner, & Rashotte, 1997.
6. Fletcher & Lyon, 1998; Shaywitz et al., 1992.
7. U.S. Department of Education, National Center for Education Statistics, National Assessment Governing Board, 1994.
8. U.S. Office of Technology Assessment, 1993.
9. National Institute for Literacy, 1998.
10. Cramer & Ellis, 1996.
11. U.S. Department of Education, National Center for Education Statistics, National Assessment Governing Board, 1994.
12. Francis, Shaywitz, Steubing, Shaywitz, & Fletcher, 1996; Stanovich & Siegel, 1994.
13. Sacramento County Office of Education, 1997.
14. National Assessment of Educational Progress, 1995.
15. Scarborough & Dobrich, 1994; Snow, Burns, & Griffin, 1998.
16. Adams, 1990; Foorman, Francis, Shaywitz, Shaywitz, & Fletcher, 1997; Snow et al., 1998.
17. Fletcher & Lyon, 1998.
18. Nicholson, 1997.
19. Brady, Fowler, Stone, & Winbury, 1994; Brown & Felton, 1990; Foorman et al., 1997; Gaskins, Ehri, Cress, O'Hara, & Donnelly, 1996; Scanlon & Vellutino, 1997; Tangel & Blachman, 1995; Tunmer & Hoover, 1993.
20. See, for example, Adams, Treiman, & Pressley, 1998; Fletcher & Lyon, 1998; Learning First Alliance, 1998; Snow et al., 1998.
21. Snow et al., 1998.
22. Stanovich, 1994.
23. See Adams, 1990; Adams, Treiman, et al., 1998; Blachman, 1997; and Pressley, 1998, for research reviews.
24. See also Brady & Moats, 1997; Moats, 1995, 1998; and Moats & Lyon, 1996.
25. See Adams, 1990, for a retrospective.
26. Adams, 1990.
27. Rayner, 1997.
28. Moats, 1995; Moats & Lyon, 1996; Scarborough, Ehri, Olson, & Fowler, 1998.

29. Moats, 1994.
30. Fletcher & Lyon, 1998.
31. Rack, Snowling, & Olson, 1992.
32. Foorman et al., 1997.
33. Bear, Invernizzi, Templeton, & Johnston, 2000; Chall, 1983; Ehri, 1994.
34. Torgesen et al., 1997.
35. Pressley, 1998.
36. Blachman, 1997; Pressley, 1998; Snow et al., 1998.

ADDITIONAL RESOURCES ON READING RESEARCH

American Federation of Teachers. (1999). *Teaching reading is rocket science* (paper prepared by L. Moats). Washington, DC: Author.

Blachman, B. (Ed.). (1997). *Foundations of reading acquisition and dyslexia: Implications for early intervention.* Mahwah, NJ: Lawrence Erlbaum Associates.

California Department of Education. (1995). *Teaching reading: A balanced, comprehensive approach to teaching reading in prekindergarten through grade three.* Sacramento: Author. (Available from State of California Bureau of Publications, 800-995-4099)

California State Board of Education. (1998). *California reading/language arts framework.* Sacramento: Author. (Available from State of California Bureau of Publications, 800-995-4099)

California State Board of Education. (1998). *Read all about it! Readings to inform the profession.* Sacramento: California Reading Initiative Center, Sacramento County Office of Education. (Available from the publisher, 916-228-2425)

Evers, W.M. (1998). *What's gone wrong in America's classrooms?* Stanford, CA: Hoover Institution Press.

Hall, S., & Moats, L. (1999). *Straight talk about reading: How parents can make a difference in the early years.* Chicago: Contemporary Books.

Learning First Alliance. (1998). *Every child reading.* Washington, DC: Author. (Available from the author, 1001 Connecticut Avenue, NW, Suite 335, Washington, DC 20036; www.learningfirst.org)

McGuinness, D. (1997). *Why our children can't read and what we can do about it.* New York: Free Press.

Osborn, J., & Lehr, F. (Eds.). (1998). *Literacy for all: Issues in teaching and learning.* New York: Guilford Press.

Patton, S., & Holmes, M. (Eds.). (1998). *The keys to literacy.* Washington, DC: Council for Basic Education.

Pressley, M. (1998). *Reading instruction that works: The case for balanced teaching.* New York: Guilford Press.

Putnam, L. (Ed.). (1996). *Readings on language and literacy: Essays in honor of Jeanne S. Chall.* Cambridge, MA: Brookline Books.

Snow, C.E., Burns, M.S., & Griffin, P. (Eds.). (1998). *Preventing reading difficulties in young children.* Washington, DC: National Academy Press.

Brief Survey of Language Knowledge

☆ PHONEME COUNTING

Count the number of speech sounds or phonemes that you perceive in each of the following spoken words. Remember, the speech sounds may not be equivalent to the letters. For example, the word *spoke* has four phonemes: /s/, /p/, /o/, and /k/. Write the number of phonemes in the blank to the right of each word.

thrill _____   ring _____   shook _____

does _____   fix_____   wrinkle _____

sawed _____   quack_____   know _____

☆ SYLLABLE COUNTING

Count the number of syllables that you perceive in each of the following words. For example, the word *higher* has two syllables, the word *threat* has one, and the word *physician* has three.

cats _____   capital _____   shirt _____

spoil _____   decidedly _____   banana _____

recreational _____   lawyer _____   walked _____

☆ PHONEME MATCHING

Read the first word in each line and note the sound that is represented by the underlined letter or letter cluster. Then select the word or words on the line that contain the same sound. Underline the words you select.

1. **p<u>u</u>sh**   although   sugar   duty   pump

2. **w<u>eigh</u>**   pie   height   raid   friend

3. **doe<u>s</u>**   miss   nose   votes   rice

4. **in<u>t</u>end**   this   whistle   baked   batch

5. **ri<u>ng</u>**   sink   handle   signal   pinpoint

17

☆ RECOGNITION OF SOUND–SYMBOL CORRESPONDENCE

Find in the following words the letters and letter combinations that correspond to each speech sound in the word. For example, the word *stress* has five phonemes, each of which is represented by a letter or letter group: s / t / r / e / ss. Now try these:

best	fresh	scratch
though	laughed	middle
chirp	quaint	

☆ DEFINITIONS AND CONCEPTS

Write a definition or explanation of the following:

1. Vowel sound (vowel phoneme)

2. Consonant digraph

3. Prefix

4. Inflectional (grammatical) morpheme

5. Why is phoneme awareness important?

6. How is decoding skill related to reading fluency and comprehension?

Comprehensive Survey
of Language Knowledge

1. From the list below, find an example of each of the following (answer will be a word or part of a word):

   Inflected verb _____

   Compound noun _____

   Bound root _____

   Derivational suffix _____

   Greek combining form _____

   > peaches incredible slowed although shameful doughnut
   > bicycle neuropsychology sandpaper vanish

2. For each word on the left, determine the number of syllables and the number of morphemes:

	Syllables	Morphemes
bookworm		
unicorn		
elephant		
believed		
incredible		
finger		
hogs		
telegram		

3. A closed syllable is one that _____.

   An open syllable is one that _____.

4. How many speech sounds are in the following words?

sigh _____	thrown _____	scratch _____
ice _____	sung _____	poison _____
mix _____	shrink _____	know _____

5. What is the third speech sound in each of the following words?

    joyful _____   should _____   talk _____

    tinker _____   rouge _____   shower _____

    square _____   start _____

    protect _____   patchwork _____

6. Underline the schwa vowels:
        telephone addenda along precious imposition unless

7. Underline the consonant blends:
        knight climb wreck napkin squished springy first

8. Underline the consonant digraphs:
        spherical church numb shrink thought whether

9. When is *ck* used in spelling?

10. What letters signal that a *c* is pronounced /s/?

11. List all of the ways you know to spell "long *o*":

12. List all of the ways you know to spell the consonant sound /f/:

13. When adding a suffix to a word ending with silent *e*, what is the spelling rule?

14. How can you recognize an English word that came from Greek?

CHAPTER 2

Phonetics

Phonetics is the study of the speech sounds that occur in each language and in all languages. It is a topic within the broader topic of **phonology,** which is discussed in Chapter 3. Speech sounds (phonemes) are the basic building blocks of words, the smallest units that make one word different from another. Linguists who study and describe an unfamiliar language usually begin by constructing an inventory of speech sounds that distinguish that language. The determination of a speech sound inventory in a language is an interesting deductive exercise; strangely, although people who know a language are constantly using the sounds in that language, few people can list all of those sounds or describe them. Thus, the linguist cannot simply ask the speakers of the language to tell him or her what the sounds are. The list must be deduced from analysis of the words in which sounds occur because these sounds are seldom spoken in isolation.

Listing the inventory of the sounds in any language is an exercise of **metalinguistic** skill, or awareness of language structure itself. Metalinguistic knowledge of speech sounds is developed through formal study and reflection. A person needs awareness that separate sounds exist within whole words (phoneme awareness) and an ability to distinguish among those speech sounds to read and write any alphabetic symbol system. Although teachers of reading and writing do not necessarily need to have extensive training in phonetics, explicit knowledge of the speech sound system will allow them to teach reading and spelling with clarity and understanding.

SPEECH SOUNDS ARE ELUSIVE

What are the sounds of English? How many are there? Very few of us can answer these questions because we learned the sounds from exposure to them in naturally articulated words, and we usually produce the sounds without conscious attention to their number, order, or other features. The speech sound inventory, even in our native language, is not something we are likely to have been taught prior to taking a class in language structure. The human brain is designed to attend to the meaning of the message between speakers, not to the specific sounds in words, so our knowledge of phonetics tends to be tacit or implicit rather than overt and formal. Although speakers of English may not be able to list all of the sounds of the language, they recognize when words do and do not conform to English phonology. For example, most people recognize that the French *tu*, the Swahili *Ngoro*, the Russian *tovarishch*, and the Japanese *tsutsumu* are not English because these words have sounds or sound sequences that are not heard in English. Speakers are also capable of inventing new words or nonwords that follow the speech sound constraints of their own language, such as *yemble*, but seldom can explain why *yemble* conforms to English word-formation rules and why *ylebm* does not. One would think that linguists would agree on the inventory of sounds in English and other languages, but the disconcerting fact is that they do not. Estimates of the number of speech sounds or phonemes in English range from 40 to 52.[1] Every reference consulted for this chapter used a different phonetic description of English and offered a somewhat different inventory of sounds![2] Only the inherent ambiguity of phoneme identity can account for such disparities.

Becoming aware of the speech sounds in our own language without being formally taught is a process similar to identifying the speech sounds in any new language to which we are exposed. We must acquire information about a level of language processing that we use constantly but that we have never had to dissect. Words and phonemes are segments in a stream of speech that flows continuously without pauses or acoustic breaks. Speech sounds are **unsegmented** in words; that is, they are not spoken as separate units. Speakers almost never say words as a series of discrete segments, and if they do, the segments in isolation do not sound as they do in the word. The segment /p/ alone is not exactly the same as the sounds in *picture, spider,* or *stoop*. The sounds we identify as /p/ are really slightly different sounds that our brains lump together in one category. In addition, individual sounds overlap in speech, or are **co-articulated.** Sounds within words are influenced in place and manner of articulation by the sounds that come before and after them. Look in a mirror. Say the words *see* and *so,* and as you anticipate the vowel that follows /s/ in each word, feel the different mouth position for the /s/ that begins each word. Say the words *tap* and *trap* and notice how different the mouth feels and looks when it shapes the sound we think of as /t/ in the beginning of both words. Now try *cheese* and *choose*. In each case, the initial consonant sound is influenced by what comes after it. Our brains know what is coming next in a word and make adjustments in articulation of individual segments so that the sequence is amalgamated into one speech gesture, a word. When we speak sounds in isolation, we are verbalizing abstract phonemes that exist in our minds but do not exist in quite the same form when they are combined to make spoken words.

PHONEME COUNTING

It is easy to demonstrate that many speakers of English have trouble identifying the discrete segments in words that constitute the inventory of speech sounds or phonemes. Try counting the number of speech sounds in familiar words and identifying the specific sounds within those words. This task will be easier if you try not to think about how the words are spelled.

☆ EXERCISE 2.1

Count the number of phonemes in the following words:

ice _____	choose _____	mix _____	soothe _____
sigh _____	sing _____	pitched _____	her _____
day _____	thorn _____	straight _____	boy _____
aide _____	quake _____	measure _____	shout _____

Compare notes with someone else who did Exercise 2.1. Did you make the same judgments? In what way(s) did you disagree? What would cause a group of educated people to disagree about the number, sequence, or identity of individual segments within English words? What causes the ambiguity of phoneme identity?

SPEECH SOUND IDENTIFICATION

If counting speech sounds, as in Exercise 2.1, is neither simple nor straightforward for adults, why should it be easy for children who are just learning to read and write? Again, several factors conspire to prevent children from developing the insight that the words *ice, sigh,* and *me* all are made of two speech sounds even though we use a different number of letters to spell each of them. Children have not spoken the sounds in isolation and have not had to break words into their component phonemes; for them the sounds exist only in combination with others, and awareness of the segments is not necessary for everyday verbal communication. Many children who enter kindergarten know letter names but do not know that those letters are used to represent the segments of their own speech. Many first and second graders, and even some older students who are poor readers or spellers, also have not acquired this essential insight. In virtually every classroom, some children will not understand this fundamental fact. The teacher may need to provide explicit phoneme awareness instruction for children before instruction in letter–sound association for reading and spelling can be effective. Phoneme awareness is the linchpin for early reading success.

The most basic building blocks of a language are the sets of consonants and vowels that make up the speech sound inventory. The terms *consonants* and *vowels* are used in this book to refer to segments of speech, not to the letters that represent them. Every language has a set of consonants and vowels; English has more than most. It is interesting to note, however, that linguists usually differ to some degree in their description of consonants and vowels, offering varying opinions about the segments and the features that describe them. The descriptions in this book may not be the same as the phonetic classifications made by other authors. Again, ambiguity appears to be a characteristic of phonetic description, because the sounds must be "recovered" from running speech. The inventory of consonants and vowels that follows is based on the classification of the linguists Fromkin and Rodman.[3]

The task of classifying sounds is complicated by the fact that no two speakers of a language form their sounds exactly the same way and by the fact that regional dialects cause quite audible differences in sound production. One of the remarkable characteristics of the speech-processing module in the brain is that speakers can understand one another in spite of regional and individual differences in speech production. We can extract from the speech of others the acoustic signals that determine what the utterance means even though we all don't talk the same way. To describe what goes on when we talk, however, we must have a standard classification system for consonants and vowels. If you are unsure of exactly what is and is not a speech sound, Exercise 2.2 is going to be a bit challenging:

☆ EXERCISE 2.2

Identify the third phoneme in the following words:

choose _____   pneumonia _____   kitchen _____

writhe _____   vision _____   square _____

sink _____   folk _____

To identify the third sound in a word, the speaker must segment and count the sounds and then know the difference between a phoneme and a written letter. In the words in Exercise 2.2, the spelling generally does not represent the sounds with a straightforward "one letter equals one sound" principle. Furthermore, speakers may not be aware of or know how to describe the third sound in some of these words, such as the /ŋ/, or /ng/, sound in *sink* or the /ž/, or /zh/, sound represented by *s* in *measure*. Learning a system for transcribing and describing the sounds in a way other than their standard orthographic spellings helps one to clarify the differences between phonemes and the symbols used for writing. When that clarification is achieved, we can make sense of children's early struggles with print far more easily.

PHONETIC TRANSCRIPTION

To represent the speech sounds in our language, standard alphabetic writing is unsatisfactory. English spelling uses several hundred **graphemes** (letters and letter combinations) to represent 40 or so speech sounds;[4] in fact, most spellings for sounds consist of more than one letter. Consider the following sentence: *Daisy weighed in on Thursday to make great strides in horse racing history.* This sentence includes six of the eight spellings of "long *a*" in standard English: *ai, eigh, ay, a-*consonant-*e, ea,* and *a* (it does not include *ey* as in *prey* or *ei* as in *vein*). Although most of the sounds of English have somewhat more predictable spellings, it is not possible to write a transcription of speech sounds unless some standard, consistent method of representation is used.

When one sound corresponds to one letter, the writing system is said to be phonetic. It is easy to illustrate again that English orthography is not an ideal tool for phonetic transcription. The word *conscience* shows why. In this word, the letter *c* stands for three different speech sounds: /k/, /š/ (or /sh/), and /s/; a **vowel team** (two vowel letters) is needed to spell the second vowel /ə/, and the final /s/ is represented by *ce*. Phonetically, the same word is written as [kɑnšəns]; there is one symbol for each speech sound. A **phonetic alphabet** represents all of the sounds in the world's languages so that speech can be described with a common symbol system. The International Phonetic Alphabet (IPA) was invented in 1888 for that purpose and was revised by a group of linguists in 1989 and in 1993.[5] The IPA is detailed enough to represent salient linguistic features in each language, but it does not—and should not—represent the minute individual variations in the way two speakers may pronounce the same word. It is sufficient for transcribing the crucial linguistic properties of sounds in English and other languages. An Americanized version of the IPA is used in this book.

Readers of this textbook may not be inclined to learn or use a phonetic alphabet and may prefer to transcribe words using the 26 Roman letters only (a phonic or dictionary system; for example, /sh/, /ng/, /th/, /o͞o/). A phonetic alphabet, however, is recommended for practice with transcription because it unambiguously represents the speech sound system separately from the alphabet symbols of conventional English orthography. Working with the phonetic alphabet requires the learner to differentiate sounds from their conventional spellings. One can use phonic or dictionary symbols to transcribe the phonetic properties of words, but the disadvantage of such a phonic representation system is that many speech sounds must then be represented with letter combinations (the initial single sound in *chair* must be represented by /ch/). With the phonetic alphabet, only one unique symbol is used for each phoneme. In this book, the major listings of consonants and vowels are given in both symbol systems (phonic representation and phonetic alphabet). Brackets [ ] are used to denote the phonetic form of a word or speech segment, and slashes / / are used to denote phonemes. The distinction between a phonetic segment and a phoneme is clarified in Chapter 3.

Speech sounds are produced with movements of the tongue, lips, and throat. Air is pushed up from the lungs through an opening in the vocal cords (the glottis) and then through the throat, mouth, and nose. Air is more obstructed in consonant production than in vowel production. Thus, we can say for instructional purposes that consonants are "closed" sounds and vowels are "open" sounds. Figure 2.1 shows the speech apparatus.

Consonants and Their Articulation

Consonants are a class of speech sounds that are not vowels and that are formed with the mouth partially closed. Not all consonants, however, involve obstruction

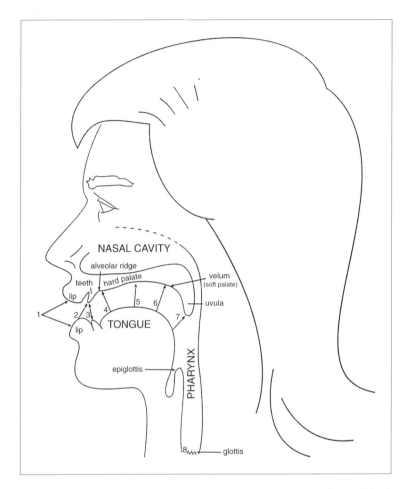

Figure 2.1. The vocal tract with places of articulation marked: 1) bilabial, 2) labiodental, 3) interdental, 4) alveolar, 5) alveopalatal, 6) velar, 7) uvular, and 8) glottal. (Figure from AN INTRODUCTION TO LANGUAGE, Sixth Edition [p. 222], by Victoria A. Fromkin and Robert Rodman copyright © 1998 by Holt, Rinehart & Winston, reproduced by permission of the publisher.)

of the air stream to an equal degree; some consonants have vowel-like qualities (for example, the [r] in *word*), which in turn cause them to be somewhat more ambiguous or difficult to identify in running speech.

You may find it helpful to fill in a blank consonant chart based on your knowledge of the speech sounds (Figure 2.2) before looking at the charts of consonant sounds that are provided in the tables on pages 28 and 29. A basic 25 consonants are identified in these two tables, classified by place and manner of articulation. Two symbol systems are given, first phonic symbols (see Table 2.1) and then phonetic symbols (see Table 2.2), which are likely to be used in classroom reading and spelling instruction. The linguistic terms that appear in these two tables are explained in the next section.

Lips	Lips/teeth	Tongue between teeth	Tongue behind teeth	Roof of mouth	Back of mouth	Throat

Figure 2.2. Chart for discovering the consonants. List as many consonants as possible, grouping them by where the sound seems to be articulated.

Table 2.1.

Phonic symbols

American English consonants listed by place and manner of articulation

Manner of articulation	Place of articulation						
	Lips	Lips/teeth	Tongue between teeth	Tongue behind teeth	Roof of mouth	Back of mouth	Throat
Stop (voiceless)	/p/			/t/		/k/	
(voiced)	/b/			/d/		/g/	
Nasal	/m/			/n/		/ng/	
Fricative (voiceless)		/f/	/th/	/s/	/sh/		
(voiced)		/v/	/th/	/z/	/zh/		
Affricate (voiceless)					/ch/		
(voiced)					/j/		
Glide (voiceless)						/wh/	/h/
(voiced)					/y/	/w/	
Liquid				/l/			
				/r/			

28

Table 2.2.

Phonetic symbols

American English consonants listed by place and manner of articulation

Manner of articulation	Bilabial	Labiodental	Interdental	Alveolar	Palatal	Velar	Glottal
Stop (oral)							
voiceless unaspirated	p			t		k	ʔ
voiceless aspirated	pʰ			tʰ		kʰ	
voiced	b			d		g	
Nasal (stop)	m			n		ŋ	
Fricative							
voiceless		f	θ	s	š		
voiced		v	ð	z	ž		
Affricate							
voiceless					č		
voiced					ǰ		
Glide							
voiceless						ʍ	h
voiced					j	w	
Liquid				l r			

☆ EXERCISE 2.3

Try to discover and label as many consonants as you can, using the blank chart provided in Figure 2.2. Categorize the consonants by the place in the vocal tract where you think they are articulated. Then, compare the consonants listed on your chart with those that appear in Tables 2.1 and 2.2. Which sounds are difficult to identify? Were any previously unknown to you?

Places of Consonant Articulation

We can distinguish consonants from one another in part because of the way the lips, tongue, teeth, and other parts of the mouth are shaped and positioned. **Labials** are made with the lips together in the front of the mouth. The **bilabial** consonants, as the name suggests, are made by bringing both lips together. Two of these, [b] and [p], are oral **stops,** and one, [m], is a **nasal (stop).** Stops are noncontinuous phonemes. **Labiodental** consonants [f] and [v] are formed with the upper front teeth on the lower lip.

Farther back in the mouth, **interdental** consonants are made with the tongue between the teeth. Two related sounds are made, one **unvoiced** (vocal cords do not vibrate) and one **voiced** (vocal cords do vibrate), both of which in English are spelled with *th:* [θ] and [ð]. The unvoiced *th,* [θ], occurs in the words *thin* and *ether;* the voiced *th,* [ð], occurs in the words *then* and *either.*

When the tongue is placed behind the **alveolar** ridge, the ridge of tissue just above the back side of the teeth, five more consonants are produced. The stop consonants [t] and [d] differ from each other only in voicing and otherwise are articulated in the same place and manner. The nasal [n] is articulated in the same position. The [s] and [z] are also alveolars, again differing only in voicing. Alveolar sounds may feel very much the same when they are articulated; thus, if a student confuses *an, and,* and *ant,* the confusion may originate with the similarity of the final phonemes (/n/, /d/, /t/) in place of articulation.

Three more consonants are made with the tongue raised against the soft palate in the back of the throat: [k], [g], and [ŋ]. These sounds are **velars** because the soft palate is called the *velum.* The [k] and [g] again differ only in voicing, which often leads to students' misspellings of the ending consonants of words such as *back* and *bag* and substitution of [k] or [g] for the nasal [ŋ]. When students write SIG for *sing,* they are not simply leaving out a letter but also may be substituting a sound for another that is made in the same part of the mouth.

The **palatals** are made with the front part of the tongue on the hard palate (roof of the mouth) behind the alveolar ridge. They include the pair [č] and [ǰ] and the pair [š] and [ž], which again differ from each other only in voicing, as in the words *chest* and *jest* and the words *fission* and *vision.* The sound [š] can be spelled with an *s* as in *sugar* and *sure* but usually is spelled with *sh* as in *sheep.* The voiced sound [ž] can begin words in French, such as *genre* and *gendarme,* but does not begin any words in English. Most people are not aware it is a phoneme because it has no unique spelling in English orthography. We usually spell [ž] with an *s* as in *vision* or *measure.* The last palatal sound is a glide, which has two permissible phonetic symbols for the same sound, [j] or [y]. Notice that [j] is different from [ǰ]. The first represents the first sound in *yes* and *usual;* the second represents the first sound in *joy* and *jester.*

Manner of Articulation

Place of articulation is only one dimension along which consonants are classified and differentiated. The other dimension is the manner in which the air stream is obstructed as it moves through the mouth. For example, the sounds [b] and [m] are voiced bilabial sounds; the manner rather than the place of their articulation distinguishes them. Likewise, the voiceless alveolars [t] and [s] are different in manner of production, so we can distinguish the words *take* and *sake*.

Stops are to be distinguished from **continuants.** Stops are aptly named because the flow of air is stopped completely for a short time. Stops may be voiced or unvoiced (voiceless) depending on whether the vocal cords are engaged and vibrate as the air passes through the larynx. The oral stops include three voiced/voiceless pairs including [b] and [p], [t] and [d], and [k] and [g]. These sounds are of short duration when spoken in isolation. They cannot be slowed down and glided into a vowel during phoneme blending (add /d/ to the beginning of *ate*). In contrast, a continuant sound can be blended smoothly without a break (add /m/ to the beginning of *an*).

Are the nasal phonemes stops or continuants? That classification depends on the definition used. The sounds [m], [n], and [ŋ] are the three nasal sounds, as in *sum, sun,* and *sung*. Most linguists call these *stops* because the air flow is obstructed in the mouth or oral cavity, but they can be sustained vocally and blended with other sounds continuously because we can say the sound as long as breath is available. Technically, the nasals are stops; for teaching purposes, they can be thought of as continuants.

All of the **fricatives** are continuants. As the name implies, significant friction is created as the air in the mouth is partially obstructed and forced through a narrow space. If you hold your hand in front of your mouth, you will feel air coming out in a continuous stream when you say [f], [v], [s], [z], [š], [ž], [θ], and [ð]. These sounds are produced with high-frequency overtones and are difficult for individuals with high-frequency hearing loss to discriminate. More than 300 years ago, during the Elizabethan period, English speakers produced a palatal fricative that remains in our spelling system as the *gh* in *knight, enough,* and *right*. This sound, which is no longer a part of English, is pronounced similar to the German *ch* in *Bach* with the tongue raised as if to pronounce a [g] but not touching the back of the throat.

Affricates [č] and [ǰ] are produced with a stop closure and then an immediate release of the air. Affricates are thus a sequence of a stop and a fricative but are noncontinuant sounds. In English there are only two affricates, which differ only in voicing, as in *etch* and *edge*. Notice that the spellings used for the sounds [č] and [ǰ] after accented short vowels, *tch* and *dge,* include the stop consonants [t] and [d], consistent with the mouth position at the beginning of the production of [č] and [ǰ].

The most problematic speech sounds for English articulation, reading, and spelling are the **liquids,** [l] and [r]. These are among the later developing sounds in the speech production of many children[6] and the most difficult to teach in speech therapy because they "float" in the mouth. The liquids have no clear beginning or end point in articulation. Furthermore, the [r] is articulated quite differently depending on whether it is in the beginning of a word or after a vowel. Usually [l] is described as a lateral liquid, with the tongue raised to the alveolar ridge and the sides of the tongue held down to allow the air to escape out to the side of the tongue.

The American English [r] is typically made with the tongue curled back or bunched up behind the alveolar ridge, but there is considerable variation from speaker to speaker and word to word. In some languages, such as Spanish, the liquid phoneme is trilled or tapped with the tongue more forward, on the alveolar ridge. In British English, /r/ may be flapped (the phonetic symbol for flapping is [ɾ]) with the tongue against the alveolar ridge, as in the British English pronunciation of *very* [vɛɾi]. In English, the liquids are voiced in most positions, but if they follow a voiceless consonant in a blend, they may be unvoiced, as in *play* or *pray.*

Some languages have no liquids at all. Others, notably Cantonese and Japanese, have only one liquid phoneme, pronounced as a flap [ɾ], and thus do not distinguish between /r/ and /l/. Speakers of these Asian languages may have difficulty articulating English words with liquids, and they may substitute [l] for [r] or vice versa.

Glides, along with liquids, have vowel-like qualities and are sometimes called **semivowels.** They include [w], [ʍ], [y], and [h]. Glides are **sonorants,** similar to vowels, but they differ from vowels in that they do not form the peak of a syllable. The beginning sounds of *yes* and *went* do not obstruct the air stream in the mouth, and the tongue quickly moves from the glide to the vowel that follows it. Glides are never followed by another consonant in the same syllable. The voiceless glide [ʍ], which is typically spelled with a *wh,* is losing its distinctiveness in American speech. Many Americans pronounce the beginning consonants in the words *witch* and *which* the same way, although British speakers tend to retain the distinction between the voiced [w] and the voiceless [ʍ]. Because [w] and [ʍ] are formed with the lips in a rounded position, they are sometimes classified as bilabial rather than velar.

As mentioned before, [y] is also represented with the symbol [j] in the phonetic alphabet. It is a **palatal glide.** The position of the tongue as the [y] is formed is very similar to the vowel [i] as in *meet,* but it is not the same as the vowel [i]. When we say [y], the tongue moves quickly into the vowel that follows and does not produce the sound for the same length of time as it does when the vowel [i] is the nucleus of a syllable. The combination of the glide [y] with the vowel [u] is very common in English, as in the words *use, refuse,* and *music,* and often is represented with one letter, *u,* in standard spelling. For our purposes, the combination of two phonemes [j] and [u] will be transcribed when phonetic symbols are used in transcriptions of words such as *unicorn* [junəkɔrn].

The glide [h] is formed with the glottis open and no other obstruction of the air stream. Usually the mouth anticipates the following vowel when [h] is formed, as in the difference between the position of the lips in *her* and *he.* Often [h] is classified as a voiceless glottal fricative instead of a glide; however, [h] is not formed with the same air obstruction as the other fricatives. The [h] is usually voiced when it is both preceded and followed by a vowel, as in *Ahab, cohabitation,* or *antihistamine.*

Glottal stops, represented by [ʔ], are **allophonic variations** in English; that is, they are not part of the standard phoneme inventory for every speaker, but they do occur in certain dialect variations and in casual American speech. For example, some speakers say the words *bottle* or *button* with a glottal stop instead of a [t] or a flap [ɾ], as in [bɑʔl] and [bʌʔan].

Syllabic consonants are the liquids and nasals that can constitute a separate syllable. Liquids and nasals, including /l/, /r/, /m/, and /n/, are continuant consonants with vowel-like features that allow them to act as syllables. The variant or allophone of /r/ that is found on the end of words such as *summer* [sʌmɚ] is written as a combination of **schwa** and /r/. These syllabic consonants are found in words such as *mitten* [mɪtʔn], [mɪtn], or [mɪtən], *rhythm* [rɪðm], *letter* [lɛɾɚ], and *bible* [bajbl]; they can also be nonsyllabic single consonants as in *need, mystery, red,* and *laugh.*

The liquids, glides, nasals, and vowels form a class of sounds known as **sonorants.** These are to be contrasted with **obstruents,** the class of sounds consisting of nonnasal stops, fricatives, and affricates. Sonorants are typically the sounds that children have the most trouble spelling, perhaps because these are more difficult to segment or pull out of the speech stream.

☆ EXERCISE 2.4

Write the symbol for first and last consonants in each word. Pay attention to how the words sound, not how they are spelled.

some _____	judge _____	wide _____
knight _____	nose _____	thing _____
clear _____	shoal _____	rhyme _____
write _____	which _____	phone _____
once _____	use _____	yawn _____
thatch _____	comb _____	hymn _____
guest _____	quest _____	gem _____
gym _____	whole _____	rouge _____
pave _____	there _____	thief _____

Vowels and Their Articulation

What is a vowel? Most people will say "*a, e, i, o, u,* and sometimes *y,*" but English has 15 vowel sounds, not 6. Vowels are a class of open, unobstructed speech sounds that are not consonants. No syllable can be without a vowel. (Sometimes the vowel is contained in a syllabic consonant, as described previously.) The vowel is the nucleus of the syllable; the syllable is formed with consonants surrounding a vowel. Vowels are what we sing. Try singing the song "America the Beautiful" without the vowels! Now try singing it with only the vowels. That should be much easier.

☆ EXERCISE 2.5

Discover and label as many vowels as you can, using the blank chart provided (Figure 2.3). Record the vowels on the chart according to mouth position. Then, compare the vowels you listed with those that appear in Table 2.3 and Figure 2.4.

The characteristics of a vowel are determined by the position of the lips, tongue, and vocal cavity. All vowels are voiced and create resonance in the head. Vowels may be **stressed** or **unstressed,** spoken with **tense** or **lax** musculature, carried out for a long or brief duration, and articulated with nasal or nonnasal quality. Tongue and lip positions determine how each vowel sounds. Differences in vowel pronunciation account in large part for dialect differences in word pronunciation, so the "standard" dialect of English that appears in Figure 2.4 may not represent the vowels produced by many Americans. At least the arrangement of vowels on the chart can give us a basis for comparing dialect variations.

The Vowel Chart

Fifteen basic American English vowels can be distinguished from one another on the dimensions of tongue position (**front, mid, back**) and tongue height (**high** to **low**). One way that linguists can tell whether certain vowel phonemes exist in a language is to find two words made with the same consonants and different vowels. This set of words is a **minimal pair.** For example, in English, most vowel phonemes can be put in the blank in [b___t] to create different words (see Table 2.3); thus, we know that these vowels exist in English.

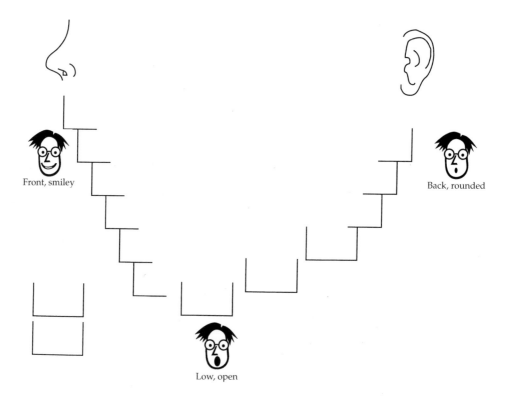

Front, smiley

Back, rounded

Low, open

Figure 2.3.   Chart for discovering the vowels. List as many vowels as possible, grouping them by mouth position.

Table 2.3.   American English vowels: phonetic and phonic symbols

Phonetic symbol	Phonic symbol	Spelling
/i/	ē	beet
/ɪ/	ĭ	bit
/e/	ā	bait
/ɛ/	ĕ	bet
/æ/	ă	bat
/aj/	ī	bite
/ɑ/	ŏ	bottle
/ʌ/	ŭ	butt
/ɔ/	aw, ô	bought
/o/	ō	boat
/ʊ/	o͝o	put
/u/	o͞o	boot
/ə/	ə	between
/ɔj/	oi, oy	boy
/æω/	ou, ow	bow

To illustrate more clearly how the vowels are distinguished by subtle changes of mouth position, Figure 2.4 shows them arranged by proximity of articulation to one another. The highest, most front vowel is [i] as in the English *meat* or Spanish *fajita*. Front high vowels are made with the mouth in a smile position. As the tongue drops step by step and the mouth opens to say each vowel in succession, [i], [ɪ], [e], [ɛ], [æ], and so forth, the jaw drops to its most open (mid) position for [ɑ], as in the words *father* and *pot*. The diphthong [aj] is placed in the sequence before [ɑ] because the mouth is in a position similar to [ɑ] when the vowel is articulated.

The next vowel [ʌ], as in *putt* and *stubborn*, is sometimes perceived as being slightly in front of [ɑ] and slightly higher. It is hard to place and is sometimes referred to as an "accented schwa" [ə], the indistinct mid vowel. As the four back vowels are spoken in order, the mouth closes slowly: [ɔ], [o], [ʊ], and [u]. All of the back vowels are made with the lips rounded.

The difference between adjacent vowels in Figure 2.4 is a small adjustment in closure of the jaw and a small shift of tongue height. Beginning with the highest front vowel, [i] as in *beet,* one can say the vowel sequence and watch in a mirror how the mouth changes little by little. All of the front vowels are unrounded in English, and the four last back vowels all are rounded. (Note that front rounded vowels occur in French, as in *tu* and *vieux*, and in German, as in *Tür* and *Müle.*)

The vowels that do not fit in the progression on the vowel chart in Figure 2.4 are the **diphthongs** [ɔj] and [æw] or [aw] (not to be confused with the phonic symbol [aw] as in *caught*) and the schwa [ə]. Diphthongs are vowels that glide in the middle. The mouth position shifts during the production of the *single* vowel phoneme. When you say the word *boy* [bɔj], notice how your mouth begins with a back, rounded position and shifts or glides to a front, smiley position. It shifts as well with *bow* [bæw] (as in *take a bow after a performance*) from a front position to a lip-rounded position. A third diphthong, [aj], is placed on the main vowel chart

Vowel Chart: Phonetic Symbols

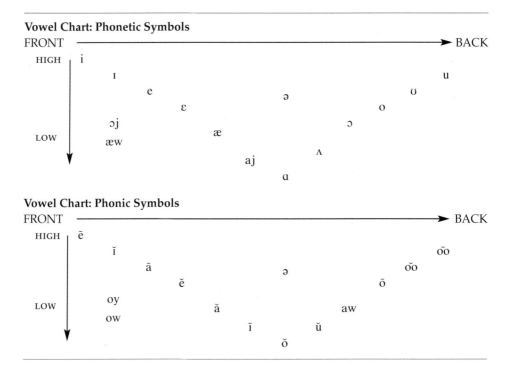

Figure 2.4. Vowel articulation: a) phonetic and b) phonic symbols. (Based on Bolinger & Sears, 1981, and Fromkin & Rodman, 1993.)

because of its relationship to [ɑ]. Children's spellings show that they perceive these vowels as being close together, so they will spell *light* [lajt] as *lot* [lɑt]. The mouth also shifts or glides at the end of the vowel [aj] as in *pie*. It is important, however, to realize that the glide is a property of the vowel phoneme [aj], not a separate vowel, as students sometimes think.

Schwa [ə] is a mid central lax vowel. In English, the vowel in an unstressed syllable often "reduces" to schwa. For example, the root word *commerce* has an [ɑ] in the first syllable, but its derivation *commercial* reduces that first vowel to schwa when the stress shifts to the second syllable. Schwa reduction presents a problem for children learning to spell because schwa can be spelled with any of the vowel letters in standard orthography (*alone, effect, definition, commence, upon*), so students must learn the identity of vowels on the basis of other, related words or by memorization. Sometimes in phonetic alphabets a schwa that sounds more like [ɪ] is represented as [i]. One way to recognize a schwa is that it cannot easily be "sounded out." The mid low vowel [ʌ] sounds similar to an "accented schwa" but is found in stressed syllables only, as in *but, butter,* and *supper,* and usually is spelled with the letter *u.*

The terms **long** and **short** are used in the terminology of phonics instruction but not in the language of phonetics. The terms, although popular among teachers, do not directly describe the physical reality of vowel duration. The terms also imply that there are only two categories of vowels, ignoring the third category, diphthongs. Linguists use the terms *tense* for long vowels and *lax* for short vowels, as follows:

Long (tense)		Short (lax)		Diphthong	
i	beet	ɪ	bit	aj	bite
e	bait	ɛ	bet	æw	bout
u	boot	ʊ	book	ɔj	boil
o	boat	ɔ	bought		
		ɑ	pot		
		ʌ	but		
		æ	bat		

Long, or tense, vowels are spoken with more tension in the tongue muscles than are the short, or lax, vowels. The actual duration of the vowel, that is, how long it is spoken, is affected by the consonant that comes after the vowel as well as by the tense/lax distinction. The vowel in *bide* is longer in duration than the vowel in *bite* is because of the voiced consonant /d/ after the vowel in *bide*. Therefore, there is no valid linguistic reason for the terms *long* and *short* to be used to label vowels. These labels have become part of our standard teaching vocabulary and will continue to be used, but they should not be interpreted literally. If we use these terms, it is important to remember that the diphthongs make up the third class of vowels and that vowels followed by *r* (**r-controlled** vowels) are a special problem for phonetic transcription.

☆ EXERCISE 2.6

1. Write your full name in phonetic transcription. Share your transcription with other people, if possible, and decode other names. For example, [luizə kʊk mots]

2. Now write the full phonetic transcription for these words:

put _____	putt _____	puke _____
coin _____	shower _____	sigh _____
should _____	thesis _____	chain _____
sacks _____	sax _____	preppy _____
critter _____	ceiling _____	cymbal _____
whether _____	question _____	measure _____

3. Translate these words into standard English spelling:

    ɔlðo ðə prɑbləm ʌv dɪslɛksiə ɪz nɑt ə kəndɪšən ʍɛrɪn pipl si θɪŋz bækwɚd ðə sɪmtəm ʌv rivɚsəlz hæz bɪn ovɚpled baj ðə prɛs

    _____

    _____

Vowels in Other Languages

Many other possibilities exist for vowel production. These possibilities are exploited by languages that use **pitch, intonation,** nasalization, and vowel duration to make different phonemes. Many African, Native American, and Asian languages are tone languages in which the register (tonal quality) of a vowel will determine different meanings. In fact, most languages in the world use tonal systems for making vowels. Thai, for example, has five tones for vowels that to an English speaker might be difficult to distinguish, remember, or use: low, mid, high, falling, and rising. One of the challenges for a speaker of a tonal language learning English is to ignore variations in vowel tone and duration.

SUMMARY

The major distinctions for understanding and teaching speech sounds and their relationship to print include the classes of consonants and vowels. Each of these classes of speech sounds has distinct features or properties, and the sounds' features can be represented by their place and manner of articulation. Identifying the existence of the speech sound inventory is not an easy or obvious task, because the sounds we think of as phonemes are buried in the continuous stream of speech that makes words, phrases, and sentences.

English spelling is not a good phonetic representation of speech because it has too few symbols (26) for the more than 40 speech sounds and because these are used in complex and varying ways. Therefore, a phonetic alphabet is useful for representing the component sounds in words.

Consonants, closed speech sounds made with an obstruction of air, share features with each other when they are spoken in the same place in the mouth or in the same manner. The major groups of consonants, classified by manner of articulation, are stops, nasals, fricatives, affricates, glides, and liquids. These sounds can be voiced or unvoiced. English has nine pairs of consonants that are produced in the same vocal place but that differ in the presence or absence of voicing. Some phonemes are oral and others nasal. English has three nasal consonants, not two. Consonants can also be described by their placement in the back (glottal), middle (velar and alveolar), or front (interdental, labiodental, and bilabial) of the mouth.

A vowel is an open speech sound that forms the nucleus of a syllable. Vowels are classified on the dimensions of front, mid, and back as well as high to low. The front vowels are unrounded, but the back vowels are made with a rounding of the lips. Vowels may be tense, lax, or diphthongs. As the next chapter discusses in greater depth, vowels also may have tone, stress, nasality, and length. English is a nontonal language, but the majority of the world's languages do produce vowels with specific pitch.

Within these general classes of sounds, there is a great deal of both systematic and random variation in how the sounds are produced. Random variation occurs from speaker to speaker depending on individual characteristics and dialect. Systematic variation occurs when **phonological rules,** shared by speakers of the language, determine how speech sounds are produced. The rule system for speech production is the subject of the next chapter.

☆ SUPPLEMENTARY EXERCISES

1. Determine what these groups of speech sounds have in common:

    a) [t], [d], [n], [s], [z]
    b) [m], [n], [ŋ]
    c) [r], [l], [y], [w], [h], [m], [n], [ŋ]
    d) [k], [g], [ŋ]
    e) [t], [g], [d], [k], [p], [b]
    f) [u], [ʊ], [o], [ɔ]

2. Write an example of the following type of speech sound:

    a) Rounded back high vowel _____
    b) Mid front lax vowel _____
    c) Voiced velar nasal _____
    d) Unvoiced interdental fricative _____
    e) Voiced affricate _____
    f) Lateral liquid _____
    g) Diphthong that begins with lip rounding _____

3. Contrast the sounds in the following minimal pairs of words. How do the sounds differ from one another, and how are they alike?

    a) tee<u>th</u>, tee<u>the</u>
    b) c<u>o</u>ne, c<u>o</u>n
    c) ri<u>ch</u>, ri<u>dge</u>
    d) lea<u>f</u>, lea<u>ve</u>
    e) <u>p</u>ap, <u>m</u>ap

4. Write the phonetic symbol for the last phoneme in the following words. (Avoid being fooled by the spelling!)

cheese _____	laugh _____	enjoy _____
attached _____	baby _____	collage _____
Xerox _____	aglow _____	
you _____	wealth _____	

5. On a separate sheet of paper, write the following poem (from "The World Is Too Much with Us" by William Wordsworth) in phonetic transcription. Brackets are optional in this exercise.

    The world is too much with us; late and soon,
    Getting and spending, we lay waste our powers:
    Little we see in Nature that is ours;
    We have given our hearts away, a sordid boon!
    This Sea that bares her bosom to the moon;
    The winds that will be howling at all hours,
    And are up-gathered now like sleeping flowers;
    For this, for everything, we are out of tune;
    It moves us not.

6. On a separate sheet of paper, translate the following poem (author unknown) from phonetic symbols to standard English spelling:

aj tek ɪt ju ɔlrɛdi no
ʌv tʌf ænd bæw ænd kɔf ænd do
sʌm me stʌmbəl bʌt nat ju
ɑn hɪkəp θʌro slæw ænd θru
so næw ju ar rɛdi pɛrhæps
tu lɛrn ʌv lɛs fəmɪljɚ træps
biwɛr ʌv hɚd ədrɛdfʊl wɚd
ðæt lʊks lajk bird ænd sæwndz lajk bɚd
ænd dɛd ɪts sɛd lajk bɛd nat bid
for gʊdnɛs sek dont kɔl ɪt did

7. Here are some spelling errors (followed by correct spellings) made by sixth-grade students. Match the spelling errors to the type of error they represent:

WOSUT/wasn't   CLORER/color   INGLISH/English   LEDR/letter
SINGIG/singing   SGARY/scary   STASUN/station   FOWD/food

a) Nasal omission or deletion _____

b) Liquid confusion _____

c) Voiced/voiceless stop substitution _____

d) Fricative substitution _____

e) Flap for a medial stop _____

f) Back vowel substitution _____

g) Front vowel substitution _____

h) Oral (nonnasal) for a nasal _____

ENDNOTES

1. Fromkin & Rodman, 1998, for example, list 25 consonants and 15 vowels in English; Owens, 1992, lists 24 consonants and 20 vowels.
2. Balmuth, 1992; Fromkin & Rodman, 1998; Owens, 1992; and Yule, 1996, all use different descriptions of sounds in English, especially for vowels.
3. Fromkin & Rodman, 1998.
4. Hanna, Hanna, Hodges, & Rudorf, 1966.
5. Fromkin & Rodman, 1993.
6. Owens, 1992.

ADDITIONAL RESOURCES

Akmajian, A., Demers, R.A., Farmer, A.K., & Harnish, R.M. (1995). *Linguistics: An introduction to language and communication* (4th ed.). Cambridge, MA: MIT Press.

Edwards, H.T. (1992). *Applied phonetics: The sounds of American English.* San Diego: Singular Publishing Group.

Fromkin, V., & Rodman, R. (1998). *An introduction to language* (6th ed.). Orlando, FL: Harcourt Brace & Co.

Ladefoged, P. (1993). *A course in phonetics* (3rd ed.). Orlando, FL: Harcourt Brace & Co.

CHAPTER 3

Phonology

Phonology is the study of the speech sound system, including the rules and patterns by which the phonemes are combined into words and phrases. The word *phonology* refers both to the sound patterns themselves and to the discipline of studying those sound patterns and their mental representations.

The previous chapter on phonetics describes and classifies the inventory of speech sounds in English, but the description of individual sounds does not account for many other phenomena that are part of the speech sound system of a language. For example, speech sounds are combined only in certain sequences within a language system. We can say [dɑks] but not [dksɑ]. The frequency with which sounds occur within syllables varies. "Short," or lax, vowels are more common in English than are diphthongs.[1] Some speech sounds occur only in certain parts of syllables and in combination with certain other sounds. For example, a glide such as /j/ or /h/ is always followed by a vowel, and /ŋ/ is always preceded by a vowel.

Speakers of a language know that some speech sound sequences seem more pleasing than others, some are "foreign," and some vary considerably from speaker to speaker. Recognizing that a word sounds "foreign" may also coincide with an inability to pronounce the unfamiliar sounds of the word, such as the last sound of *Bach* in German. When we make up new words in our own language, such as words for new products, they are likely to sound similar to words we already know. In contrast to how we say isolated words, in continuous speech we change certain sounds automatically without thinking about what we are doing and without changing the meaning. For example, if you say the words *would you* in a normal sentence such as, "Would you run to the mailbox for me?" you probably would say something like [wʊju rʌn]. Finally, we are aware that stress patterns affect the meaning of words such as *contract* and *reject,* which can be either nouns or verbs (for example, cóntract versus contráct). This kind of knowledge includes more than the ability to pronounce the individual speech sounds (phonetics); it also encompasses awareness of the sound patterns and the rules by which the speech sounds are combined and spoken (phonology).

Knowledge of phonology is very important for teachers of reading, spelling, or writing as well as for students of foreign languages, teachers of diction and singing, and academic linguists. Phonological processing ability, the ability to identify, manipulate, and remember strings of speech sounds, accounts for much of the difference between older good readers and poor readers and between novices who will learn to read easily and those who will struggle. Teachers need to be able to identify problems in this domain. To teach phoneme awareness, for example, the teacher needs to judge which stimuli to use, how to interpret student errors, and how to give corrective feedback to students who are confused. To teach reading and spelling, teachers must understand the indirect relationship between speech and print. Otherwise, they will have trouble guiding students through the sound–symbol learning process with explicit, accurate information about the spoken and written units that are being connected. This chapter focuses on the concepts that are most applicable to teaching written language.

THE PHONEME IS A PSYCHOLOGICAL ABSTRACTION

When we hear speech, the incoming signal is an unsegmented, continuous stream of sound. A spectrogram recording (Figure 3.1) of spoken words shows the production of speech sounds as a co-articulated unit without any actual acoustic divisions between one phoneme and the next. However, we *perceive* discrete segments. To perceive phonemes, our brain must translate an unsegmented acoustic signal into segments that are perceived categorically. For example, we hear one burst of sound if someone says [bɪd], but we classify the acoustic signal as a sequence of three separable speech sounds. The classification process is a consequence of **central linguistic processing,** a special capability of the human brain.

PHONEMES AND MINIMAL PAIRS

The phoneme, again, is the smallest segment that is used to create a new word. When words differ only in one speech sound and all of the others are identical, they are called a *minimal pair.* For example, the following are minimal pairs for the sounds /t/ and /d/:

damper	reteam	rode
tamper	redeem	wrote

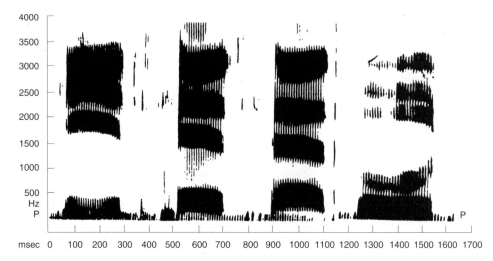

Figure 3.1. Spectrogram of the words *heed, head, had,* and *who'd,* as spoken by a person with a British accent. (Figure from AN INTRODUCTION TO LANGUAGE, Sixth Edition [p. 364], by Victoria A. Fromkin and Robert Rodman copyright © 1998 by Holt, Rinehart and Winston, reproduced by permission of the publisher.) (*Key:* Hz = hertz, msec = milliseconds)

Notice that the term *minimal pair* refers to the sequence of speech sounds, not the conventional spellings; the sounds may be similar although the spellings differ. Phonemes distinguish words or determine the difference between one word and another. As mentioned previously, the linguist's first test for whether a sound is a phoneme is to identify a minimal pair of words in which a target sound replaces a sound in one word to make a different word.

Phonemes are described by linguists as having sets of **distinctive features.** Each distinctive feature is a controllable aspect of articulation that a phoneme either has or does not have. For example, the feature *voiced* is either present (shown by a plus sign) or not present (shown by a minus sign). The phoneme [b] is [+voiced] and the phoneme [p] is [–voiced]. Both [b] and [p] share the features [+labial] and [+consonantal]. The phoneme [m] shares the features [+labial], [+consonantal], and [+anterior] with [p] and [b] but is also [+nasal], whereas the others are [–nasal]. Each phoneme is essentially a combination of features such as these and others. A partial description of the phoneme [s] is [–syllabic] [+consonantal] [–sonorant] [–voiced] [+continuant] [–nasal] [+strident] [–lateral] [+anterior]. Here are more examples of minimal pairs and minimal sets of words in English:

Consonant voicing	Place of articulation	Continuancy	Lateral/central
teeth	leaf	leash	seer
teethe	lease	leech	seal

Vowel placement

bowel	bought	pin	cot	put
bile	boat	pen	caught	putt
boil	boot	pan	cut	pout

PHONETIC VARIATION

The difference between phonology and phonetics, the psychological perception of speech segments and the actual physical production of them, can be illustrated with the concept of **phonetic variation.** Allophones are phonetic variants or versions of a phoneme that are produced differently according to where they are in a word and what sounds precede or follow them. These variations, however, do not create new words.

To illustrate, the words *table, swept, bitter,* and *tray* all have the phoneme /t/; that is, if you were asked to identify the sound represented by the letter *t* in those words, you would say /t/. All of the sounds that we identify or classify as /t/ in our minds are in fact spoken slightly differently. The first sound in *table* is aspirated, or articulated with a push of breath that does not characterize the articulation of the [t] on the end of *swept,* and is notated as [t^h] to indicate the aspiration. The letters *tt* in *bitter* are pronounced as a tongue flap [ɾ] with the tongue coming up behind the teeth; the tongue taps the alveolar ridge only briefly, and the vocal cords keep vibrating throughout. The /t/ before an /r/, as in *tray,* is pronounced with affrication, close to the sound of [č]. Many children in fact will spell *tray* as CHRA until they are deliberately taught that *tr* blends sound as though they should be spelled *chr* but are to be recognized as *tr.* But we would not think that the word *tray* pronounced with [t] was a different word from the *tray* pronounced with a beginning sound close to [č]. We would not think that the word *swept* pronounced with an aspirated [t^h] was a different word from the *swept* pronounced without an aspirated [t^h].

Much variation in individual speech patterns is **systematic,** or driven by a set of rules for the production of sounds in words. Some phonetic variation is **nonsystematic.** That is, not all speakers of a language change the phonemes in the same way. For example, in northern New England, some people say [ɛ́ləmɛnteri] instead of [ɛləméntri] for *elementary,* but whether the word is pronounced that way is a matter of choice (nonsystematic variation). Still, regional variation in speech is usually attributable to slightly varying phonological rule systems that are shared by speakers in that region or group. The variations do not affect our understanding of the meaning of the word being spoken. Many people in Boston say [pæk] for *park.* Many people in Texas say [pɪn] for *pen. Britches* was a western American version of the English *breeches,* but both words still refer to pants. If a child puts a glottal stop in the middle of the word *little* and says [lɪʔl], the meaning is understood. If you say [t^{h}omɑto] and I say [t^{h}omeɾo], the conversation will continue and we will have the same referent in mind. Such variation in utterance is often determined by dialect or by a subtly varying rule system.

ALLOPHONES

Variation that is systematic and rule based is called *allophonic variation.* Allophones are phonetic variants, or **phones,** that are produced in a **predictable** way by the speakers who share a language system. The predictable, rule-based changes in pronunciation are **surface** expressions (allophones) of **underlying** phonemes. To clarify the difference, slashes / / indicate phonemes and phoneme representations, and brackets [ ] denote allophones or phonetic realizations of those phonemes. The phonological rules that govern the translation of phonemes into allophones are unconscious and applied automatically by speakers who acquired the language naturally. Several predictable allophonic variations are important for interpreting spelling and reading behavior because they explain the systematic ways that speech often varies from print, as well as the reasons that certain sounds and symbols are confusable. When these are understood, children's speech, reading, and spelling errors make much more sense.

SYSTEMATIC VARIATION IN SPEECH SOUND PRODUCTION

As discussed in the previous section, speech sounds can be described at several levels, ranging from an abstract, psychological level to a concrete, physical level. On the abstract level, each speech sound that contrasts with other speech sounds has an identity that is determined by a set of features, such as voicing, nasality, or stopping. For example, the final sounds of *his* [hɪz] and *hiss* [hɪs] share some overlapping features: Both are alveolar fricatives. They differ, however, in the critical feature of voicing. The same is true of the plural in *cubs* [kʌbz] and *cups* [kʌps]; however, in this case, we must account for the fact that the plural units represented by *s* have the same meaning and different phonetic forms. To account for this phenomenon, we could state that there is a plural morpheme, {PLU}, whose form is similar to an abstract phoneme /s/. The realization of the spoken plural, however, depends on the application of a rule that governs how this plural morpheme is pronounced when it follows specific sounds. A phonetic description is one that describes how the abstract plural form /s/ is spoken in *cats*, *dogs*, and *wishes*. The phonetic production of a plural ending is the result of a systematic phonological translation process that converts an abstract linguistic construct (or category of features that distinguish a phoneme) into a physical reality, as in

$$cat + \{PLU\} = /kæt/ + /z/ \text{ or } /s/ = [kæts]$$

We choose which pronunciation to use automatically by rule. For example, we add a voiceless ending, [s], to words that end in a voiceless consonant, such as [t]. Several of these regular phonological alternations come up again and again in teaching language skills to children. Some of the most significant are discussed here in more detail.

Reduction of Vowels to Schwa

In words of more than one syllable, one syllable gets primary stress and the others are either unstressed or given secondary stress. Often, vowels will be pronounced as a neutral schwa [ə] with its allophones or as unaccented [ɨ] as in *picnic*, especially in words of Latin origin. The schwa is the most commonly spoken vowel in English, accounting for 20% of all vowels uttered.[2] Schwa is spoken with neutral pronunciation, as in *about*, *definition*, and *upon*, and has no special letter in spelling, although the letters *o, a,* and *i* are used most often for the sound.[3] When the phonemes in the word *tempest* are spoken as [tʰɛmpəst], the second syllable is unaccented and the second vowel becomes a schwa. This occurs by phonological rule; we do not have to think about where to place stress or how to pronounce the vowel.

Consider the differences among the following words: *photograph, photography,* and *photographic.* The stress pattern in each word shifts to accommodate the new syllable structure. When we speak, we apply the changes in stress automatically because we know not only the specific words but also the way the pattern of stress works in English. If we were asked to read nonsense words that follow the same pattern, we would apply stress and reduce vowels to schwas by the same set of stress rules: *milograph, milography,* and *milographic.*

☆ EXERCISE 3.1

Underline the unaccented vowels that have lost their distinctiveness in pronunciation (schwas). Write other forms of the words, if any, in which the vowels recover an identity. Your perceptions may be different from someone else's.

imitate _____   expository _____

blossom _____   argumentative _____

about _____   orthographic _____

application _____   competent _____

complexity _____   deleterious _____

narrative _____   beautiful _____

Vowel Nasalization

Every time a vowel is spoken before a nasal consonant, that vowel is nasalized. Vowel nasalization is nondistinctive in English; that is, nasalization of a vowel does not create a different phoneme and a different word. It is difficult, however, to avoid nasalizing the vowel before a nasal consonant because we do this so automatically. With each pair of words in the following list, you should be able to feel the channeling of resonance through the nose on the vowels preceding nasal consonants, and the lack of nasal resonance on the other vowels that are not followed by a nasal consonant. To detect this phenomenon, hold your nose and say the following pairs of words:

and	add
limb	lib
bunk	buck
went	wet
gang	gag
don't	dote

The nasalization phenomenon becomes important in understanding one of the most common characteristics of children's early spelling and the spelling errors of children who are not good spellers. Frequently, these children omit the nasal consonant in a word when the nasal comes before a final stop consonant and after a vowel, as in WOT for *want*, FED for *friend*, SAD for *sand*, SIG for *sing*, and JUP for *jump*. These omissions often occur even in compositions in which the nasal consonants /m/, /n/, and /ŋ/ are spelled correctly in the beginnings or ends of words.

Why does the omission of nasals after vowels and before final consonants occur? In essence, the nasal phoneme in the spoken word becomes absorbed by the vowel before it and the final consonant after it, especially when the final consonant is a voiceless stop. Say the word *can't*. Phonemically it is /kʰænt/; phonetically it is [kʰæt] (the tilde [˜] over the vowel denotes nasalization). There is no separate, distinct speech gesture for the nasal phoneme /n/. The nasal quality becomes part of the preceding vowel because that vowel is automatically nasalized by a phonological production rule, and the place of articulation for [n] was unified with the articulation of the final consonant [t]. Thus, if a child were to spell the word *can't* as CAT, the child's phonetic spelling would be very close to phonetic reality. Note that the presence of a nasal consonant before a vowel has no effect on the vowel that follows it. For example, the word *net* does not have a nasalized vowel.

Consonant Aspiration

Experienced teachers know that children make more errors with consonants at the ends of words than with other consonants during phoneme awareness, reading, and spelling instruction. But why should the endings of words be more difficult? The answer may have more to do with the properties of sounds at the ends of words than with the fact that the consonants are the last letters of a sequence.

Aspiration is characteristic of voiceless stop consonants in certain positions only. That is, voiceless stop consonants /k/, /p/, and /t/ have at least two allophonic forms: an aspirated form, [kʰ], [pʰ], and [tʰ], and an unaspirated form, [k], [p], and [t]. The aspirated forms of these sounds are detectable if you put your hand about an inch from your mouth. When a consonant is aspirated, you should feel a small explosion of breath against your palm. Say the following phrases, and try to detect where that push of breath occurs:

> *Candy canes make good presents.*
> *Let's play Star Trek.*

The push of breath can be felt at the beginning of *Candy, canes, presents, play,* and *Trek,* as denoted in the phonetic transcription of the sentences:

> [kʰæ̃ndi kʰẽnz mek gʊd pʰrɛzɵ̃nts]
> [lɛts pʰle stɑr tʰrɛk]

It is possible to determine when aspiration occurs and whether it is a predictable variation—one that occurs by phonological rule in the speech of anyone who uses the language. We can do this by observing what is similar about all of the occurrences of an aspirated /p/, /t/, or /k/ and what is true about the instances when /p/, /t/, and /k/ are not aspirated:

Aspirated	_Unaspirated_	
(beginning of syllable)	(second consonant)	(word-final)
place	spend	soap
appalled	scare	sock
clean	stable	knot
accountant		
tame		
attend		

These observations could be summarized as follows. When a voiceless stop consonant occurs in the beginning of a stressed syllable, it will be aspirated. Under other conditions, these stops are not aspirated, such as when they are the second sound in a blend or when they come after the vowel in a syllable. The alternation of these allophones is _predictable;_ they are thus said to be in **complementary distribution** because each of the two never occurs in the phonemic environment as the other. Predictably, the aspirated and unaspirated forms of the consonants occur in specific places in a word.

The unaspirated forms of the unvoiced stops can sometimes sound or feel like their voiced equivalents. That is, /p/ can be confused with /b/, /t/ with /d/, and /k/ with /g/. Children's spelling errors often show their tendency to confuse these sounds. It is common to see such substitutions as the following: SBOYDR for _spider,_ CUB for _cup,_ SGOL for _school,_ HOSBIDL for _hospital,_ and SIG for _sick._ Notice that these confusions are much more likely to occur when the sounds are in the second part of a blend or in word-final position, that is, when they are not aspirated.

☆ EXERCISE 3.2

Write these words phonetically, using the aspiration sign [ʰ] for aspirated voiceless stops, the schwa [ə] for unaccented vowels, and the tilde [˜] above nasalized vowels that precede nasal consonants.

kitchen_____	steam _____
purchase _____	challenge _____
tender _____	approve _____
problem _____	snap _____
skate _____	threat _____
spirit _____	solution _____

Vowel Lengthening

The terms "long" and "short" to describe the sets of vowels in English are misnomers. There is such a thing as vowel length, but it is not synonymous with the _duration_ of vowel articulation, that is, how many milliseconds are needed to pronounce a vowel. Consider the following words:

seize	cease	sped	speck
bed	bet	live	lift
keel	keep	hag	hack
heed	heat	rise	rice

In these pairs, the vowels in the first column are actually spoken with slightly longer duration than the vowels in the second column. Can you determine what causes this variation?

The consonant in front of the vowel obviously has nothing to do with the length of the vowel sound because each of these pairs begins with the same consonant. The consonant after the vowel, however, does determine its length. As you may have guessed, the voicing of the consonant following the vowel determines its length. It is therefore important to tell children that the labels "long" and "short" are quite arbitrary. At one time in history, the labels were directly descriptive of vowels as they were spoken in Middle English, but many of those distinctions have since been lost. The vowels have changed so much that the labels have little meaning. But the lengthening of a vowel in co-articulated words is another predictable phenomenon, governed by phonological rule, that pertains to the sequences of sounds in words and the effect of some sounds on others.

Flapping of Medial /t/ and /d/

Say the following words naturally, as you would say them in a phrase or a sentence:

putting	pudding	tally	dally
writer	rider	temple	dimple
little	Liddy	latter	ladder
tire	dire		

The sounds /t/ and /d/ in the first two columns are pronounced very similarly to one another, differently from the initial /t/ and /d/ in the words of the last two columns. In each of the first two columns, the medial /t/ and /d/ are pronounced as an alveolar flap, or tongue flap, [ɾ]. This is not lazy speech because most American English speakers change these sounds in medial position by a predictable phonological rule. The /t/ and /d/ are pronounced as a tongue flap when they occur between two vowels and the second vowel is not stressed, as in *photograph* [forəgræf]. Notice that flapping does not automatically occur in words such as *rooster* and *panda* because the /t/ and /d/ in those words occur between a consonant and a vowel.

Affrication

The affricates are the phonemes [č] and [ǰ] that comprise two vocal gestures: a stop of breath followed by a fricative. In some phoneme environments, /t/ and /d/ are affricated; that is, before certain speech sounds, [t] is articulated like a [č] and [d] is articulated like a [j] because of the influence of the phoneme that follows. Say the following words:

take	train	attack	actuary
desk	dress	actor	furniture
addict	educate	could he	could you

In each of the words in the right-hand column, the [t] or [d] that is affricated is followed by an [r] or the glide [j]. The mouth must pucker in anticipation of the [r] or the [j]. The glide after the [č] or [j] in the examples *educate, actuary,* and *furniture* is hidden. Spelling does not show the presence of [j] directly; the letter *u* in those three words stands for the combination of the glide [j] and [u], as it does in the word *you.* Sometimes this combination is called "long *u*" in phonics texts; sometimes the combination is classified as a diphthong in phonics systems. At any rate, the affrication of alveolar stops before [ju] is automatic for most American English speakers. When children spell words with *tr* or *dr* blends, such as *train* or *dress,* or when they spell words such as *educate,* they are likely to write CHRAN, JRS, or EGUKAT until they learn consciously to ignore the concrete phonetic details of speech. Teachers can reassure children that their perception is correct: Their mouths do say what they are writing, but pronunciation is not spelled so literally.

Vowel Raising Before a Velar (Back) Consonant

Say the following words:

Lax vowel	*Lax and raised vowel*
bat	bag, bank
etch	egg, Engle
icky	igloo, ink

In the first column, the words contain front, lax ("short") vowels in their pure form. In the second column, the vowels sound slightly different. The subtle changes in the vowels in the second column occur because the tongue is raised to anticipate the velar consonants [k], [ŋ], and [g]. Thus, in each word in the second column, the lax vowel comes out sounding more like the tense vowel next to it on the diagram showing vowel articulation (see Figure 2.4). When children write the word *bag* as BAEG, the word *egg* as AG, or the word *igloo* as EGLOO, they are demonstrating awareness of the literal phonetic characteristics of the words. They have yet to learn about the more abstract nature of English orthography.

☆ EXERCISE 3.3

What phonological principle is shown in children's spelling of each set of words below (invented spelling in capital letters before the target word)?

1.   LAG/leg   ENK/ink   EGLU/igloo
2.   CHRIK/trick   GRAK/drink   CHRA/tray
3.   SWEDR/sweater   PUDING/putting   PEDE/pretty

SEQUENCES, SYLLABLES, AND STRESS

When a teacher plays Hangman with a class of children who already know some-thing about spelling, some children will make logical guesses and some will not. The children who make logical guesses not only are better at keeping track of which letters have been asked already but also have a better sense of the order in which sounds and letters occur in words. The words in any language are limited to cer-tain permissible sequences of phonemes. These possibilities are influenced by ease of pronunciation, but often the sequences are arbitrary and simply part of the grammar of the language. Suppose that you were asked to create possible or pro-nounceable words in English using only these four phonemes:

/ŋ/   /l/   /ɛ/   /b/

The only sequence that would be possible is [blɛ̃ŋ]. No words in English can start with /ŋ/; no blends start with /l/; no beginning blends have /ŋ/ as the second phoneme; and there is no sequence [ŋb] or [bŋ] in English syllables, so the only pro-nounceable option is [bl] in the beginning, with [ɛ] and [ŋ] following.

When words begin with an affricate, a liquid, a glide, or a nasal, the next sound must be a vowel. In English we cannot create words such as *yburtz, lgas,* or *chwot* for this reason. There can be no more than three consonant sounds at the beginning of a word, and these are limited to the following possibilities in first, second, and third position: /s/ + /p, t, k/ + /l, r, w, y/. Thus, we have the words *sprain* [sprẽn], *strain* [strẽn], *square* [skwer], and *spew* [spju] beginning with these three-consonant sequences. Not all sequences of these elements are possible, however; we can say the word *strict* but not the word *stlict.*

Homorganic Nasal Rule

Although the **homorganic nasal rule** has a rather strange name, the pattern is uni-versal in the construction of syllables with a nasal phoneme preceding another consonant. Consider these words (note that the [ŋ] in the third column of words is spelled with *n*):

[m]	[n]	[ŋ]
jump	gentle	jungle
jumble	gender	junk
symbiotic	sentinel	singular
sympathy	send	sink

Can you determine which consonants follow each of the nasal consonants [m], [n], and [ŋ]? Once again it is easy to be fooled by spelling, and it is important to think only of the sound sequences represented in these words. Sound sequences must be arranged so that the sounds are articulated in the same place. Therefore, bilabial [m] must precede the bilabials [p] and [b], alveolar [n] must precede the alveolars [t] and [d], and velar [ŋ] must precede the velars [k] and [g]. When children say "punkin" [pãŋkĩn] for *pumpkin,* they are applying this rule automatically in creating their version of the word.

☆ EXERCISE 3.4

Find at least 10 more examples of words that demonstrate the homorganic nasal rule. Sort them into those that have /m/, /n/, or /ŋ/ after a vowel, and look at the consonant that follows each nasal sound. Does the principle of sound sequencing hold?

Syllables

As mentioned before, phonemes are an abstraction. We do not pronounce separate phonemes when we speak. We pronounce syllables or clusters of phonemes grouped around a vowel. Syllables may be **simple** or **complex.** A simple syllable has a vowel that may be preceded or followed by a single consonant; a complex syllable has two or more consonants in a cluster before or after a vowel. Syllables may have any of the following combinations of consonants (C) or vowels (V), in progression from most simple to most complex:

Syllable structure	Example
V	I
CV	me
VC	ice
VCC	ask
CVC	sack
CCV	ski
CCVC	skin
CVCC	cans
CCVCC	stops
CCCVC	scream
CCCVCC	squeaks
CCVCCC	starts
CCCVCCC	scrimped

Note again that the structures listed here pertain to phoneme sequences, not letters; therefore, *ice* [ajs] is two phonemes.

The complex syllables that contain consonant clusters (blends) are more difficult for children to read and spell than are the simple syllables. We know that this is the case because many of children's errors involve the omission or substitution of sounds in consonant clusters, especially the internal sound in a cluster.[4] When consonants exist in clusters before or after vowels, they are difficult to segment because the phonemes tend to be stuck tightly together in articulation. That is, phonetically, the duration of consonant pronunciation is often shorter within a cluster. Phoneme awareness of consonant clusters tends to develop after reading instruction is started, after kindergarten for many typical 5- and 6-year-olds.

Therefore, the complexity of syllable structure is important to consider in design-
ing phoneme awareness, decoding, and spelling tasks for students. The word *blast*
is not simply one with more sounds than the word *bat,* it is linguistically more difficult to pronounce and learn because of the presence of two blends.

Most people who understand the definition of a syllable will have little trouble
identifying how many syllables there are in a word. The **boundaries** between syllables, however, may be cause for disagreement because the natural breaks between
syllables do not correspond to the syllable division rules used by editors and in dictionaries and because syllable boundaries are simply ambiguous, even to linguists.
The word *yell* is one syllable, and the word *yellow* is two, but where is the boundary
in the second word? Is the [l] part of the first syllable, part of the second, or part of
both? (The doubled letter is a spelling convention, not a reflection of phonological
reality; there is only one segment [l] in *yellow.*) There are rules that tell us where to
divide words in print (see Chapter 5), but our judgment—and that of linguists—
about where spoken words divide often differs from those conventions.

Although scholars may disagree about where syllables begin and end, they do
agree on a few basic ideas about these natural linguistic units. Every syllable must
have a vowel, and each separate vowel constitutes the peak of a syllable. When two
vowel sounds are adjacent, as in *idiot, poetry,* or *idea,* there is a syllable division
between the vowels (*id-i-ot; po-et-ry; i-de-a*). Second, consonants tend to cluster at
the beginning of a stressed syllable rather than at the end of an unstressed syllable.
In the word *astringent,* the *str* begins the stressed syllable; therefore, speakers who
are asked to find the natural boundaries in the word are likely to divide the word
like this: *a-strin-gent.* Finally, sequential order rules for allowable consonant sequences govern our perceptions of syllable boundaries. The word *only* has to be
divided between the /n/ and the /l/ because these two consonants cannot form a
cluster within a syllable; they can only be adjacent across a syllable boundary. Similarly, *pumpkin* has to be divided between the /p/ and the /k/ because /pk/ is not an
allowable consonant cluster. The existence of these phonological properties of syllables can assist children in deciding where the boundaries of multisyllabic written words are located.

Syllables are much more than strings of phonemes. They have an internal
structure composed of an onset (what, if anything, comes before the vowel) and a
rime (the vowel and what comes after it). Words do not always have an onset; for
example, the words *egg* and *itch* do not have an onset and are structured as rimes.
A word always has a rime because it includes the vowel. The vowel belongs to a
part of the rime called the **peak.** The peak is the part of the syllable with the most
sonority or resonance. The consonants that follow the vowel in the rime are usually called the **coda.** For example, the syllable *trust* has an onset [tʰr] and a rime
with a peak [ʌ] and a coda [st], as shown in the following tree diagram:

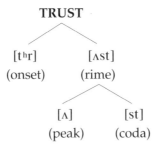

TRUST

[tʰr]   [ʌst]
(onset)   (rime)

[ʌ]   [st]
(peak)   (coda)

Linguists debate whether a sonorant consonant following a vowel can also be part of the syllable peak. In the word *went* [wĕnt], the vowel is nasalized and the nasal consonant is closely bonded to the vowel. Some argue that the nasal consonant coheres with the vowel so much that it, too, is part of the syllable peak, not the coda, which would be /t/ alone. In contrast, the /t/ in *wet* does not adhere to the vowel and is clearly the coda, not part of the peak. Thus, the internal structure of the word varies according to the features or properties of the phonemes and their sequences. The syllable peak includes an inseparable combination of a vowel and a following consonant when the consonant is a liquid /l/ or /r/, such as in *bell, will, fur, her,* and *bird.* That is why children so often confuse the letters in words such as CLOD for *cold,* BRID for *bird,* and GRIL for *girl.* The vowel and the following liquid operate as a unit in the syllable peak, and the printed form of words containing such sound combinations is deceptive. Vowels followed by /r/ are even more cohesive units than those followed by /l/ because the sonority of /r/ is only slightly less than the sonority of a vowel and is greater than that of any other consonant.[5] Nasals seem to adhere both to the peak and to the coda of the rime, spreading out their features in both directions, but other consonants (stops, fricatives, affricates) adhere clearly to the coda.

Even if this discussion seems somewhat abstract, it will make more sense when children's spelling and reading are analyzed closely. When a child spells BRID for *bird* or GRIL for *girl,* the child is making a very sensible linguistic choice. There is no auditory discrimination problem in such instances; the child is writing what, in fact, is in the word—a vowel and a liquid consonant that have become one unit. Therefore, in instruction, the teacher cannot say, "Sound it out," and expect to get better results. The teacher must teach the spellings of *r*-controlled vowels as units (*er, ir, ur, ar, or*) and teach groups of words with each spelling pattern while offering students much practice reading and writing the words in meaningful sentences.

Prosodic Features: Stress and Intonation Patterns

The phonological layer of language also encompasses intonation, phrasing, and stress patterns on words, phrases, and sentences. English does not have a tonal system for vowel production, but the intonation of a phrase does help determine its meaning and resolve any ambiguity that may ensue from the order of words. These sentences may illustrate the importance of intonation and phrasing:

> Marcia did say she was going, didn't she?
> Marcia did say she was going, didn't she.
>
> I *expect* her to show up later.
> I expect *her* to show up later.
> I expect her to show up *later.*

The phrase stress in a sentence will determine which of a number of possible meanings is intended by a single word string. Stress will occur on the nouns, verbs, adjectives, and/or adverbs that should carry the central meaning. Whole phrases and sentences are changed by stress and intonation patterns in which one syllable (usually the most meaningful word) is stressed more than the others. That a sentence ends with a downward contour in English statements can affect how well children remember or process sentences during writing or speaking. Sometimes a child's writing will contain clear examples of his or her "losing" the unstressed parts of words and phrases (see Figure 3.2).

Any multisyllabic word will have a primary stress and sometimes a secondary stress applied as part of the word's form. Individuals with phonological processing weaknesses often have trouble achieving awareness of stress in a word, a phrase, or a sentence, even though they speak with standard intonation patterns. Some stress patterns may vary according to region or dialect, but most are standard enough to merit a preferred pronunciation by writers of dictionaries. A few are a matter of choice; *élementary* and *eleméntary* are two accepted versions of this word. How do you say the word *address*? Especially challenging for students with a weak sense of phonology is the pronunciation of morphologically related words, such as *philosophy* and *philosophical,* that shift the stress from one syllable to the next. More is said about patterns with phonological shifts in Chapter 4.

SUMMARY

Phonology is the study of the speech sound system of a language. It includes but is not limited to the study of phonetics, the physical description of the inventory of speech sounds. Speakers of a language actually produce many subtle variants of phonemes called *allophones.* Allophonic variation occurs according to phonological rules. Phonemes are really groups or classes of speech sounds that are perceived to be similar because they share distinctive features. When those segments are spoken in patterns governed by systematic rules, they are in complementary distribution and their forms are predictable according to their place in words and phrases. For example, /t/ and /d/ are always affricated before /r/ and /j/ but not before other consonants. A phoneme can be used in combination with others to make a word. Its existence is verified by the existence of minimal pairs of words that differ only in one phoneme.

The syllable is a **suprasegmental**, or overarching, unit with a hierarchical internal structure. Every syllable must have a vowel that serves as the syllable nucleus. Syllables may have an onset, or a consonant or consonant cluster before a vowel, and must have a rime, or the vowel and any consonants that follow it. These

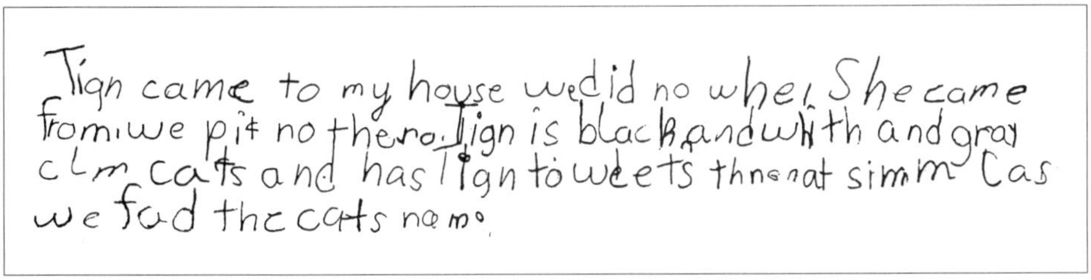
Tign came to my house we did no whe. She came
from we pit no thero. Tign is black and whith and gray
clm cats and has Tign to weets thnenat simm Cas
we fad the cats namo.

Figure 3.2. Writing sample from K.T., a second-grade student. When asked to read her writing aloud, K.T. said (with some difficulty deciphering her own writing), "Tiger came to our house. We did not know what to do. We put it on the radio. Tiger is black and white and gray colored cat and has tiger. For two weeks then at swimming lessons we found the cat's owner."

are natural segments that have psychological reality. The vowel and sometimes a following consonant form the syllable peak. A consonant or consonant cluster following the vowel sometimes form the coda.

The phonological system of any language includes rules or constraints about the order and place of speech sounds in words and the specific ways they should be articulated. Languages differ not only in their inventory of phonemes but also in the rules that specify how these phonemes can be combined. Pitch, stress, and intonation all are part of the phonological system.

☆ SUPPLEMENTARY EXERCISES

1. Reverse the sequence of speech sounds in each of these words, or say them backward. Think of the sounds, not the letters.

teach	lip	palm
sigh	easy	cash
cuts	judge	snitch
pitch	speak	face

2. Do this exercise with an adult partner. Say each word. Then ask your partner to say the word again without the part marked in parentheses ("Say the word *man*. Now say it again without the [m]").

(m)eat	ma(ke)	st(r)eam	off(er)ing
(b)and	(s)kill	sc(r)am	dri(v)er
sol(d)	(g)lass	boa(s)t	in(ve)stigate

3. In each of the following minimal pairs of spoken words, two phonemes contrast to form different words. Identify by number, from the right-hand column, the primary feature by which each contrasting phoneme pair differs:

tick, chick _____	a) voicing
seek, sick _____	b) nasalization
rich, ridge _____	c) front/back placement
keel, cool _____	d) tenseness/laxness
whet, when _____	e) affrication

4. Automatic aspiration of /p/, /t/, and /k/ in the beginning of words is the result of an unconscious phonological rule in action. When does aspiration occur? What difference might aspiration, or lack of it, make to the ease with which students learn to decode and spell these phonemes?

5. Write concise definitions for the following terms:

    Phonology

    Phonetics

    Phoneme

    Allophone (phone)

6. Think of minimally contrasting pairs of words that differ only in the
    target sounds in initial, medial, and final position.
    Example: /p/, /b/   pest, best   scrapple, scrabble   cap, cab

                     Initial   *Medial*   *Final*

    /k/, /g/

    /ǰ/, /č/

    /t/, /n/

    /s/, /š/

    /f/, /v/

    /ŋ/, /n/

7. Given these four phonemes, how many possible words (real and
    nonsense) can you make with the set that conform to the order rules
    of English phonology? (Words should be pronounceable.) Which
    words have complex syllable structures?

                   /r/, /s/, /k/, /a/

    Example: [raks]

8. a) Some consonant sounds in English never begin a word. List
        them.

    b) List the consonants in English that must always be followed by
        a vowel if they are in the beginning of a syllable. These conso-
        nants would never be followed by another consonant to make
        a blend. (Look back at the consonant inventories in Tables 2.1
        and 2.2.)

9. Here are some phonological rules that affect word production in English. Find a spoken word that is an example of each of these rules:

    a)   Automatic nasalization of a vowel before a nasal consonant

    b)   Reduction of an alveolar stop to a voiced flap when preceded by a stressed vowel and followed by an unstressed vowel

    c)   Elongation of a tense vowel before a voiced final consonant and shortening of a tense vowel before a voiceless final consonant

    d)   Raising of a lax vowel before a voiced velar consonant

10. What do the three words in each of these sets of spelling errors have in common? What phonological processing weaknesses might they represent?

    a)   JELE for *chili*, GARASH for *garage*, SBENT for *spend*

    b)   POIT for *point*, KINCHEN for *kitchen*, FRUT for *front*

    c)   SPEAS for *spears*, COLOL for *color*, TEE for *tree*

ENDNOTES

1. Edwards, 1992.
2. Hanna et al., 1966; Yule, 1996.
3. Hanna et al., 1966.
4. Kibel & Miles, 1994; Treiman, 1997.
5. Treiman, 1997.

ADDITIONAL RESOURCES

Lederer, R. (1990). *Crazy English.* New York: Pocket Books.
Pinker, S. (1999). *Words and rules: The ingredients of language.* New York: Basic Books.
Treiman, R. (1993). *Beginning to spell: A study of first-grade children.* New York: Oxford University Press.

CHAPTER 4

Morphology

The terms *morpheme* and *morphology* are much less familiar to educators than are the terms *phoneme* and *phonology*. Yet, a morpheme is the smallest unit of meaning in language. There have been fewer studies of the role that morphological knowledge plays in reading, vocabulary, and spelling development than there have been studies of the role of phonology. Especially since the demise of Latin in the high school curriculum, it has been uncommon for instructional materials in word recognition, vocabulary, and spelling to systematically explicate the structural components of words and morphological relationships among words. Yet knowledge of word meaning, rapid word recognition, and spelling ability greatly depend on knowledge of word structure at the level of morphemes. Familiarity with morphology is essential for teachers who give instruction in advanced word recognition, vocabulary, and spelling from third grade on.

People who read, spell, and comprehend well typically are aware of the distinctions among words that sound similar, such as *fiscal* and *physical, illicit* and *elicit,* and *specific* and *pacific*. Good readers attend to the parts of words, both spoken and written. They use strategies to distinguish and remember the meanings of words that sound alike, including recognition of meaningful parts. For example,

Portions of this chapter are adapted by permission from Moats, L.C., & Smith, C. (1992). Derivational morphology: Why it should be included in language assessment and instruction. *Language, Speech and Hearing Services in Schools, 23,* 312–319; © American Speech-Language-Hearing Association.

someone with a deeper knowledge of word structure might know that *il-* in *illicit* means "not" and that *e-* in *elicit* means "out of." Furthermore, students with better awareness of morphemes can recognize when words might be related even when the words are pronounced differently, as in *resign* and *resignation, legal* and *legislate, litigate* and *litigious,* and *please* and *pleasant.* With morphological knowledge, a good reader can guess at a definition for a word first encountered in text, such as *exposition:* It comes from *expose,* which has two morphemes, *ex-*meaning "out of" and *pose* meaning "put or place." Thus, an exposition puts out information.

Incomplete knowledge of morphology accounts for some of the most amusing speech and spelling errors that children produce. Children between the ages of 5 and 7 commonly use word parts creatively and inaccurately as they are trying to learn the rules and components of word building:

- After going to the circus, a child said "That was a great deformance!"

- Leaving the class for tutoring in Intensive Phonics, one student said, "It's time for Offensive Phonics!"

- After being asked about his aspirations about creating things, a boy said, "I want to be a preventor!"

- Complimenting her mother who complained about feeling pudgy, a girl said, "Mom, you're a completely unpudgable person! My stomach is unholdable inable!"

The ability to use words well depends on levels of linguistic knowledge that are gained slowly with much exposure to text: knowledge of words' sound structures, grammatical categories, meanings, and spellings. This chapter discusses units of meaning called *morphemes*—linguistic entities that may be whole words, parts of words, or single phonemes.

MORPHEMES: THE SMALLEST MEANINGFUL UNITS

A *morpheme* is the most elemental unit of grammatical form that has both sound and meaning. *Morphos* means "form" or "structure" in Greek; *eme* means an "element" or "little piece" of something. A morpheme may be one or more syllables (*red, indigo, crocodile*); a morpheme may or may not be a word (*full* versus *-ful* as in *wonderful*). **Free morphemes** can stand alone as words and do not have to be combined with other morphemes (*spite, woman, elephant*). They may be made up of one or more syllables. Free morphemes are assigned to a few broad categories that govern how we remember and use the words. They may be **function words,** including **conjunctions** (*but*), **prepositions** (*below*), **pronouns** (*he*), **auxiliary verbs** (*was*), and **articles** (*a, an*), that are limited in number, learned early, and commonly used as the grammatical glue of sentences. The other class of free morphemes is **content words,** including nouns, verbs, adjectives, and adverbs. Unlike function words, content words are invented regularly as a language evolves. Most of the new words we encounter during reading are content words. **Compounds,** which are generally composed of Anglo-Saxon words, are combinations of two free morphemes, such as *tattletale, lighthouse,* and *yellowfin.*

Bound morphemes work as meaningful units only in combination with other morphemes. These include the suffixes that are grammatical endings (**inflections**) such as *-ed, -est, -er,* and *-ing;* bound **roots** (primarily from Latin); and **prefixes** and **suffixes,** including parts such as *peri-, ex-, bi-, -fer, -tract, -ject, -ity, -ible,* and *-ment.* Bound morphemes must be combined with others and never stand alone (*spiteful, womanly, elephantiasis, incredible, defected, amorous*). See Figure 4.1 for a tree diagram of the different types of morphemes. The terms in the diagram are discussed in greater detail later in this chapter.

How to Identify a Morpheme

Identification of morphemes in words without reference to a dictionary is often more challenging than one would expect. After all, the identification of meaningful parts in words seems as though it would be more straightforward than counting elusive phonemes. If one attempts to identify morphemes without a dictionary at one's elbow, two quick tests are helpful: 1) Can the linguistic unit be defined or paraphrased, and 2) can another word be identified in which the morpheme is used? For example, we know that there is no definable part *flow-* in *flower* but that *-spire* in *conspire* does work as a meaningful part in *inspire, perspire, respiration,* and so forth. The relatedness of word parts and their function within words are not always transparent; words sometimes contain a letter or sound combination that can be a morpheme in some words but that is not a morpheme in others, such as *sub-,* which is not a morpheme in *subtle.* One must think of the structure and meaning of a whole word before deciding whether a word part is a morpheme. When questions arise, the dictionary usually yields information about a word's origin, structure, and meaning.

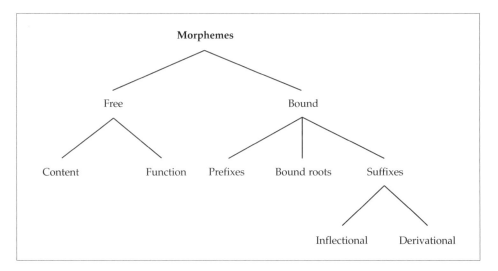

Figure 4.1.   Morpheme types.

☆ EXERCISE 4.1

1. Underline the base word (free morpheme) from which each longer word is constructed:

   tearful   antidisestablishmentarianism

   humorous   warmly

   fortunate   kingdom

   unlike   knighthood

   return   misspell

2. Identify all of the morphemes in these words:

   watchdog   telemarketing   contract

   mistletoe   odometer   injection

   piped   prevaricate   biodegradable

   dodgers   illegal   power

Even though the words in Exercise 4.1 are fairly easy to divide into morpheme units, the complexities of morphology begin to appear as soon as one begins morphological analysis. First, the identity of morphemes is not always obvious. How does one divide the word *telemarketing*, a relatively new entry into the English language? There is such a thing as *telemarking*, a type of turn in skiing, but the word *market* does not divide into two morphemes. (*Telemarking* is named after a county in Norway; *telemarketing* is a Greek combining form [a Greek morpheme that combines flexibly with others] *tele*, added to an Anglo-Saxon noun *market*, which is transformed into a gerund with the addition of the grammatical morpheme, *ing*.) Finding morphemes is not the same as "finding the little words in the bigger words" as children are sometimes urged to do. The word *illegal* has a prefix *il-* (*in-*), a root *leg*, and a suffix *-al*, but the root is the same as that in *legislate* and is unrelated to the Anglo-Saxon word for a lower extremity of the body.

Complex Relationship Between Form and Meaning

The relationship between language form and meaning in English can be complex and variable, just as the relationship between sound and symbol is complex and variable. The word *power* has an *-er* ending, but the ending is not a morpheme in this word; the word *power* is one free morpheme with two syllables. The word *mistletoe* does not have a prefix *mis-*; neither does the word *period* have a prefix *peri-*. The word *contract* would appear to have the combined meaning of the prefix *con-* and the root *tract*, which literally would mean "pull against," but instead the word means "pull with" in Latin. As it happens, the prefix *con-* in *contract* does not mean "against" as it does in *contrary*; the prefix is simply an alternate spelling for *com-*, meaning "with" or "together," changed so that it can be pronounced more easily in front of *tract*, which begins with an alveolar consonant.

☆ EXERCISE 4.2

Identify the number of morphemes in these words:

softer _____	delirious _____	felt _____
teacher _____	higher _____	serious _____
water _____	fire _____	
butter _____	melt _____	

The grammatical rules of English limit the number of words to which we can add certain prefixes and suffixes. Thus, we can say that morphemes are only **partially productive.** Their use is confined to specific words or specific types of words. We can add the suffix -*ment* to verbs to create nouns such as *enjoyment, refinement,* and *endearment,* but the words *rejectment* and *acceptment* do not exist. We can have *equality* but not *equalness, reddish* but not *cloudish,* and *beautification* but not *uglification* (although this is now a word in some unabridged dictionaries). Some **derivational morphemes** are more widely applied than others, such as *non-* to negate an adjective, adverb, or noun, but few are applied to all possible base or root forms.

Finally, morpheme combinations do not always mean what the parts suggest. We can say that an event is *unlikely* or that we *dislike* someone, but there is no word *dislikely,* and if one thing is *unlike* another, that word means something quite different from an *unlikely* occurrence. *Apartment* may be derived from *apart,* meaning "divided," but the relationship between the word and its root is not as obvious to most speakers as that of *place* and *placement.* From *syllabify* we can *syllabificate;* from *syllabicate* we get *syllabication,* and each form seems to be acceptable—all four of these words exist. Language evolves, so meanings change over time, word forms are added and deleted, and derivational constructions that were once transparent assume other meanings. Consider the word *unspeakable.* An unspeakable event is often talked about a great deal because it is uncommonly horrific.

Several researchers have estimated that more than 80% of derived words do mean what their parts suggest,[1] as long as multiple meanings of the roots are taken into account. For example, *disengage* does mean "uncouple" but not in the sense of ending a marriage or an engagement. *Scripture* connotes holy or spiritual text, not just any kind of writing, a meaning that is easier to grasp with the historical knowledge that *scribes,* people who could write, translated or copied the Bible and other religious texts. The word *incredible* would be interpreted literally to mean "not to be believed"; however, its connotation is great superiority, as is that of the word *matchless.*

☆ EXERCISE 4.3

Create some possible and some impossible words from the following menu by mixing and matching word parts:

Prefix	Root	Suffix	Word	Impossible word
inter	spir(e)	(a)tion	_____	_____
dis	cred	icate	_____	_____

Prefix	Root	Suffix	Word	Impossible word
non	sect	(i)able	_____	_____
pre	var	arian	_____	_____
in	rupt	ed	_____	_____

Meaning, Pronunciation, and Word Relatedness

Morphological knowledge allows us to judge when words are related in meaning even when they are pronounced differently, as in *wild* and *wilderness, judge* and *judicial,* and *logic* and *logician.* To a great extent, our knowledge of morphology develops as we learn to read and spell. We would be able to see that words such as *wild* and *wilderness* are related even if we had not thought about this from hearing or saying the words. English orthography often delineates for us the meaningful parts of words, preserving them in spelling even though the pronunciation of the morphemes varies as in *phone, phonetics,* and *phonics* or in *define* and *definition.*[2]

Words that share a morpheme base may be closely or distantly related in meaning. Whether words are related in meaning can be determined by the collective judgment of a community of language users. When speakers of a language are asked to judge whether words come from each other or are connected in meaning, their opinions generally converge because they are members of a language community. Both semantic and phonetic similarity between words affect whether adults judge the words as related. Whether a meaningful connection between words is perceived as close, distant, or nonexistent is influenced as much by spelling knowledge as it is by sound similarity.[3] For example, literate adults know that *wise* and *wisdom, doubt* and *dubious, number* and *numerous,* and *please* and *pleasant* are related word forms. They can overlook the differences in pronunciation between the word pairs when deciding whether the words have meaning in common. Exposure to both spoken and written language accounts for the development of the ability to tell whether words are indeed related to one another.

☆ EXERCISE 4.4

Place the number 1, 2, 3, or 4 next to the word pairs that follow, according to the degree of relatedness or similarity you perceive. Words with 1 are definitely related in meaning, words with 2 are related but somewhat less closely, words with 3 seem to have a more distant connection, and words with 4 do not have a meaningful connection.[4]

_____ doubt, dubious

_____ deep, depth

_____ ham, hamburger

_____ bomb, bombard

_____ holy, holiday

_____ joy, join

_____ sheep, shepherd

_____ scribble, scripture

_____ iris, iridescence

_____ amnesty, amniotic

_____ serene, serenity

_____ hand, handkerchief

_____ catch, ketchup

_____ cap, capture

Inflectional and Derivational Morphology

Inflections and morphemes are two kinds of morpheme units that operate differently in word formation.

Inflections: Learned Early

Inflections are bound morphemes that show possession (*hers*), gender (*alumna*), or number (*wishes, crises*) if the word is a noun; tense (*talked*), voice (*he was driven*), or mood if the word is a verb (*she could have been driving*); and comparison (*softer, softest*) if the word is an adjective. Possession and degree can be expressed either morphologically or syntactically. One can say, "That boat was hers," or, "That was her boat"; one can say, "He wanted more curls," or, "He wanted curlier hair." Typically developing children first use inflectional morphology as soon as they begin to combine words into sentences, usually by 2 years of age.[5] For example, children quickly learn to inflect some verbs with the progressive tense marker -*ing* or to mark the concept of more than one with -*s* or -*es*. The rules of grammatical inflectional morphology in speech typically are mastered between the ages of 4 and 7 years.[6]

Most preschoolers have learned the basic inflections for speech purposes before they enter school and before they begin to learn to read and spell, whereas most of their awareness about derivational processes in word building will come from learning to read and spell.[7] Inflections are everpresent and obligatory in the oral language patterns to which children are exposed early on, so it should not be surprising that inflections are learned many years before the derivational forms that children will read, often for the first time, in fourth grade or later. Children learn the system by which the inflections are added before they learn all of the specific inflected forms. Because children are overgeneralizing from an apparent rule, they produce regular or predictable inflected forms before they learn the exceptions. Thus, they are likely to say "goed" for *went*, "taked" for *took*, "keeped" for *kept*, and "mans" for *men* until they learn the specific **suppletive** (irregular) forms that are a legacy from Middle English. As with other dimensions of child language, regular patterns can temporarily overrule the production of unusual forms. The generation of past, plural, and comparative words, such as *bringed, mices,* and *bestest,* dominate before children come to terms with the exceptions, such as *brought, mice,* and *best.*

Inflections do not change the part of speech of the word to which they are added. The word continues to be a noun, verb, or adjective even with the inflection. The plural of *wish* (*wishes*) is still a noun; the past tense of *dance* (*danced*) is still a verb; the superlative of *hard* (*hardest*) is still an adjective. Derivational morphemes often, but not always, change the part of speech of the word to which they are added.

Anglo-Saxon Compounds

English words in use today from the oldest layer of English, Anglo-Saxon, often were formed by compounding and inflecting. Compounding remains a common strategy in modern English for coinage of new words. Many combinations of word types are allowed:

Adjective with adjective: *bittersweet*
Adjective with noun: *hotdog*
Noun with noun: *barnyard*
Noun with verb: *sea-kayaking*
Verb with verb: *sleepwalk*

The grammatical category of the compound will be determined by the last word, not the first. *Hotdog* is a noun, *sleepwalk* is a verb, and so forth. Compounds are characterized more by their stress pattern than by their spelling. Stress almost always occurs on the first word of the compound. Spelling may include a hyphen or a space. There are no hard and fast rules about spelling, and often there is more than one acceptable way to write a compound. *Ice cream* and *White House* are compounds by pronunciation but not by visual joining of the components. Sometimes more than two words make a compound, such as *two-time winner, mother-of-pearl,* and *six-dog sled.*

☆ EXERCISE 4.5

The meaning of a compound is not always the same as the sum of its parts. Define the following words and think about how the meanings of the compounds and their parts compare:

redcoat

laughing gas

looking glass

blackboard

turncoat

bigwig

rubbernecking

Although the meanings of compounds often are different from the meanings of their parts, many compounds are self-defining, such as *turnstile, hardwood,* and *tap dance.* Many languages, especially German, use compounding as a word generation strategy, although the Latin and Greek layers of English contributed other devices for vocabulary building, including the use of roots and combining forms.

Derivational Suffixes

Derivational word-building processes in English are characteristic of the Latin (Romance) layer of English; Latin-derived words along with Greek-derived words compose about 60% of all words used in text.[8] Latin-based words are constructed around a root whose meaning is modified through the addition of prefixes and suffixes (*pro* + *ject* + *ion*). Words derived from Latin roots are most common in expository text of a somewhat formal or nonconversational nature. Again, a major difference between inflectional and derivational morphemes is that inflections added to verbs, nouns, or adjectives do not change the grammatical role or part of speech of the base words. In contrast, most derivational suffixes change the grammatical class of the word. For example, *philosophy* is a noun; *philosophize* is a verb; *philosophical* is an adjective; and *philosopher* is a noun.

Some derivational suffixes are **neutral,** such as *-able* and *-ly*, because they do not change the stress or vowel quality of the word to which they are added.[9] Others are **nonneutral,** such as *-ity*, because they often cause shifts in pronunciation of the base word when the suffix is added (*generous, generosity; curious, curiosity*). The prevalence of nonneutral suffixes accounts for the frequency with which vowels in unaccented syllables are reduced to schwa [ə]. The more complex relationships between words with nonneutral suffixes and the words from which they are derived in turn affect the ease with which children learn to read, spell, and use them in speech.[10]

☆ EXERCISE 4.6

Identify the part of speech of each word in these pairs (noun = n, verb = v, and adjective = a). Some words may serve more than one grammatical role.

preside _____   president _____

legislate _____   legislature _____

compete _____   competition _____

invent _____   inventor _____

sign _____   signify _____

peril _____   perilous _____

disturb _____   disturbance _____

active _____   activity _____

type _____   typify _____

face _____   facial _____

All of the derivational suffixes added to the second column of words in Exercise 4.6 change words predictably from one part of speech to another, and all tend to be used with certain kinds of base words. Words that end in *-er, -or, -cian,* and *-ist* are people nouns; words that end in *-sion* and *-tion* are thing nouns. Nouns can also be made by adding *-ment* and *-ity*. Verbs are made by adding *-ize* and *-ify*, and adverbs are created with *-ly*. The endings *-ar, -ous, -ive, -al,* and *-ful* make adjectives. Morphemic knowledge, which may be largely unconscious, includes awareness of the grammatical function of suffixes.

☆ EXERCISE 4.7

First, identify the parts of speech of the words in the left of the following list (noun = n, verb = v, and adjective = a); then, add suffixes to create derived forms that serve the grammatical functions indicated. You may need to alter the spellings of the original words when adding the suffixes.

generous _____   noun _____

decide _____   adjective _____

successive _____   noun _____

extent _____   verb _____

depend _____   adjective _____

occur _____   noun _____

teach _____   noun _____

pretense _____   verb _____

revise _____   noun _____

intend _____   adverb _____

When a word with a derivational ending is made plural, past, comparative, or possessive, the inflectional suffix is always added to the end of the word and does not come before any derivational suffix. The rule for production is derivation first, inflection last. Thus, we have *remediated, unretreadables,* and *summarizing,* with the inflectional marker at the end of each word. We would not produce words such as *handsful* to mean *handfuls* or *generaledize* to mean *generalized.*

In Middle English, many more inflections were pronounced than are produced in modern English. Some of our odd spellings are legacies from more than three centuries ago; for example, *kept, wept,* and *slept* are contracted forms of old inflectional patterns that at one time were spoken as separate syllables. The form of each word is abstract and includes a base and a past-tense morpheme, such as in this example:

$$/kip/ + \{past\ tense\} = [k^hɛpt].$$

☆ EXERCISE 4.8

Underline all of the inflections, and notice where they occur:

inducements	higher	singing	unhappiest
legalizing	disentangled	tardiest	misunderstood
productions	factors	shoed	lost

Greek Combining Forms

Modern scientific and mathematical terms incorporated into English in the past 500 years have most often been constructed from Greek morphemes. Greek-derived words are constructed somewhat differently from Latinate words. Greek-derived morphemes are not necessarily assigned specific roles as prefixes, suffixes, or roots; many can combine with other bound morphemes of equal importance in flexible order. So, for example, we can have *psychoneurosis, neuropsychological, parapsychology,* and many other words with *psych.* Although *psych* has not been a free morpheme in the past, it is becoming a verb in American English, as in "I'll *psych* him out before making the offer." *Photograph* is a Greek compound; so are *graphology, lithograph, photosynthesis,* and *telephoto,* which use the morphemes in variable order or position.

☆ EXERCISE 4.9

Give yourself 3 minutes to generate as many words as you can on a separate sheet of paper that use any one of these Greek-derived morphemes:

chrom   cycle   therm

To summarize, children use inflections and simple derivational morphemes before they enter school. Complex derived forms and their alternation patterns are learned much more gradually over a period of many years. Mastery of derivational morphemes is influenced by the frequency with which words are encountered in text; the complexity of the derivational relationships that characterize the words; and whether spelling is a clue to a word's structure, meaning, and origin. After children acquire phonemic awareness and phonic knowledge, they can attend more easily to this additional layer of language organization.

Derivational Complexity

Derivational complexity is a term that characterizes the number and type of changes that have been made in the base word or root when it is combined with other morphemes. Some derived words are created without any sound or spelling changes in the base form, as in *forget/forgetful, employ/employment,* and *embark/embarkation.* But more often, changes occur in the way the stem is pronounced, the way it is spelled, or the way it is stressed. The types of phonological changes that can occur between a stem and a derivation include **syllable regrouping, vowel alternation, consonant alternation,** and **stress alternation.** Syllable regrouping describes what happens when *differ* becomes *different,* vowel alternation describes what happens when *sane* is changed to *sanity,* consonant alternation explains the difference between *electric* and *electricity,* and stress alternation describes the changes that occur between *philosophy* and *philosophical* and is a common result of derivational word building.

Vowel alternation can occur in many forms. A tense (long) vowel is reduced to schwa in *define/definition* and *compete/competition.* A tense vowel becomes an accented lax (short) vowel in *extreme/extremity, precise/precision,* and *profane/profanity.* A schwa becomes an accented lax vowel in *industry/industrious, final/finality,* and *brutal/brutality.* A schwa becomes an accented tense vowel in *labor/laborious* and *injure/injurious.* If words in a derivational family are taught together in a vocabulary or spelling lesson, students are likely to perceive the words' relatedness in spite of these changes in pronunciation.

Consonant alternation is exemplified by each of the following word pairs. Note how consonants change in pronunciation from one form of a word to another, even though most of the base words stay the same in spelling:

> bomb/bom<u>b</u>ardier
> crumb/crum<u>b</u>le
> paradigm/paradi<u>g</u>matic
> malign/mali<u>g</u>nant
> anxious/an<u>x</u>iety
> incredible/incre<u>d</u>ulous
> perceive/perce<u>p</u>tion
> medic/medi<u>c</u>ine
> definite/defini<u>t</u>ion
> repress/repre<u>ss</u>ion

Changes can also occur between the spelling of the base when it occurs alone and the spelling of the base when endings are added to it. Changes that occur by spelling rule are called orthographic changes in the base form. They include dropping final *e* when the suffix begins with a vowel, changing *y* to *i* before a suffix unless the suffix begins with *i*, and doubling the final consonant before a suffix that begins with a vowel. More is said in Chapter 5 about the structure of English orthography and the specific constraints of each rule, but examples of these orthographic change rules are as follows:

Drop e	*Change* y *to* i	*Double the consonant*
sense/sensible	happy/happiest	win/winning
compete/competition	fury/furious	occur/occurrence

☆ EXERCISE 4.10

1.   From the derived form of the word given, write the base word, and underline any part of the word that is pronounced or written differently in the derived form.

Example: division   *divi<u>de</u>*

reference _____

precision _____

dramatic _____

theatrical _____

possession _____

sanity _____

originality _____

ridiculous _____

sociology _____

political _____

ritual _____

2. Decide what kind of change has occurred between the base form and the base in the derived form of these words (1 = no change, 2 = orthographic [spelling] change only, 3 = phonological [sound] change only, 4 = both phonological and orthographic changes).

Example: grow/growth __1__

bat/batty __2__

human/humanity __3__

wide/width _____

differ/difference _____

sun/sunny _____

athlete/athletic _____

personal/personality _____

propel/propeller _____

combine/combination _____

idiot/idiotic _____

usual/usually _____

extend/extension _____

ration/rational _____

define/definition _____

assist/assistance _____

Derivational complexity does affect how easily students learn Latin-based words. One study[11] examined the relationships between oral knowledge of derivational morphology and the spelling development of fourth, sixth, and eighth graders. Ninth graders with learning disabilities were compared with typically progressing fourth, sixth, and eighth graders on both oral and written word generation. Clear developmental trends showed that up to and beyond eighth grade, students continued to learn about derivational rules and relationships. At all age levels the ability to generate derived forms orally preceded the ability to spell these forms. Furthermore, the complexity of the relationship between the base and the derived form of a word pair affected the ease of spelling. Those pairs with only phonological changes (usually with nonneutral suffixes) and those with both phonological and orthographic changes evoked the most spelling errors at all levels of development. For example, pairs such as *decide* and *decision* evoked more errors than did pairs such as *enjoy* and *enjoyment*.

INDIVIDUAL DIFFERENCES IN
USE OF DERIVATIONAL MORPHOLOGY

The language proficiencies of good readers and the language weaknesses of poor readers extend beyond phonology to other levels of language organization, including morphology. To understand individual differences in morphological skill, it is necessary to appreciate the connectedness of words to one another.

How We Remember Words

There is considerable evidence that words, both spoken and written, are remembered in relation to other words and that word meanings are not stored in our memory as isolated wholes that resemble separate entries in a dictionary. Whenever possible, we learn words in connection to others that we already know. Each word is part of a network of related meanings. One of the ways that word family networks are constructed in memory is by their morphological relationships.[12] When one word in the family is encountered, the other words in the family are activated for possible retrieval. The stem of words in a known high-frequency word family, such as *decide, decision, decided, undecided,* and *decisive,* will be recognized more quickly during reading than will the stem of words in a low-frequency word family, such as *amnesia, mnemonic,* and *amnesty.*[13] These connections between words in memory are not dependent simply on matching letter strings; knowledge of *code,* for example, will not facilitate retrieval of an unrelated word such as *cod.* Related words are activated in memory when they have meaningful connections and when they share structural elements at the morpheme level, especially when spelling reveals those connections.

Awareness of morphemes helps us understand and remember the differences among homophones (words that sound the same but have different meanings). The spelling of a homophone can make sense if the word is known in relation to other words with a similar structure. *Site* is related to *situation* and means "place"; *cite* is related to *citation* and means a "reference in text." *Sight,* of course, is in that group of Anglo-Saxon words that refer to our senses. *Rite* and *ritual; wright, boatwright,* and *playwright; write, written, writing;* and *right* and *righteous* are more likely to be remembered if their origin and meaning connections are understood.

Networks of semantically related morphemes are established in the memories of adults. How these networks become established is of considerable relevance to the issue of language instruction. How children learn about morphological relationships and how much they know at certain developmental stages have been topics of limited investigation, primarily in studies involving either reading and spelling tasks or a combination of oral and written tasks.[14] We know from cognitive experimental research that people with morphological awareness organize their mental dictionaries so that related words are associated and are more readily retrieved.[15] In general, the mind is always seeking pattern recognition to reduce the load on memory and facilitate retrieval of linguistic information. When we see the word *postscript,* the whole network of familiar *script* words is activated. If we were to think quickly of all of the words we know that have the morpheme *audi* in them, we could easily call up *auditory, auditorium, audit, audition, audible,* and *audience* for starters. We would be able to retrieve this list more quickly than a series of morphologically unrelated words because they all share a root morpheme and use prefixes and suffixes that are familiar. Therefore, it should be productive to teach words in association with their morphological networks and to teach novice learners the derivatives of one root morpheme at a time.

Morphological Awareness of Good and Poor Readers

In the small number of studies that have attempted to map the development of morphological knowledge in typically progressing children, substantial individual variation has been the norm. Rough developmental trends have been established, but separating the effects of reading from the causes or characteristics of limited reading ability is challenging. Children do learn a great deal about word structure from reading and writing itself, so text exposure alone may account for substantial individual variation in word knowledge.

On both oral and written language tasks, good verbal learners have been shown to be more sensitive to derivational relationships and to use this knowledge more productively than have poor verbal learners.[16] Phonological awareness facilitates morphological awareness in younger children,[17] and both are associated with stronger reading skills. Better readers with excellent language abilities in fourth through eighth grade are able to talk about word structure and word meaning in a precise, decontextualized manner that reveals conscious knowledge of phonology and morphology.[18] Linguistically superior fifth graders do better than typical eighth graders with identification and generation of derivational morphemes.[19] Fifth-grade students with superior verbal learning ability also are more able to detect and use word structure when deciphering word meanings than are typical, older students. Adults who read accurately and fluently have accumulated wide networks of word families for ready access and cross-referencing in the **lexicon**.[20] In contrast, adults who read poorly have less information in their mental dictionaries as well as less ability to organize and gain access to words using morphological relationships.[21]

Children who read poorly, when tested orally with a morpheme-generation task, have difficulty applying morphological rules to unfamiliar base words as well as good readers can.[22] These problems are attributable in large part to more basic weaknesses in phonological processing.[23] Because morphemes are units of both sound and meaning, deficits in phonological processing contribute to confusion of similar-sounding words and word parts, failure to recognize similarities of structure, and failure to either store or retrieve word form with precision. Similarly, differences between good and poor spellers are associated with significant differences in sensitivity to word structure at the morphological level. Children with specific written language and spelling disorders have been shown to misuse, substitute, or omit inflected endings more than typical children.[24] Insensitivity to morphological aspects of word structure also characterizes adults who spell poorly.[25]

By sixth grade, typical students have an understanding of *stem constancy* that is reinforced by seeing words in print.[26] That is, they notice the parts of words that mean the same thing and the letters that spell those morphemes. Well-designed spelling and vocabulary programs make use of morphological structures in word study, making explicit the kind of understanding that good spellers tend to get on their own from seeing words in print. Good spellers and people with larger vocabularies search for and notice in new words letter sequences that can give them a clue to meaning. Thus, it makes sense to organize the presentation of vocabulary in this manner after the third grade.

DERIVATIONAL MORPHOLOGY: INTERVENTION

Knowing meaningful word parts, knowing the ways in which they are combined, and knowing how they are represented in spelling help children acquire vocabulary. Knowledge of roots and affixes facilitates rapid, efficient, and accurate reading of unfamiliar vocabulary, as well as reading comprehension. Knowing that one word is derived from another helps children spell words, especially because written English is a system that preserves meaningful relationships in its orthography.[27] Awareness of word structure and the ability to use derivational relationships productively in turn is nourished by exposure to words in written text. Thus, the development of oral language competence is closely intertwined with the development of reading and writing. This interaction is particularly important for the learning of derivational patterns and rules, as many of the members of related word families may be encountered first in written text.

Primary Grades

Word structure at the morpheme level should be addressed as early as first grade. In first through third grade, we typically either expect children to gain and use knowledge of inflectional and derivational morphology without explicit instruction or teach them about word parts in a cursory way, perhaps in one or two circumscribed spelling lessons. Children who are at risk for reading failure and who are not learning to spell because of deficits in linguistic awareness, however, would probably benefit from explicit instruction. Direct instruction about inflections and simpler derivatives could be incorporated into daily language lessons. Morphology could be addressed through listening, speaking, reading, and writing of inflected and derived words in lists, phrases, and sentences. Direct teaching of the concepts of speech sounds, syllables, and meaningful word parts would enable students to recover stems from inflected and derived words, combine word parts to form new words, and use them in spoken and written form. For example, in the primary grades, children could be taught to recognize that many words are built from other words and to differentiate between the structures of words such as *money* and *funny, wise* and *pies, winner* and *winter,* and *pinned* and *wind.*[28]

Fourth Through Eighth Grade

According to one analysis, if students receive direct instruction in the meanings of the most commonly used prefixes (*un-, re-, dis-, in-/im-/il-/ir-*), the removal of the most common suffixes (*-able/-ible, -ly, -ness*), and the spelling changes associated with the addition of inflections beginning with vowels (*-es, -ed, -ing*), they can successfully analyze 250 new printed words per year through morphological analysis.[29] Great differences among good and poor verbal learners' ability to use derivational relationships, however, can be expected.

Between third and seventh grade, most children learn anywhere from 2,800 to 26,000 words.[30] Most new words are encountered through reading; only a limited number will be taught directly. The greatest benefit from instructional time spent on word study can be gained from exploring Latin roots, prefixes, suffixes, and networks of related words.[31] Words with affixes outnumber single-morpheme words

Table 4.1.   Proposed content and order for morpheme instruction

Language layer	Element of language	Examples
Anglo-Saxon	Compounds	*doghouse, ballgame, blackbird*
	Inflected and derivational endings with no spelling change	*feeding, teacher, puppy, sadly, hits, wanted*
	Inflected and common derivational morphemes with spelling changes	
	Final consonant doubling	*shipping, robber*
	Drop final *e*	*hoping, likable, mover*
	Change *y* to *i*	*cried, happiness, sillier*
	Double final consonant of accented syllable	*occurrence, beginner*
	Prefixes and suffixes	*under-, over-; -hood*
Latin (Romance)	Roots	*port, rupt, script, tract, cept, spect, ject, struct, dict, mit, flex, cred, duc, pend, pel, fac, vert*
	Prefixes	*un-, re-, non-, dis-, in-, pre-, ex-, mis-, en-, con-, per-, inter-, super-, trans-, sub-, circum-, intra-, bi-, mal-*
	Suffixes	*-ly, -ful, -ness, -less, -ment, -ible/-able, -ent/-ant, -ous, -ic, -al, -ity, -tion/-sion, -teen, -ian, -ence/-ance, -tious, -cial, -ture*
	Assimilated prefixes that change form to match the root	*in- (immigrate, illegal, irregular) ad- (address, approach, aggressive) ob- (obstruct, opportunity) sub- (subtract, suppose, surround) com- (commit, collide, corrode) dis- (dissuade, difference) ex- (extinguish, emit, eccentric, efficient)*
Greek	Combining forms	*micro, scope, photo, graph, tele, phon, geo, -meter, -ology, -itis*

From Moats, L.C., & Smith, C. (1992). Derivational morphology: Why it should be included in language assessment and instruction. *Language, Speech and Hearing Services in Schools, 23,* 319; © American Speech-Language-Hearing Association. Adapted by permission.

four to one in English written text;[32] however, derived words with affixes are relatively more numerous among less common content words. For example, the word *demoralization* might be found infrequently in a history textbook about the Civil War but might be a key concept in understanding the consequences of a battle, and its meaning should be clear from morphological analysis. Listening, speaking, reading, and writing such words should be interwoven. Even older students with good verbal skills can benefit from direct instruction in derivational morphology.

Instructional Content and Strategies

Derivational relationships are complex and irregular; therefore, memorizing suffix meanings in lists, for example, may have little purpose. In the absence of experi-

Table 4.2.   Steps for teaching morpheme groups to individuals who need a systematic, structured approach

1. Establish metalinguistic awareness at the syllable and phoneme level. Present and talk about sounds and syllables in the word. Relate the *spoken* form to the *written* form. Have students say the word.

    Examples: quickly (2 syllables, 6 sounds)
    conclude (2 syllables, 7 sounds)

2. Identify, pronounce, and define roots and affixes through word comparison and sorting. Group and contrast with other words of similar sound or appearance.

    Examples: donkey, sunny; best, pressed; ugly, lovely
    seclude, include, conclude
    physician, physical, physiology

3. Generate a formal definition based on this model: A/An _____ (word) is a/an _____ (superordinate category) that _____ (restrictive attributes).

    Example: A *micrometer* is an *instrument* that *lets us measure in small units.*

4. Talk about relationships with other words or concepts.

    Example: conclude, conceal, convince

5. Use in analogies, cloze activities, or other meaningful contexts.

    Examples: conclude: _____ *(begin)*
    include: _____ *(exclude)*

6. Use in reading activities appropriate for level.

7. Introduce spelling and spelling rules appropriate for level.

From Moats, L.C., & Smith, C. (1992). Derivational morphology: Why it should be included in language assessment and instruction. *Language, Speech and Hearing Services in Schools, 23,* 319; © American Speech-Language-Hearing Association. Adapted by permission.

mental validation of a content, sequence, and method of instruction in morphology, instruction could be designed to follow developmental trends suggested by existing studies. Instruction would progress logically from the most transparent and common prefixes to the more complex, nonneutral suffixes that cause phonological and orthographic changes in spoken and written words. The greater the phonological difference between the base form and the stem of the derived word (*anxious/anxiety; preside/president; philosophy/philosophical*), the less recognizable the word connections might be for students with verbal learning difficulties. Print itself, however, is a very helpful aid in acquiring morphemic knowledge because spellings for morphemes usually remain stable even when pronunciation changes. Students can be taught to recognize them using multisensory approaches.

Table 4.1 lists morpheme groups to be taught explicitly across oral (listening/speaking) and written (reading/writing) language. The general order reflects the natural order of difficulty, which in turn is evident across many studies of morpheme knowledge in developing students. The sequence moves from early acquired grammatical morphemes (inflectional and contracted forms), to more transparent neutral morphemes (prefixes and suffixes) that do not change the base word, to complex derived forms that produce phonological and orthographic changes to the root. Latin and Greek roots are emphasized in fourth grade and beyond because they appear frequently in the vocabulary of math, science, and social studies. Oral and written language learning are presumed to be interdependent and reciprocal; that is, the one will benefit the other, and vice versa.

Table 4.2 proposes instructional procedures for teaching morpheme groups to children with language learning problems. Intervention programs often begin with aural and visual recognition of meaningful word parts because these cognitive skills appear necessary for analysis of increasingly complex structural aspects of words in spoken and written form. Explicit instruction of roots and affixes could be done through presentation and creation of oral and written examples in context. Students can engage in a variety of activities, including grouping related words, searching text for examples of words, generating definitions, using words in analogies, and creating maps of related words.

In 1970, Carol Chomsky, after observing that English orthography is a **morphophonemic** rather than phonetic transcription of speech, suggested that we should teach derivational word relationships to school children. Her advice should, at last, be heeded.

☆ SUPPLEMENTARY EXERCISES

1. Divide these words into morphemes. Use a dictionary if necessary.

misspell	stimulate	insanely
sensible	attached	forgettable
inoperable	beautifully	continuity
psychology	excitement	dismiss
preferring	inspiration	recommend
morphemic	pacify	television

2. The Greek combining form *psycho* means "mind." How many words can you generate that include *psycho*? Make a list on a separate sheet of paper, and then organize the words into a web, picture, or map showing how they are related.

3. Divide these words twice, once to show the syllables and again to show the morphemes. The two are not always in agreement because different language structures are involved at each layer of language organization:

	Syllables	*Morphemes*
competition	_____	_____
precision	_____	_____
scaling	_____	_____
tractor	_____	_____
invasive	_____	_____
gentle	_____	_____

4. Words like *remain, finger,* and *hamburger* look as though they might have separate morphemes but do not in modern English usage. They cannot be divided into meaningful parts. Think of three more words

that look on the surface as though they could be made of separate morphemes but (at least in modern use) are not.

5. Make up five new words, composed of common prefixes, roots, and suffixes, that could be real words but that are not established words in English, such as *unpudgable*.

6. Below is list of correct and incorrect spellings of words. English spelling often retains the spellings of meaningful parts even when pronunciation changes, so the correct spellings of the words listed can be affirmed by knowing the pronunciation and spelling of another form of the word. Determine the correct spellings. Then, to the right of these lists, write a form of each word that can help you remember the correct spelling.

> *Example:* practice   practise   *practical*
>   desine   design   *designation*

		Other word
compitition	competition	_____
persperation	perspiration	_____
physician	physision	_____
restiration	restoration	_____
pleasure	plesure	_____
resign	resine	_____
publisity	publicity	_____
electrisity	electricity	_____
demacratic	democratic	_____
president	presedent	_____
comprable	comparable	_____
history	histry	_____
janiter	janitor	_____
managor	manager	_____
majer	major	_____
industry	indistry	_____

7. Match the terms in column B to one of the words in column A:

A	B
incredible	1. Assimilated prefix (changed to match root's beginning)
credits	
accredit	2. Derivational noun suffix
cred	3. Inflectional suffix
creditor	4. Bound root morpheme
	5. Derivational adjective suffix

ENDNOTES

1. Nagy & Anderson, 1984; White, Power, & White, 1989.
2. Derwing, Smith, & Wiebe, 1995.
3. Ibid.; Derwing & Baker, 1979.
4. Based on Derwing et al., 1995.
5. Brown, 1973.
6. Ibid.; Berko, 1958; deVilliers & deVilliers, 1973.
7. Derwing et al., 1995.
8. Henry, 1997.
9. Tyler & Nagy, 1989.
10. Ibid.
11. Carlisle, 1987, 1988.
12. MacKay, 1978; Nagy, Anderson, Schommer, Scott, & Stallman, 1989.
13. Nagy et al., 1989.
14. Carlisle, 1987; Derwing & Baker, 1979; Freyd & Baron, 1982; Rubin, Patterson, & Kantor, 1991; Templeton & Scarborough-Franks, 1985.
15. Schreuder & Baayen, 1995.
16. Rubin, 1988; Shankweiler, Lundquist, Dreyer, & Dickinson, 1996; Stolz & Feldman, 1995.
17. Carlisle & Nomanbhoy, 1993.
18. Snow, 1990.
19. Freyd & Barron, 1982.
20. Nagy et al., 1989.
21. Cunningham & Stanovich, 1997; Leong, 1989; Shankweiler et al., 1996.
22. Carlisle, 1987, 1988.
23. Fowler & Liberman, 1995.
24. Bailet, 1990; Moats, 1996.
25. Fischer, Shankweiler, & Liberman, 1985; Liberman, Rubin, Duques, & Carlisle, 1985; Shankweiler et al., 1996.
26. Templeton, 1989.
27. Holmes & Brown, 1998.
28. Rubin, 1988; Rubin et al., 1991.
29. White et al., 1989.
30. Wysocki & Jenkins, 1987.
31. Henry, 1997.
32. Nagy & Anderson, 1984.

INSTRUCTIONAL MATERIALS FOR TEACHING MORPHOLOGY

Bebko, A.R., Alexander, J., & Doucet, R. (1998). *LANGUAGE!: Roots.* Longmont, CO: Sopris West.

Danner, H.G., & Noel, R. (1996). *Discover it!: A better vocabulary the better way.* Occoquan, VA: Imprimis Books.

Greene, J.F. (1998). *LANGUAGE!: A reading, writing, and spelling curriculum for at-risk and ESL students at grades 1–12.* Longmont, CO: Sopris West.

Henry, M., & Redding, N.C. (1996). *Patterns for success in decoding and spelling.* Austin, TX: PRO-ED.

Kleiber, M.H. *Systematic study of Latin and Greek roots.* New York: Decatur Enterprises. (Available from the publisher, Post Office Box 1355, Bronx, NY 10471)

CHAPTER 5

The Structure
of English Orthography

Humans have communicated with spoken language for more than 30,000 years, long enough for linguistic capability to be "hard wired" in the brain. Every human society has spoken language; every human being, except those who have neuro- logical impairments or who are totally deprived of vocal contact with others, learns to speak. In people from all cultures, development of spoken language includes the unfolding of similar grammatical structures along a predictable sequence.[1] The predisposition to perceive, categorize, recognize, and learn the lan- guage of caregivers is observable in the youngest infants. Acquisition of spoken language, within a range of ability, is an expected consequence of evolutionary development in human beings.

Humans have only recently invented writing systems to represent spoken lan- guage; that is, writing is a much later evolutionary attainment than speaking. Our biological predisposition for mastery of spoken and written language differs con- siderably. Speech is learned early without direct instruction; it is difficult to *prevent* children from learning to use oral language. The few individuals who have been prevented from doing so have been scrutinized by scientists because of their uniqueness. In contrast, writing is acquired incrementally after oral language com- petence is attained. The majority of the world's languages have no writing system at all; in those languages, the speakers' tradition, history, and knowledge all are preserved through oral memorization.[2] The invention of written symbols enabled humans to record their culture and science and is thus one of the most important innovations of the human race.

A BRIEF HISTORY OF WRITING

Although many literate cultures have created myths about the invention of writing, attributing the origins of their symbol systems to the gods, writing systems probably evolved from early drawings. The first written communication, dated to approximately 20,000 years ago, contained signs and pictures (**pictograms**) that portrayed literally the objects, events, and ideas of daily life without any arbitrary assignment of either meaning or sound to a symbol. Pictograms are used today as signs in parks or public places that cater to an international population because they can be understood by anyone.

Ideographic writing systems evolved simultaneously in China and in Sumeria more than 5,000 years ago. Ideograms were stylized pictograms that were used as representations of ideas and words rather than as literal records of events. The first standardization of 3,000 basic Chinese characters was decreed by Li Si in 213 B.C., which was necessary to eliminate redundancies and simplify the complex system then in use throughout China. Each ideogram had to be memorized, however, because it did not bear a direct relationship to a sound.

The Sumerians of Mesopotamia left an archive of clay tablets with commercial and historical records written in cuneiform script, a system that also developed from ideograms (see Figure 5.1). Cuneiform symbols were stylized, simplified representations of words and ideas that had once been pictograms and were later adopted from Sumeria by the conquering Assyrians and Persians. When adopted by other languages, the Sumerian symbols were designated as syllable units and became the first **syllabaries,** systems that represented each syllable but not each separate phoneme in speech.

The **hieroglyphics** of the Egyptians developed in parallel with cuneiform writing and flourished around 4000 B.C. Gradually hieroglyphics came to symbolize the syllables of the words in Egyptian. Many other people who had trading contact with Egyptian and Sumerian civilizations borrowed hieroglyphic symbols to use in their writing systems. The Phoenicians, who resided on the eastern shore of the Mediterranean Sea, created a system of 22 syllabic symbols that represented consonant and vowel combinations and some consonants alone. (Figure 5.2 shows examples of syllabic symbols in Cherokee.) The Greeks then borrowed the Phoenician writing system around 1000 B.C. but found that it worked inefficiently for the more complex syllable constructions in Greek. Taking the final step toward the creation of a true **alphabetic** writing system, the Greeks assigned a symbol to each consonant and vowel of their language. (*Alpha* and *beta* were the first two letters of the Greek symbol system.) The Romans, who were given the Greek alphabet by the Etruscans, then adopted and refined it, used it to transcribe Latin, and spread it throughout the world.

Thus, the alphabetic writing system of English represents a late evolutionary development and a form of writing that humans generated over millennia. (Figure 5.3 is a schematic of the different types of writing systems throughout history.) Only gradually did humans become aware of the separate phonemes that could be

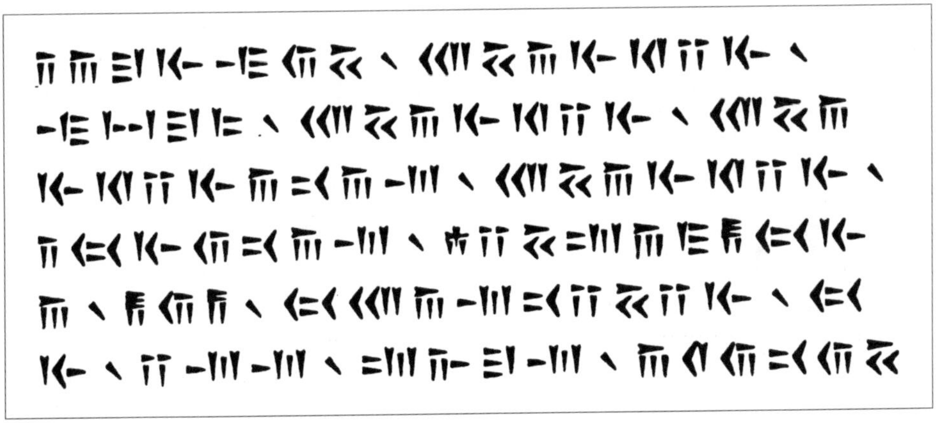

Figure 5.1. Ideographic script (Sumerian cuneiform). (From Pedersen, H. [1959]. *Linguistic science in the 19th century.* Cambridge, MA: Harvard University Press.)

represented in a writing system. In many ways, the individual development of children who are discovering the alphabetic principle in English writing recapitulates human history and reflects the unnatural and effortful learning process that underlies learning to write.

THE NATURE OF ENGLISH ORTHOGRAPHY

Alphabetic writing systems, including English, vary in the accuracy and fidelity of speech sound representation. Finnish and Serbo-Croatian are among the most phonetically predictable written languages, in that each symbol of their alphabetic systems corresponds to one speech sound. English, however, is known as a *deep orthography,* one in which the spelling units correspond not only to sounds (phonemes and syllables) but also to meaning (morphemes) and is most accurately described as a morphophonemic system.

Chomsky and Halle[3] even described English as an optimal system because it represents both sound and meaning. For example, we know that the words *educa-tion* and *induction* share a meaningful root that is preserved in spelling even though the spoken forms of the words differ considerably. The alphabet also represents sound units in an abstract manner, purposely avoiding the kind of detailed phonetic representation that might, for example, be used to show whether the /d/ in *educate* is affricated (pronounced like [j̆]). Our orthography is phonemic, not phonetic; as discussed in Chapter 2, that it does not represent the actual features of speech compelled linguists to invent the IPA to better represent the sounds heard in English and other languages. Our Greco-Roman orthography, however, is alphabetic, as are Greek and Russian.

HISTORICAL LAYERS IN ENGLISH ORTHOGRAPHY

One logical way to categorize the spelling patterns of English is by their language of origin (Anglo-Saxon, Latin, and Greek) and the sounds, syllables, and morphemes that are represented systematically in each base language (see Table 5.1).[4]

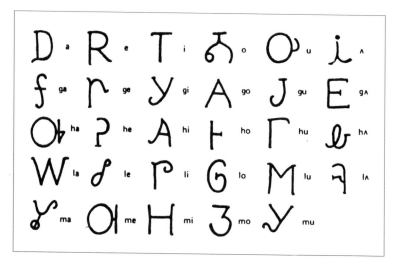

Figure 5.2. Syllabic script. (From Akmajian, A., Demers, R.A., Farmer, A.K., & Harnish, R.M. [1995]. *Linguistics: An introduction to language and communication* [4th ed., p. 542]. Cambridge, MA: MIT Press; reprinted by permission.)

Anglo-Saxon and Its Roots

The most common, frequent words of English are preserved from its oldest layer, Anglo-Saxon. In turn, Anglo-Saxon evolved from primitive Indo-European and primitive Germanic roots. Indo-European languages are believed by historians to have come from a common ancestral language in existence more than 20,000 years ago, spoken by tribes residing in Eastern Europe, which then developed into different languages as migrating groups were isolated from one another. Similarities in the vocabulary, grammatical patterns, and phonological features of all of the Indo-European languages attest to their common origin.[5] Words for animals, family members, numbers, emotions, and universal daily activities tend to be similar across related language groups that evolved from the same ancestral language.[6] A Germanic language family comprises one group of languages with such similarities, including Danish, Dutch, English, German, and Swedish; a Latin language family comprises another, including French, Italian, Portugese, Romanian, and Spanish.

The Proto-Germanic language from which Anglo-Saxon evolved was spoken in a territory around Denmark somewhat before the first century A.D. Certain words in modern English, including *rain, drink, broad,* and *hold,* are not similar to those in the Latin family and are believed to have come from Proto-Germanic. The language was highly inflected and included derived forms similar to our present day *heal/health, hold/held, sell/sold,* and *bake/baked,* some of which included a vowel shift and all of which included an ending with the tongue behind or between the teeth. Gradually, the unaccented inflections on verbs became shorter in duration; eventually, they were dropped altogether. *Ride/rode, stand/stood,* and *choose/chose* are Proto-Germanic descendants in which a vowel shift was maintained in the past-tense verb form after a final inflection was dropped. Proto-Germanic words were always stressed on the first syllable with the exception of compound verbs such as *abide* and *begin.* The evolution of Indo-European languages is depicted in Figure 5.4.

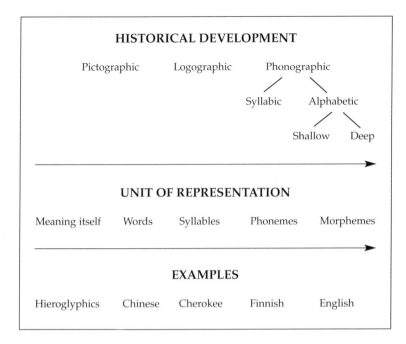

Figure 5.3.   Classification of orthographies. (From Seymour, P.H.K. [1992]. Cognitive theories of spelling and implications for education. In C. Sterling & C. Robson [Eds.], *Psychology, spelling, and education* [p. 53]. Clevedon, England: Multilingual Matters, Ltd.; adapted by permission.)

West Germanic, an offshoot of Proto-Germanic, had evolved by the fourth century A.D.[7] The isolation of migrating tribal groups again led to the evolution of more branches of Germanic, including, by the sixth century, dialects spoken by Angles, Saxons, and Jutes living on the west side of the waters separating what are now the British Isles from Germany and Denmark. During the fifth and sixth centuries, Germanic tribes steadily invaded Britain, pushing to the west the Celtic peoples who lived there. The absorption of Celtic and Latin forms into the Low West German languages brought by the Germanic invaders resulted in the birth of Old English, or Anglo-Saxon. This language was subsequently preserved in the writings of King Alfred and the Augustinian monks who were sent to reestablish Roman Christianity in Britain during the ninth century.

Anglo-Saxon words in English include those for work (*shepherd, plough, work*), those for numbers (*one, hundred*), those for body parts (*heart, knee, foot*), those for basic sentiments (*love, hate, laughter*), and those for animals (*sheep, goat, horse*). Of the 100 words used most often in English, all can be traced to Anglo-Saxon origins. The grammatical glue words, or function words, are almost uniformly Anglo-Saxon (*the, a, and, you, to, would*). They are often one-syllable words. In Anglo-Saxon, compound forms were stressed on the first syllable, as in *mother*.

Anglo-Saxon vowels were spelled as they sounded, with *a, e, i, o, u, y, ea, eo, ie,* and *ae* each corresponding very predictably to two pronunciations, one long and one short in duration. (Duration of vowel production is the actual length of time that it takes to produce a vowel in a word.) In Anglo-Saxon spelling, lengthening of vowel duration was indicated by doubling the letter (as in *aa*) or by adding a diacritical mark. As mentioned previously, the labels "long" and "short" that we use today to describe the qualities of vowel sounds are of quite different meaning and

Table 5.1.   Features of layers of English orthography by language of origin

	Sound	Syllable	Morpheme
Anglo-Saxon	*Consonants* Single Blends Digraphs *Vowels* Short/long *R*-controlled Teams Diphthongs	*Six types* Closed Open *R*-controlled Consonant-*le* Vowel team Vowel-consonant-*e*	Compounds Inflections
Latin (Romance)			Prefixes Suffixes Roots Plurals
Greek	*y* = /ɪ/ *gym* *ch* = /k/ *chorus* *ph* = /f/ *sphere*		Combining forms (scientific vocabulary) *micro + meter* *psych + ology* Plurals *crises*

Based on Henry (1999).

in fact do not have the same direct relationship to vowel length that characterized Old English spelling. "Short" vowels are sometimes long in duration, and "long" vowels are sometimes short in duration. The "short" vowel in *bend* is spoken for a longer duration than the "long" vowel in *beat*. Our descriptions and labels for vowels descend from Old English concepts rather than from modern speech patterns.

Because of the vowel shift patterns and inflection changes that occurred as Old English became Middle English and then Modern English, spoken and written word forms such as *foot/feet, tooth/teeth, goose/geese, climb, told,* and *find* have been preserved. These words, however, are exceptions to the most common patterns for word formation and spelling.

From the Anglo-Saxon layer of language came most of our consonant and vowel sound–symbol correspondences; only a few additional phonic correspondences were adopted from Greek spelling patterns (*y* for /ɪ/ as in *gym; ph* for /f/ as in *philosophy;* and *ch* for /k/ as in *chorus*), and no new correspondences were contributed by Latin. As Modern English adopted words from many other languages, however, spellings from those languages were often assimilated as well (*barbecue, plaza, marijuana,* and *chocolate* from Spanish; *bayou, butte, levee,* and *picayune* from French; *pizza* and *cello* from Italian).

Latin Layer of English

The Latin-based vocabulary incorporated into Anglo-Saxon after the Norman invasion of Britain in 1066 was the language of scholars, nobles, and those of high

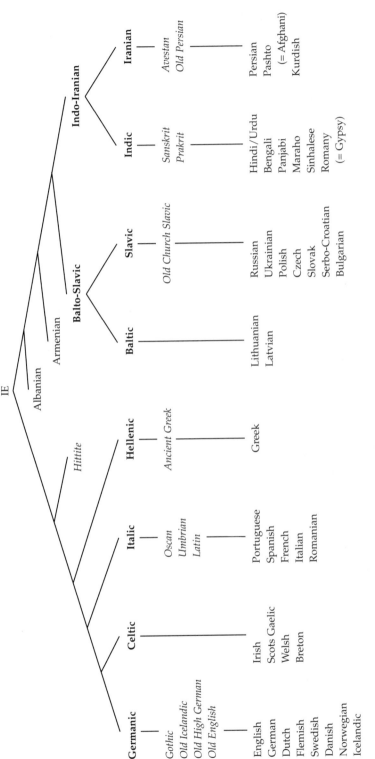

Figure 5.4. The Indo-European (IE) language family. Families are listed in bold type. The oldest attested forms of each family are given in italics, and currently spoken languages are listed in plain roman type. (From Akmajian, A., Demers, R.A., Farmer, A.K., & Harnish, R.M. [1995]. *Linguistics: An introduction to language and communication* [4th ed., p. 311]. Cambridge, MA: MIT Press; reprinted by permission.)

social class. The Normans, led by William the Conqueror, were a French-speaking people whose cultured literati wrote in French and Latin, closely related members of an Indo-European language family. These languages contributed thousands of words to English that were often used in the language of text and scholarship, such as *amorous, malevolent, fortitude, maternal,* and *residence.* After the monarchies of France and England officially separated in the 13th and 14th centuries, the up-swing in patriotic sentiment in England led to a new embrace of Middle English by the upper classes, who previously had regarded English as the crude language of the uneducated masses. English was adopted by all Britains by the beginning of the 14th century. Shortly thereafter, the first great works of English literature were written, including those of Geoffrey Chaucer, and by the early 15th century, English became the official language for written communication during the reign of Henry V. Close to Modern English, the form of the language used then was an amalgam of Anglo-Saxon, Latin, and French that had undergone rapid evolution and several major shifts of pronunciation.

The Evolution of Spelling

During the linguistic change of the 14th and 15th centuries, scholars adopted spelling habits that added to the confusion and lack of consistency in vowel representation. Middle English had seven diphthongs, that is, vowels pronounced with a glide in the middle, that were spelled with letter combinations, including *au/aw, ai/ay, ei/ey, u/eu/ew, oi/oy,* and *ou/ow.* Ten vowels were pronounced without a glide, sometimes long and sometimes short in duration. Doubled letters *aa, ee,* and *oo* were sometimes used to show vowel lengthening. Unaccented vowels were reduced to schwa in pronunciation but most often were spelled with *e* or *i.*

Where did "silent *e*" come from? Several change processes account for the final *e* on the ends of syllables with tense vowels. Old English included many more inflections than Middle English that over time were dropped or reduced, leaving only an unaccented neutral vowel pronounced at the ends of the Middle English equivalent of words such as *time, stake,* and *before.* Scribes also added a final *e* to some words that did not have reduced inflectional endings, just for appearance's sake or for orthographic consistency. *Home* and *bride* are such words. By the 16th century, final silent *e* had become a convention of spelling used as a pronunciation guide not only for tense vowels but also to mark soft *c* and *g* (*chance, page*) and to prevent words from looking like plurals (*false, else*).

After 16th-century spelling conventions developed, rapid pronunciation changes continued, including a phenomenon known as the Great Vowel Shift.[8] During the 15th and 16th centuries, it became customary to pronounce tense vowels (now represented in the phonetic alphabet as /e/, /i/, /aj/, /o/, and /u/ to match the way they were spelled and pronounced in Middle English) with a higher tongue position. The shift resulted in our Modern English tense vowel and diphthong pronunciations, but spellings were preserved from eras during which pronunciation was considerably different from today's speech.

Modern English spelling has been fairly stable since the middle 17th century. In 1690, the first American primer for children, the *New England Primer,* was published in Boston and was reprinted and used for more than 100 years. Its spelling patterns were very similar to conventional English spelling that has endured over the past 300 years, with several exceptions, such as use of the letters *i* and *j*, and *u* and *v*. A long history of letter confusion accounts for the interchangeability of these letters until Webster's 19th-century dictionary. The Romans had adopted the letter *I* from the Greeks but began to use it not only to represent a vowel sound /aj/ but also to spell two consonants: /j/ as in *bunion* and /ǰ/ as in *jump*. When the letter was adopted into English after the Norman invasion, scribes elongated it to make a *j*. The letter *y* was also used in Middle English for [i] at the ends of words. Thus arose the custom of changing *y* to *i* when suffixes were added to words such as *stories* and *beautiful*. The *u* and *v* were confused because at one time, a rounded uppercase *U* was the Latin version of *v*; this single letter *U/V* represented both a consonant and a vowel, and the letters were not clearly separated in spelling until about 1700.

By the early 1700s, Jonathan Swift and other literary figures began a movement to preserve and defend the integrity of English against the rampant experimentation and assimilation of the Elizabethan period. Writers were literally afraid that their works would find their way to oblivion because English lacked standard usage and was so vulnerable to rapid change. A committee of the Royal Academy was assigned the duty of rendering English pure by declaring right and wrong usage. Although the Royal Academy never accomplished that task, Samuel Johnson volunteered to bring order to chaos by single-handedly writing a dictionary of English with definitions for 40,000 words. Johnson worked for 9 years, finally publishing his work in 1755. This was the first document of standard, modern English that fixed orthographic patterns, usage, origin, and meanings of words.

The Greek Influence

The Italian Renaissance reached England in the mid-16th century, bringing with it a renewed cultural interest in classical Roman and Greek language, art, and literature. The Greek influence on English actually began in Canterbury during the 10th century with the residence of St. Augustine, who used words such as *disciple, apostle,* and *psalm,* religious terms with Greek roots. Contact with Greek culture had been maintained by followers of the Greek Orthodox religion, who entered into commercial and cultural exchanges with the Italians in the 14th and 15th centuries and began exporting Greek vocabulary, scholarship, and aesthetics. Scholars who migrated west from Constantinople stimulated interest in the study of language, an academic discipline that had flourished in ancient Greece. Tudor scholars in the mid-16th century deliberately borrowed words from classical vocabulary to embellish and elevate their prose. Words such as *catastrophe, lexicon,* and *thermometer,* of Greek origin, became English words in this way.

During the Renaissance, scientific inquiry flourished and the printing of scholarly works proliferated. Many new words were needed to describe concepts, inventions, and discoveries such as *atmosphere, pneumonia, skeleton, gravity,* and *encyclopedia.* Anatomical and physical scientists needed to coin words such as *chronology, excrement,* and *paradox.* Of course, the reliance on Greek roots and combining forms continues today in science, mathematics, and philosophy; recently acquired words include *synthesizer* and *cryptogram.* Greek words can be recognized by their use of combined elements that are analogous to English compounds: Each part has equal value in determining the meaning of the word but must exist in combination with others before it can make a word in English. As mentioned previously, Greek words often use the letter *y* for the sound /ɪ/, *ph* for /f/, and *ch* for /k/.

The coinage by 16th-century scholars of "inkhorn" terms—those borrowed directly from another language to refine or embellish one's writing—continued at a great rate, initially with opposition and controversy but later with greater acceptance. As a consequence, English vocabulary was enlarged by thousands of words that enhanced writers' ability to communicate meaning with flair and precision. For this reason, English remains the language with the richest vocabulary and the most options for expressing a range of abstract ideas and shades of meaning.

☆ EXERCISE 5.1

Identify whether the following words are likely to be Anglo-Saxon (AS), Latin (L), Greek (G), or other (O) without looking them up in a dictionary. You may want to refer to Table 5.1.

hemisphere _____   dealt _____

inducement _____   stadium _____

groundhog _____   etymology _____

gnocchi _____   suffix _____

arms _____   knight _____

kaput _____   wanted _____

SOUND–SYMBOL CORRESPONDENCES IN AMERICAN ENGLISH: HOW THEY WORK

On the face of it, the alphabet is insufficient for English spelling: The 26 Roman letters are insufficient for representing the more than 40 phonemes of English. Letter combinations are thus necessary to spell some consonants (combinations such as *th, wh, sh, ch, ng*) and many of the 15 vowels (combinations such as *oo, ee,* and *i*-consonant-*e*). In this book, the term *grapheme* is analogous to *phoneme,* referring to any written letter or combination of letters (as many as four) that corresponds to one phoneme in a word. The *eigh* in *weight, ough* in *though,* and *tch* in *batch* are multiletter graphemes that each spell a single phoneme in these words. The letter combinations *ea, ei, ie, ee, ey,* and *e*-consonant-*e* all are used for "long *e*" [i]. Although many graphemes have unsounded letters, the letter groups form a stable configuration that corresponds to a speech sound in a predictable manner, and most "silent" letters are part of these stable configurations used in discrete sets of words. These silent letters are an indispensable part of the grapheme unit, not extraneous letters as some phonics systems teach.

More than 250 graphemes are used to spell the 40 phonemes of English. Reading is thus a convergent process whereby a limited set of sounds are mapped onto various ways of spelling them. Spelling, on the other hand, is a more divergent and difficult symbolic activity because often several ways to spell the same sound must simply be memorized. The units of spelling from which words are constructed include single consonants, **consonant digraphs,** consonant blends, and silent consonants (see Tables 5.2 and 5.3), as well as single vowels, vowel-consonant-*e* patterns, vowel teams, and *r*-controlled vowels. To complicate matters, some letters are used as markers; that is, they have no direct relation to sound but signal the sound of other letters. Examples include the *k* in *picnicking* that keeps the *c* from sounding like /s/; the *e* in *continue* that keeps the word from ending in a plain *u*; the *u* in *guess* that keeps the *g* from sounding like /ǰ/; and, of course, the *e* in *date* that marks the quality of the vowel represented by the letter *a*.

English orthography also uses some letters and letter combinations in ways that differ from the typical pattern of letter–sound correspondence. These letters, *x, w, u,* and *y,* are sometimes called *chameleon letters,* for the following reasons:

- The letter *x* can correspond to [z] as in *Xerox,* to [ks] as in *mix,* or to [gz] as in *exact.* The voiceless correspondence [ks] occurs when the *x* occurs between a stressed and an unstressed vowel (*taxi, excellent*), and the voiced equivalent [gz] occurs when the *x* is between an unstressed and a stressed vowel (*examine, exist*).

- The letter *u* has three roles. It is used as a consonant when it corresponds to /w/, as in *quack, assuage,* and *language.* It is used as a vowel unit by itself (*cut, unknown*) or as part of a vowel team (*sausage, blue, fruit*). It also serves as a marker in *guest* and *vague,* keeping the *g* from being softened by the *e*.

- The letter *w* acts as a consonant when it represents /w/, as in *water* and *beware.* It can be part of a vowel team spelling as in *snow, few,* or *saw,* but it is never a vowel by itself.

- The letter *y* is a consonant when it represents /j/ as in *yes* and *beyond.* It can represent one of three vowel sounds when it is used alone (/i/, /ı/ or /aj/), as in *baby, gym,* and *cry.* Or, it can be part of a vowel team spelling as in *toy, key, buy,* and *stay.*

Vowel spellings are more variant than consonants. The lax vowel spellings are generally more predictable than the tense vowel spellings. In Figures 5.5 and 5.6, vowels are arranged by place of articulation, from front to back and high to low, with an example of common spellings for each vowel.

☆ EXERCISE 5.2

Identify the letters or letter combinations (graphemes) that correspond to the phonemes in the following words. Each grapheme should correspond to a phoneme. For example, the graphemes in *shriek* are sh / r / ie / k.

s o w	s h o v e	p r a i s e
b a t c h	j e l l o	p e o p l e
e i g h t	q u i e t	

What Determines Predictability in English Spelling?

English sound–symbol correspondences are not as capricious or unpredictable as critics assert. Rather, the correspondence system used to spell the individual

Table 5.2. Consonant and vowel graphemes

Consonant Graphemes

Single	Blends	Digraphs/trigraphs	Other
p b t d *k c g* *f v s z x (/z/)* *h* *m n* *w y* *r l* *j*	**Beginning** *bl- br- cl-* *cr- dr- fl-* *fr- gl- gr-* *pl- pr- sc-* *scr- shr- sk-* *sm- sn- sl-* *sp- spl- spr-* *squ- st- str-* *sw- thr- tr-* *tw-* **Ending** *-nd -nt -nk* *-ft -pt -st* *-mp -lk -sk* *-sp*	*-ch/-tch -ck -ge/-dge* *-gh -ng ph* *sh th wh*	Combinations with silent letters *-bt gn- kn- -lk* *-lm -mb -mn ps-* *rh- wr-* Oddities *qu* = /kw/ *x* = /ks/ or /gz/

Vowel Graphemes

Lax vowels, single letters	Tense vowels, single letters or vowel-consonant-*e*	Letter teams for tense vowels	Diphthongs	R- or l-controlled
a = mad	*table*	*ai, ay, ei, eigh, ey*	*oi/oy, ou/ow*	*air, are (hair)*
e = pet	*secret, baby*	*ee, ea, ei, ie, ey*		*ar (car)*
i = bid	*digraph, cry*	*ie, igh*		*er, ir, ur*
o = rob	*robot*	*oa, ow, oe, ough*		*(herd, bird, turn)*
u = cut	*pupil*	*ue, ui, ough*		*ere, ear (hear)*
u = put	*made*	*oo, ou*		*or, our (short)*
y = gym	*complete*	*au, aw, augh*		*al (halt, all)*
	bide			
	robe			
	cute			

speech sounds in words is predictable to a great extent.[9] At the same time, it is complex because several factors determine the spelling that is used for each sound in a word. Such factors include the language from which the word came (*charade* is from French, *spaghetti* from Italian, and *mosquito* from Spanish), the position of a sound in a syllable ([f] cannot be spelled with a *gh* at the beginning of a syllable but can be at the end, as in *rough*), the meaning and morphological structure of the word (the past tense of *play* is not spelled *plade*), and the sounds that come before or after a given sound (the [f] in *sphere* must be spelled with a *ph* because it comes after [s]). The system is variant because even within these constraints, there are spelling "choices," or different ways to spell the same sound. The most notoriously variable sound–spelling relationship in English is probably the phoneme /š/, as in *sherry, sugar, mission, conscious, special, chef,* and *objection,* although in many cases the ambiguity in spelling this sound can be reduced by knowing the word's origin and meaning (*sh* is the most common spelling for /š/, but many words borrowed

Table 5.3.   Consonant sound–symbol correspondence units

Phonetic symbol	Phonic symbol	Examples	Graphemes for spelling[a]
/p/	p	pit, spider, stop	p
/b/	b	bit, brat, bubble	b
/m/	m	mitt, slam, comb, hymn	m, mb, mn
/t/	t	tickle, mitt, sipped	t, tt, ed
/d/	d	die, loved, handle	d, ed
/n/	n	nice, knight, gnat	n, kn, gn
/k/	k	kite, crib, duck, chorus, walk, quiet	k, c, ck, ch, lk, q
/g/	g	girl, Pittsburgh	g, gh
/ŋ/	ng	sing, bank, English	n, ng
/f/	f	fluff, sphere, tough, calf	f, ff, gh, ph, lf
/v/	v	van, dove	v, ve
/s/	s	sit, pass, science, psychic	s, ss, sc, ce, ps
/z/	z	zoo, jazz, cheese, Xerox	z, zz, s, x
/θ/	th	thin, breath, ether	th
/ð/	th	this, breathe, either	th
/š/	sh	shoe, sure, mission, charade, conscience	sh, s, ss, ch, sc
/ž/	zh	measure, azure	s, z
/č/	ch	cheap, etch, future	ch, tch, t
/ǰ/	j	judge, wage, residual	j, ge, dge
/l/	l	lamb, call, single	l, ll, le
/r/	r	reach, wrap, singer, bird, turn	r, wr, er/ir/ur
/j/, /y/	y	you, onion, use, feud	y, i, u, eu
/w/	w	witch, shower, queen	w, (q)u
/ʍ/	wh	where, when	wh
/h/	h	house, rehab	h
Phonetic segment (allophone)			
[ɾ]	t, d	writer, butter, ladder	t, tt, dd

[a]Graphemes are spellings for individual phonemes; those listed are among the most common spellings, but the list does not include all possible graphemes for a given consonant. Hanna, Hanna, Hodges, and Rudorf's (1966) tables are recommended for lists of all possible spellings.

from French preserved the *ch* spelling for the phoneme, as in *Charlotte, chagrin,* and *Cher*).

The idea that English spellings are either predictable or unpredictable is an oversimplification of linguistic reality. The psychological or cognitive factors that enable people to remember a word include the following: the intensity of emotional associations with a word (*sex*), its frequency in an individual's writing (*they, of, said*), whether it follows a pattern (*colonel*), and whether it is so unusual that its oddity makes it memorable (*ski*). In addition, some word spellings are less probable in the overall rule system but are members of a small family of common words that are just as learnable as words that conform to a primary rule of correspondence. For example, *he, she, be,* and *we* all share the spelling for [i] and are among the most common words in the language, even though they violate the rule for spelling [i] at the ends of words (*ee* is used more often, as in *bee, fee, glee, thee, tree, free, knee, agree, tee, flee, scree*). A predictability scale representing a continuum of

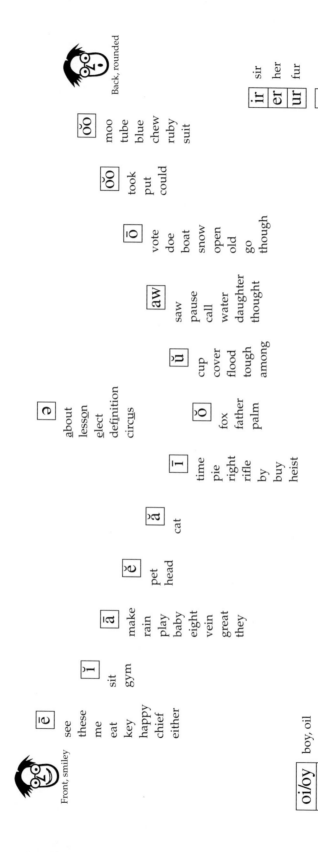

Figure 5.5. Spellings for vowels positioned by place of articulation (phonic symbols).

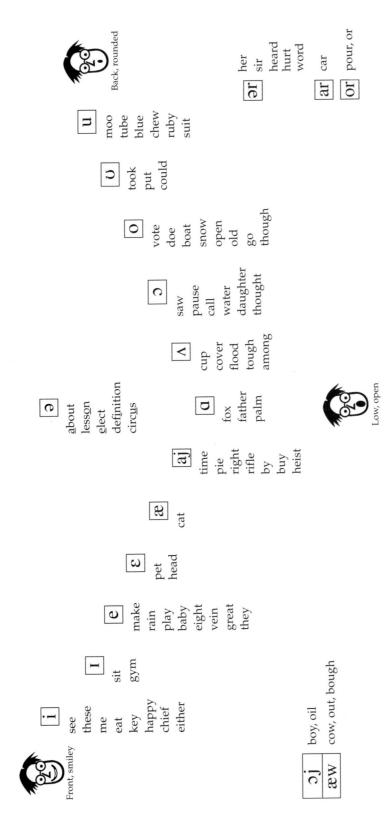

Figure 5.6. Spellings for vowels positioned by place of articulation (phonetic symbols).

absolutely predictable spellings (0) to spellings that recur as part of a family but are less common graphemes for the same sound (5) might look like this:

0	1	2	3	4	5
tin	quit	care	catch	pie	hurt
pup	beck	hope	dodge	tea	weigh
bad	crab	kite	child	put	feud

The words in Column 0 must be spelled with the letters they have; there are no other ways to spell them. The words in Column 5 have low-frequency vowel spellings that do occur in some other words. In Columns 1–4 are words that use conditional or variant spelling patterns for sounds such as -ck for [k], -are for [er], -tch for [č], and -u for [ʊ].

How faithfully, though, does the English spelling system represent speech sounds, given all the "rules" of correspondence that can be identified? The first definitive analyses of English orthography were accomplished by Venezky and by Hanna, Hanna, Hodges, and Rudorf, who were commissioned by the U.S. Office of Education to resolve the question of regularity in the English spelling system.[10] Venezky wrote a classic paper on the structure and nature of English orthography, explaining the linguistic levels at which correspondences operate. Hanna and colleagues selected the 17,000 words used most often in English print and analyzed them by computer for sound–symbol regularities. Hanna and colleagues identified 52 speech sounds, including r-controlled vowel variations; coded the words by their constituent phonemes; and then asked the computer to list the spellings for each sound by the position of the sound in the word. More than 170 spellings for phonemes in specific positions in words were identified.

Hanna and colleagues demonstrated that at least 20 phonemes had spellings that were more than 90% predictable and that 10 others were predictable more than 80% of the time. Spellings of vowels collectively were less consistent than those of consonants. Only 8 phonemes of 52 that were analyzed had individual predictability of less than 78%, and 5 of these were vowels.

If multiple layers of language organization are taken into account, English is a predictable and rule-based spelling system. Using the 17,000 most common words, the researchers analyzed the ways that speech sounds were spelled according to the positions of the phonemes in the word. After cataloging the spellings for sounds, they then reversed the process and asked the computer to create a rule system that would be able to spell whole words when phonemes are specified. For example, the phoneme sequence [kʰot] generated coat because a [k] that is followed by [o] is most often spelled with c, and an [o] followed by [t] is most often spelled with oa. Hanna and colleagues found that 50% of English vocabulary could be spelled with no errors and that another 36% could be spelled with one error on the basis of phoneme–grapheme correspondences alone. Only 14% of the words were "irregular" in that the sound–symbol algorithm spelled them with two or more errors, but many of those errors could be easily corrected by a person (or computer) who knew the word's origin and meaning. These findings can be summarized as follows:

- About 50% of English words were spelled accurately by the computer on the basis of sound–symbol correspondence rules alone.
- Approximately 36% more were spelled with only one error.

- About 10% more were spelled accurately when word meaning, origin, and morphology are considered.
- Less than 4% were true oddities.

A few sound–symbol relationships in English are predictable and invariant. The computer algorithm produced correct spellings for these sounds almost every time. These include the spellings for [ʍ] and [θ], which are always spelled with *wh* and *th*. In addition, the sound [v] is always spelled with a *v*, except in the word *of*, and a *v* is always followed by a silent *e* at the ends of words such as *dove*, *have*, and *live*.

As you might predict, the computer did not do well at spelling compound forms, such as *caretaker* and *daybreak* (they became *cartaecer* and *dabrake*). The sound–symbol algorithm did not account for morphological structure such as assimilated prefixes in *irrational* and *abbreviate*. Word families that represent spelling generalizations, such as the "*f*, *l*, and *s* doubling rule" (*mess*, *stiff*, *grass*), and those that use *-old*, *-ild*, *-ind*, or *-ost* patterns also were missed by the computer. Adopted foreign language spelling patterns, such as *chaise*, *buffet*, *beige*, *croquet*, and *machete* also caused mix-ups because they do not conform to the English orthography system.

A few words in the Hanna and colleagues experiment had spellings that were unique or truly unpredictable. Some were compounds, affixed forms, or foreign words. Others were of Latin or Greek derivation with complex morphological structure, such as *philosophize*, *psychology*, *semicircular*, *officiate*, *schizophrenia*, *polysyllabic*, and *accommodating*. Others were the high frequency, Anglo-Saxon words for common things and ideas, including *said*, *does*, *were*, *who*, *one*, *two*, *their*, *lose*, *gone*, and *done*. Most of these were at one time pronounced in a way that is consistent with their spelling today.

The computer algorithm generated lists that showed how the position of a phoneme and the stress of its syllable affect the spellings of its sounds. For example, the spelling of /k/ is variable but is constrained by the sounds and letters surrounding the /k/ phoneme.

☆ EXERCISE 5.3

Consider these words, and explain the spellings for /k/:

counter	kickball	stack	question
cattle	ketchup	mock	queen
cup	keep	fleck	quit
comb	kind	bucket	quandary

Pattern:

At the end of a syllable following a lax vowel, *ck* is the preferred spelling for /k/ (*decks*, *sticker*, *bucket*). The *qu* combination, when it represents /kw/, always occurs before a vowel. (Words ending in *-que* have been adopted from French, and their French spellings have been retained.) Whether the letter *k* or *c* is used to spell /k/ at the beginnings of syllables depends on the letter or phoneme that follows it. When /k/ is followed by vowels spelled with *a, o,* or *u,* the letter *c* is used (*cat, cushion, cozy*); when /k/ is followed by vowel letters *i* or *e,* the letter *k* is used (*kite, ketchup, keen*). In consonant blends, /k/ followed by /r/ or /l/ is always spelled with a *c* (*clean, crazy*). To add one more layer of complexity, word origin also determines spelling: *ch* for /k/ is used almost exclusively in words of Greek origin, such as *chorus* and *orchestra.*

The complexity and variance of some sound–symbol correspondences can also be illustrated with the vowel /o/. When we learn to spell words like *potato, tomato; toe, foe, Joe, woe; snow, stow, bow,* and *throw,* part of what we learn implicitly is the probability of certain spellings for sounds in certain positions.[11] According to Hanna and colleagues, of all of the words ending in /o/ in the 20,000 English words used most often, a plain *o* spelling is used 140 times, *oe* is used 13 times, and *ow* is used 74 times. Only two words analyzed with unaccented final syllables ending with /o/ are spelled with *oe: mistletoe* and *oboe.*[12] Just for good measure, it is also interesting to note that when /t/ and /d/ follow /o/, the preferred spelling is *oa* (*boat, float, goad, load*); finally, /o/ in the middle of accented syllables at the ends of words is most often spelled *o-consonant-e* (*abode, enclose, alone*). This is the sort of information that most of us learn by exposure to multiple examples rather than through conscious memorization of a rule system.

Clearly, then, memorizing all of the correspondences for sound–symbol relationships would be fruitless and overwhelming. Language teaching should encourage students to search for the consistent speech–print mappings that exist in English. Word study activities, however, must also respect the diversity, complexity, and multilayered nature of language organization. They should allow for the fact that spellings for sounds are influenced by phoneme identity, position of a phoneme in a word, stress on the syllable, phoneme surroundings, language of origin, orthographic units, and morphological structure.

ORTHOGRAPHIC CONVENTIONS

In addition to the sound–symbol rule system, the orthography of English itself embodies constraints on permissible letter sequences and letter uses, many of which were settled by the writers of dictionaries and primers for children in the 18th and 19th centuries. Some letters can never be doubled within a syllable or between syllables in English, such as *j, y, i* (exception: *skiing*), and *k* (exception: *bookkeeper*). Consonant *digraphs* (*sh, th, wh, ch, sh, ng, ph, gh*) act as relational units and spell single speech sounds; they also cannot be doubled. A doubled consonant or its substitute must intervene between a stressed lax vowel syllable and an inflected ending beginning with a vowel (*grabbing, drugged*). The complex spellings *ck, dge, tch,* and *x* replace or act similar to doubled consonants after lax vowels, in words such as *picnicking, dodger, pitching,* and *boxer,* signaling that the preceding vowel is lax. (The grapheme *tch* is used for /č/ after lax vowels. Exceptions to the *tch* generalization include *much, rich, which, sandwich, such,* and *bachelor.*) Tense vowel sounds can never be spelled with single vowel letters before complex consonant units.

Some letters in English are never used in word-final position, particularly *j* and *v.* Thus, the permissible spellings for word-final [j] are *dge* and *ge.* In words ending with [v], such as *love, have, sieve, live, dove, leave,* and *salve,* the marker *e* is placed at the end of the word so that it does not violate the "*v* rule," regardless of the pronunciation of the vowel. In this way, then, all of the words ending in [v] are predictable, not necessarily because of sound–symbol correspondence, but because of orthographic convention.

The letter *e* has several uses in orthography. Sometimes it acts as a relational unit—that is, it represents phonemes directly (*we, bet*)—and sometimes it acts as a marker within a larger orthographic pattern (*rose, enrage*). The letter *e* indicates when a vowel is tense, as in *drape* and *probe*. It indicates when *c* or *g* should have its "soft" sound, as in *stooge, receive*, and *nice*. As mentioned before, the letter *e* also is placed at the ends of words ending with [s] to keep them from looking like plurals, not to mark the vowel (*please*, not *pleas*; *horse*, not *hors*; *mouse*, not *mous*).

Six Types of Syllables

Six basic syllable configurations can be identified in English spelling; Samuel Webster regularized these to justify his 1806 dictionary's division of syllables. The syllable types (see Table 5.4) are useful to know and teach because they encourage students to notice similar chunks of print when they are developing automatic word recognition and spelling skills. Our print system does not represent separate syllables directly; it represents phonemes and morphemes. The syllable "chunks" that students can be taught to identify are a contrivance of scholars, a tool for attacking longer unknown words. The six syllable types are organized around the vowel in the nucleus of the syllable. The closed syllable is the most common spelling unit in English.

☆ EXERCISE 5.4

Classify the underlined syllables in these words by syllable type, and also record syllables that don't fit. List the syllables according to these seven types. The first six are done for you.

<u>hu</u>mor	con<u>sent</u>	bu<u>gle</u>	<u>ail</u>ment
ab<u>surd</u>	phon<u>eme</u>	im<u>pale</u>	<u>vi</u>tal
<u>mi</u>nor	<u>ta</u>ble	re<u>mark</u>	com<u>bine</u>
in<u>spect</u>	bi<u>ble</u>	com<u>pete</u>	<u>boast</u>ful
fes<u>tive</u>	eag<u>er</u>	<u>few</u>	<u>hair</u>cut
<u>ab</u>scess	<u>fur</u>niture	a<u>mong</u>	na<u>tion</u>

Closed	Open	Consonant-*le*	Vowel team	R-controlled	Vowel-consonant-*e*
-sent	*hu-*	*-gle*	*ail-*	*-surd*	*-eme*

Other: _____

Table 5.4.   Types of syllable units

Syllable type	Examples	Definition
Closed	*dapple* *hostel* *beverage*	A syllable with a lax vowel, ending in a consonant
Open	*program* *table* *recent*	A syllable that ends with a tense vowel sound that is spelled with a single letter
Consonant-*le*	*bible* *beagle* *little*	An unaccented final syllable containing a consonant plus [l] and silent *e*
Vowel team (and diphthong)	*awesome* *trainer* *congeal* *spoilage*	Syllable with tense or lax vowel sounds that uses a vowel combination for spelling (diphthongs *ou/ow* and *oi/oy* are included in this category)
R-controlled	*spurious* *consort* *charter*	Any syllable in which the vowel is followed by [r] (vowel pronunciation often changes before [r])
Vowel-consonant-*e*	*compete* *despite* *conflate*	Single vowel, a consonant, then silent *e*

The integrity of the syllable types explains, in many cases, why letters are doubled across syllable boundaries or why two consonant letters appear at the juncture of two syllables (*les/son, nap/kin, pun/dit*). Consider the differences between the words in Column 1 and the words in Column 2:

1	2
writing	written
prefix	suffix
Mabel	marble
maple	apple
super	supper
libel	little

When the vowel in a syllable is lax, the syllable will be closed and will end in a consonant. Therefore, if a closed syllable is connected to another syllable that begins with a consonant, a doubled consonant will result (*little*). If a syllable is open, it will end with a tense vowel sound; there will be no consonant to close it and "protect" the vowel (*libel*). When a syllable containing a single tense vowel is followed by another syllable, there will not be a doubled consonant between the syllables. Samuel Webster regularly applied this definition of syllable form to his divisions of words in his dictionary.

The identification of syllables and how they join together becomes very important to students in about third grade, when they must independently decode words of greater length. If they are not taught to perceive the larger chunks of written words and to associate vowel pronunciation with syllable structure, they will be quite stymied by longer words encountered in reading. If they are aware of syllable units and where to divide them, however, they can read words such as *detective, insulation,* and *accomplishment* with no trouble.

Orthographic Ending Rules

Three major orthographic rules govern addition of endings to words with certain syllable types. The rules apply to both reading and spelling. They are much easier to teach and are much easier for students to learn when students already understand syllable constructions.

Consonant Doubling

When a one-syllable word with one vowel ends in one consonant, double the final consonant before adding a suffix beginning with a vowel (*wettest, sinner, crabbing*). Do not double the consonant if the suffix begins with a consonant.

☆ EXERCISE 5.5

Fill in the blanks.

pat + _____ = patted

_____ + er = runner

step + _____ = stepped

_____ + ing = skipping

begin + ing = _____

sad + ness = _____

beg + er = _____

bad + ly = _____

Advanced Consonant Doubling

When a **multisyllabic** word has a final syllable that is accented and has one vowel followed by one consonant, double the final consonant when adding an ending beginning with a vowel (*transferred, embedded*).

☆ EXERCISE 5.6

Why is the consonant doubled or not doubled in these words?

occur	occurrence	occurred	occurring
commit	commitment	committee	committed
excel	excellent	propelled	propeller
legal	legality	legalization	legalese

Drop Silent e

When a root word ends in a silent *e*, drop the *e* when adding a suffix beginning with a vowel (*blaming, pasted*). Keep the *e* before a suffix beginning with a consonant (*confinement, extremely*).

☆ EXERCISE 5.7

Fill in the blanks.

Base word + suffix = affixed word
Example: fame + ous = *famous*

wise + ly = _____

flake + y = _____

close + ness = _____

blame + ful = _____

ice + y = _____

joke + ing = _____

late + est = _____

state + ment = _____

grade + ed = _____

Change y *to* i

When a root ends in a *y* preceded by a consonant, change *y* to *i* before a suffix (*tried*), except when adding *-ing* (*crying, hurrying*). Note that *y* changes to *i* even if the suffix begins with a consonant (*happiness*). If the root word ends in a *y* preceded by a vowel (*ay, ey, uy, oy*), just add the suffix (*playing*).

☆ EXERCISE 5.8

Take the following words apart into the base word and the suffix, and explain what happened to make these spellings:

studious	sillier	buying
keyed	praying	studying
uglier	stories	happiness
beautiful	sorriest	partying

Pattern:

Morphology and Orthography

For a reader of English to decode unknown words accurately, morpheme boundaries often must be detected. Across morpheme boundaries, adjacent letters do not behave the ways they do when they are within a single morpheme. For example, *ph* does not correspond to /f/ in *shepherd*, *uphill*, and *topheavy*. The homorganic nasal principle discussed in Chapter 3 does not necessarily apply across a morpheme boundary; for example, the *n* in *ingrain, ingratitude,* and *ingratiate* is not changed to /ŋ/ before a new morpheme beginning with /g/ or /k/ as it is within morphemes such as *finger, congress,* or *anchor.*

The English spelling system at all language layers represents morphemes as integral units. In many words, morpheme structure takes precedence over phonology in spelling. Anglo-Saxon words use consistent spellings for inflections, including the past tense *-ed,* the plural *-s* and *-es,* the comparatives *-er* and *-est,* and the *-ing* added to form gerunds (*Walking is not strenuous*) and the present tense (*I am walking ahead*). Meaning is preserved in spelling; pronunciation varies and is not transcribed in perfect detail. The past tense is pronounced variously as [d], [t], and [əd], and only the last form constitutes a syllable. Thus, the relationships among sound, meaning, and spelling in these constructions are particularly complex.

☆ EXERCISE 5.9

Write the sound of the ending ([d], [t], or [əd]), then count the number of syllables in the word. Remember, a syllable is a spoken unit organized around a vowel sound.

Example: talked   [t]   1

Word	[d], [t], [əd]	Number of syllables
instituted		
spelled		
opened		
popped		
offended		
exhumed		
breathed		
approached		
enraged		
prevented		

Now, list together all of the words that share a common pronunciation of *-ed,* and determine why some words have a voiced [d] at the end, some have an unvoiced [t], and some have a syllabic [əd].

The linguistic complexity inherent in the spellings of inflections, as well as the requirement that the user of written English grasp the multiple levels of language organization on which these spellings are based, accounts for the frequency of inflection errors in children's reading and writing. Students with language insensitivity are especially likely to omit, misread, substitute, or phonetically spell the past tense and plural endings (see Figure 5.7).

English is replete with examples of spelling that preserve morpheme identity. In other words, from looking at the word, we can begin to decipher its meaning if we can identify morphemes that recur in other known words. For example, it is advantageous to spell *health* like *heal* and to spell *anxious* like *anxiety*. Some related words look similar in spelling but are pronounced differently, as in *prevent/prevention, press/pressure, machine/mechanic,* and *magic/magician*. Other spellings preserve vowel identity in spelling even though the spoken vowel alternates between a tense vowel and a schwa (*compete/competition, perspire/perspiration*), between a schwa and a lax vowel (*theatre/theatrical, human/humanity*), or between a tense vowel and a lax vowel (*describe/description, sincere/sincerity, phone/phonic, induce/induction, sane/sanity*).

Silent letter spellings are sometimes cases of suppressed phoneme identity in root words; when derivations are created, the "silent" letter is spoken. Some of the words in English whose spellings do not correspond directly to sound, such as *bomb, sign, damn, autumn,* and *hymn,* have related word forms in which the silent consonants are pronounced: *bombard, signal, damnation, autumnal,* and *hymnal*.

In many Latin- and Greek-based words, the stress pattern shifts in their derived forms. Vowels may alternate between schwa and the sounded vowel with a clear identity. Consider these pairs, in which the stress systematically shifts to the syllable before *-tion*, sometimes with a change in vowel quality as well as stress:

Stress change but no vowel change		*Stress and vowel change*	
aggravate	aggravation	admonish	admonition
consecrate	consecration	infest	infestation
dedicate	dedication	compete	competition
prevaricate	prevarication	inspire	inspiration

The prefix-root-suffix structure of many Latin-based words accounts as well for the prevalence of doubled consonants where first and second syllables are joined. Many prefixes have alternate forms. When the prefixes are added to roots, their form changes to match the beginning sound of the root. These changes have occurred mainly for ease of pronunciation. It is much easier to say "ap-proached" than to say "ad-proached" or to say "sup-pose" than to say "sub-pose." The process of changing the consonant at the end of a prefix to match the consonant at the beginning of a Latin or Greek root is called **assimilation.** Doubled consonants near the start of a word often, but not always, signify an **assimilated prefix.**

☆ EXERCISE 5.10

1. Separate the prefixes from the roots of these words, and identify the form of the prefix before it was assimilated. You may want to look back at Table 4.1.

   Example: assemble = *ad + semble*

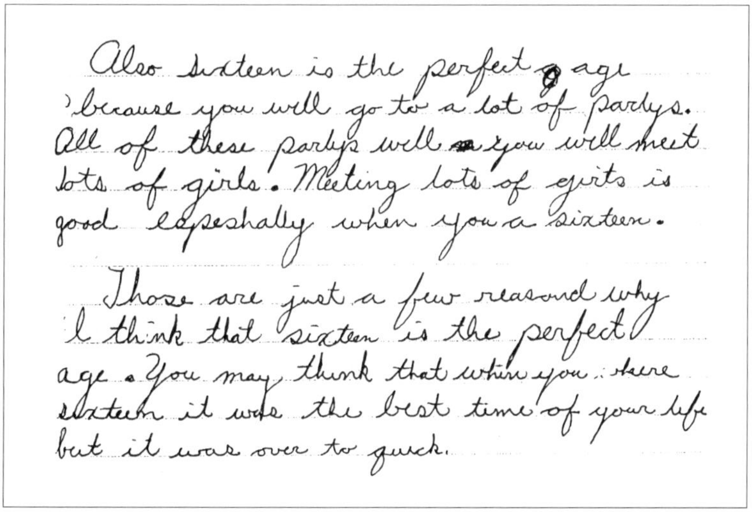
Also sixteen is the perfect age
because you will go to a lot of partys.
All of these partys will you will meet
lots of girls. Meeting lots of girls is
good espeshally when you a sixteen.

Those are just a few reasond why
I think that sixteen is the perfect
age. You may think that when you were
sixteen it was the best time of your life
but it was over to quick.

Figure 5.7. Inflection errors in a 16-year-old's writing (*partys* for *parties*, *reasond* for *reasons*).

irregular = ______________	attract = ______________
colleague = ______________	accommodate = ______________
support = ______________	apprehend = ______________
immigrate = ______________	surrogate = ______________
different = ______________	

2. Now, fix these spelling errors, which were created by using the original prefix prior to assimilation:

inlegal ______________	comrelated ______________
adsertion ______________	adpendix ______________
inmeasurable ______________	subpress ______________
adgression ______________	inluminate ______________

Dialect and Its Relation to Orthographic Knowledge

Regular shifts in pronunciation found in regional dialects are predictable; they are part of a speaker's phonological system. Many phonological forms of words, however, refer to the same meaningful entity. For example, southerners say the word *hear* as [hiə], not [hir]. This shift is predictable in words with [ir]; the link between sound and symbol can be consistent and predictable even though the person pronounces the vowel plus *r* differently from how they are pronounced in standard American English. The same could be said for the Bostonian who says [pʰæk] instead of [pʰark]. Much dialectical variation occurs on vowels, especially *r*-controlled vowels. There is some evidence that teachers who speak the same dialect as their students can reinforce and teach the sound–symbol linkage system more successfully than teachers who pronounce the words differently from their students.[13] What matters when students are learning the spelling system, however, is the constancy, accuracy, and automaticity of sound–symbol connection while learning words; predictable dialectical variation among students and teachers may not be an impediment in that process. When the sound associated with a symbol is referenced vocally and visually in a consistent way, there is a better chance for the linkage to be made.

A second type of dialectical variation involves regular shifts of standard English phonology and grammar that are part of a deeper structural difference in the speaker's language system. These differences often produce a lack of correspondence between the written system of standard English and the sounds of speech. For example, in African American English Vernacular (AAEV) [θ] and [ð] become [t] and [d] in the beginnings of words ([tʰɪ̃ŋ], [dæt]); there are no phonemes [θ] and [ð]. Furthermore, words with medial or final *th* may be pronounced with an [f] or [v] as in [wɪf] or [brʌvɚ]. Therefore, the speaker of AAEV may have more trouble remembering the presence of medial and final *th* in printed words.

A feature of many southern dialects as well as AAEV is deletion of final consonants, as in [čajl] for *child*, [pʰæwn] for *pound*, or [sɔl] for *salt*. Consonant deletion is a regular feature in AAEV. To date, there is very little research on how these dialectical variations affect children's ability to read and spell.[14]

Learning to Read and Spell: The Content Domain

To learn English orthography, the reader and speller must grasp a number of concepts about the relationships between print and speech, the organization of the orthography, and the various levels at which words and the writing system are structured. Regardless of whether students are taught explicitly, their acquisition of reading and writing skills involves understanding the orthographic system in a number of dimensions. These follow in an outline form and delineate the content knowledge appropriate for study of orthography:

I.   Phoneme–grapheme correspondences (Grades K–1)   *Examples*

   A.   Predictable spellings

      1.   Consonants   *him, napkin*

      2.   Lax (short) vowels   *wet, picnic*

      3.   Digraphs   *chin, fish*

      4.   Blends   *dragon, scraps*

   B.   Variant/conditional correspondences (Grades 1–3)

      1.   Single consonants   *dress, edge, result*

      2.   Tense (long) vowels   *grown, light, explain*

      3.   *R*-controlled vowels   *dear, port, bird*

      4.   Diphthongs   *toil, boyfriend; tower, bout*

      5.   Consonant blends   *blink, square, scary*

      6.   Consonant digraphs   *which, kitchen*

      7.   Silent letters and oddities   *knew, walk*

II.	Irregular (odd) spellings of high frequency words (Grades 1–3)	*of, one, enough, said*
III.	Compounds (Grades 2–4)	*breakfast, fifty-one*
IV.	Syllable Patterns (Grades 2–4)	
	A. Closed (lax [short] vowel, syllable ends with consonant)	*si<u>ster</u>, <u>Sep</u>tember*
	B. Open (tense vowel, no consonant ending)	*<u>be</u>hind, <u>no</u>body*
	C. Vowel team (vowel spelled with two or more letters)	*gr<u>ea</u>t; w<u>eigh</u>; b<u>ay</u>*
	D. Consonant-*le* (at the ends of words)	*bu<u>gle</u>, treat<u>able</u>*
	E. *R*-controlled vowel	*<u>por</u>ter, <u>hur</u>dle*
	F. Vowel-consonant-*e* (tense vowel)	*com<u>pete</u>; sup<u>pose</u>*
	G. Idiosyncratic	*ac<u>tive</u>, atom<u>ic</u>; vill<u>age</u>*
V.	Inflections (plural, past tense, and so forth) (Grades 2–3)	*walk<u>ed</u>, want<u>ed</u>; dog<u>s</u>, wish<u>es</u>*
VI.	Orthographic rules and syllable juncture (Grades 2–5)	
	A. Word-final [v]: *-ve*	*have, give, love*
	B. The *f, l, s* doubling rule	*hell, guess, off*
	C. Doubling final consonant rule	*running, inferred*
	D. Change *y* to *i* rule	*studious, beautiful*
	E. Drop silent *e* rule	*baked, coming*
VII.	Homophones (Grades 2–5)	*their, there; to, two, too*
VIII.	Latin-based affixes and schwa (Grades 4–8)	*predict, protection; vision, enjoyment; attend, appearance*
IX.	Greek combining forms (Grades 6–8)	*microscope, psychobiology*
X.	Contractions (Grades 1–6)	*you've, I'll, don't*
XI.	Possessives, plurals (Grades 1–8)	*night's; oxen; alumnae, crises*
XII.	Abbreviations (Grades 1–8)	*etc., St., P.M.*
XIII.	Consonant alternation (Grades 6–8)	*mischief, mischievous; medic, medicine*
XIV.	Vowel alternation (Grades 6–8)	*hostile, hostility; explain, explanation; define, definition; serene, serenity*

SUMMARY

The spelling patterns of English are predictable and logical when one takes into account several major layers of language represented in the orthography. The many factors that determine predictability in spelling include sound–symbol correspondences, syllable patterns, orthographic rules, word meaning, word derivation, and word origin. The idea of predictability is an oversimplification, and it would be erroneous to try to classify English vocabulary in a dichotomous fashion (predictable/unpredictable). Only a few sound–symbol correspondences work all of the time regardless of sound sequence, such as in *that, must,* and *pan.* Other correspondences are predictable but are determined by position of a phoneme in a word, syllable stress, and phonemic environment. These conditional or variant correspondences are much more common than invariant correspondences. Correspondences can be predictable and frequent; they characterize a large set of spellings in the vocabulary. Others are predictable but infrequent; they belong to a limited but distinctive family of words that share a spelling pattern, such as the group including *find, blind, kind, rind, hind,* and *mind.* Odd and truly unpredictable spellings, such as *of, aunt,* and *does,* are only a small percentage of English and are mostly leftovers from our Anglo-Saxon heritage, although those words are overrepresented among the words used most often for writing. Finally, spelling often preserves and visually represents meaningful word parts and meaningful relationships between words and often reflects the language from which a word originated.

☆ SUPPLEMENTARY EXERCISES

1. Find the grapheme that corresponds to each phoneme in the words below. Note that the number of graphemes should equal the number of phonemes.

    s e a   w r e t c h   c h r o m e

    s l i n g   w h o   r a n k

    v i l l a g e   b e a r d   p s y c h o l o g y

2. Underline the consonant blends (not every word has a blend):

    dumb   first   squawk   shrink

    known   muskrat   scotch

3. Underline the consonant digraphs (not every word has a digraph):

    whether   shepherd   daughter

    church   wrack   physic

4. Group the following syllables according to syllable type. Combine each syllable with others (listed or not) to make a real word:

    pete   se   po   ple

    com   ble   ment   ate

    tor   ploit   fer   rain

Vowel

Closed Open Consonant-*le*   team   R-Controlled Vowel-consonant-*e*

5. Sort the following words into groups by the sound of the letter *c*.
    Explain when the letter *c* has a "soft" /s/ sound and when it has a
    "hard" /k/ sound:

    /s/   /k/

    caught

    cereal

    receive

    pecan

    sauce

    incidence

    coagulate

    cuff

    civilization

    Pattern:

6. Explain what happens to "silent *e*" when suffixes are added to base
    words such as the following:

careless	lately	driving	invitation
basement	useless	rising	using
homely	ninety	cloned	simply

    (Some exceptions include *advantageous, noticeable, awful,* and *judg-
    ment;* you need not explain these exceptions).

    Pattern:

7. What are the two phonemes represented by the letter *n* in the follow-
    ing words?

    English   bank   ingot   trunk   _____
    Ecklund   band   input   trundle _____

8. Are the vowel sounds in these word pairs the same or different?

few   feud

grief   sheaf

meadow   better

build   gild

cruise   crucial

boil   boy

9. Make observations about the structure of these words that you could point out while teaching the words to children:

messy

incredulous

solemn

ENDNOTES

1. Owens, 1992.
2. Fromkin & Rodman, 1998.
3. Chomsky, 1970; Chomsky & Halle, 1968.
4. Henry, 1998; Henry & Redding, 1996.
5. Yule, 1996.
6. Ibid.
7. Balmuth, 1992.
8. See Chapter 15 in Balmuth, 1992, for more detail.
9. Hanna et al., 1966.
10. Ibid.; Venezky, 1967.
11. Venezky, 1967.
12. Hanna et al., 1966.
13. Foorman, Francis, Fletcher, Schatschneider, & Mehta, 1998.
14. Labov, 1995. See also discussions in Snow et al., 1998.

ADDITIONAL RESOURCES

Balmuth, M. (1992). *The roots of phonics: A historical introduction.* Timonium, MD: York Press.
Bryson, B. (1990). *The mother tongue: English and how it got that way.* New York: Avon Books.
Chall, J.S., & Popp, H. (1996). *Teaching and assessing phonics: Why, what, when, how. A guide for teachers.* Cambridge, MA: Educators Publishing Service.
Fischer, P.E. (1993). *The sounds and spelling patterns of English: Phonics for teachers and parents.* Morrill, ME: Oxton House.
Ganske, K. (2000). *Word journeys.* New York: Guilford Press.
Hull, M.A. (1981). *Phonics for the teacher of reading.* Columbus, OH: Charles Merrill.
McCrum, R., Cran, W., & McNeil, R. (1986). *The story of English.* New York: Viking.
Moats, L.C. (1995). *Spelling: Development, disability, and instruction.* Timonium, MD: York Press.
Orton, J.L. (1976). *A guide to teaching phonics.* Cambridge, MA: Educators Publishing Service.
Ouaknin, M. (1999). *Mysteries of the alphabet: The origins of writing.* New York: Abbeville Press.

CHAPTER 6

Semantics

Reading is typically defined as deriving meaning from print. Ironically, however, the nature of meaning is the least understood, most abstract area of linguistics. We know when words make sense to us, yet the challenge of unraveling the nature of meaning itself has occupied philosophers for several thousand years. Meaning in language resides in several places simultaneously: in words and their morphemes, in sentence structure, and in the context of the communication. **Lexical semantics** is the study of word meanings, **sentential semantics** is the study of sentence meanings, and pragmatics is the study of context and its effect on meaning interpretation. This chapter has more to say about lexical semantics than about the other topics, but these other topics are touched on as well.

Meaning construction is also individual and personal. You and I might say we comprehended a newspaper editorial we both just read, but if asked to summarize it, we might give significantly different responses depending on our backgrounds, expectations, prior knowledge, and verbal reasoning skills. The sense we have of our own understanding or misunderstanding drives the process of **comprehension monitoring.** An important aspect of comprehension is knowing when and what we have not comprehended. If we are adaptive, we reread, rethink, search for more information, ask for explanation, or engage in other strategies until we do understand. No two people are exactly alike in the way they go about deriving meaning from a text.

The basic organization of lexical (word) and sentential (sentence) knowledge still can be explicated and should constantly inform our instruction. This chapter discusses the meaningful relationships among words, phrases, and sentence structure, and ties information about language to recommendations for teaching vocabulary. The theme of this chapter is that verbal knowledge is organized in networks of associations that have definable structures. Words and concepts are known in relation to one another, not as isolated units. New verbal information is learned in accordance with prior knowledge. Effective teaching elaborates various connections among better-known and lesser-known words, deepens and enriches existing knowledge, and seeks to build a network of ideas around key concepts that are well elaborated.

VARIETIES OF WORD MEANING

Word meanings are, for the most part, completely arbitrary verbal signals for things and ideas. There is no particular reason that the word *scar* means one thing and *scare* means another. Norton Juster portrayed the arbitrary nature of word meaning in *The Phantom Tollbooth* when the main character Milo found himself wandering in a strange land called Dictionopolis and noticed that letters were hanging off the tree branches:

> "I didn't know that words grew on trees," said Milo timidly.
> "Where did you think they grew?" shouted the earl irritably. A small crowd began to gather to see the little boy who didn't know that letters grew on trees.
> "I didn't know they grew at all," admitted Milo even more timidly. Several people shook their heads sadly.
> "Well, money doesn't grow on trees, does it?" demanded the count.
> "I've heard not," said Milo.
> "Then, something must. Why not words?" exclaimed the undersecretary triumphantly.[1]

Words have meanings that are agreed on by speakers of a language. Although word meanings are constantly evolving, individual speakers are not free to use words in any way they like or to make up words at will because others may not understand the words. Meanings are shared and meanings evolve by agreement. Each of us has a lexicon, a mental dictionary residing in the brain that contains more information about words than a published dictionary would be able to print.

Denotative and Connotative Meanings

Words have denotative meaning and **connotative meaning.** Denotative meaning is embodied in formal definitions and describes the theory, quality, action, or relationship denoted by the word. Connotative meaning triggers the network of associations to other words and ideas. For example, the denotative meaning of the word *prejudice* is "judgment before the truth is known" (*pre* and *judi* are the Latin prefix and root meaning *before* and *to judge*, respectively), usually resulting in unfair treatment of the person or group being judged. This denotative meaning, however, does not include the instantaneous reaction most of us have to the mention of the word *prejudice,* which in our society has become associated with injustice to social and racial groups, political movements, and legal actions. Those associations, learned from reading or hearing a word in context repeatedly, are connotative. Connotative meanings may be rich and are tempered by individual experience. They comprise many other concepts and experiences that together compose a **semantic field** (see Figure 6.1). Semantic fields are constructed gradually over time on the basis of many encounters with words in context. As we read, we constantly add to the information in our semantic fields.

Definitions and Semantic Features

Denotative meaning is concisely stated in dictionary definitions. Definitions may include an alternate phrase or synonym, the category to which the idea or thing belongs, and the characteristics or features of meaning that distinguish the word from others similar to it. For example, a *train* is a *transport vehicle* that *travels on a rail system.*

Content words, which are nouns, verbs, adverbs, and adjectives, are defined by or embody the category to which they belong and the properties of the object or idea, including its grammatical class. Content words have essential and peripheral attributes—**semantic features**—that define them and cause them to be distinct from or to overlap with other words. The essential attribute of the word *knee* is that it is a joint; the essential attribute of the verb *race* is that of competition involving speed; the essential attribute of *red* is that of primary color, and so forth.

☆ EXERCISE 6.1

Practice making your own definitions for words by stating 1) a synonym or category for each word and 2) its most important properties, distinguishing characteristics, or semantic features. For example, *to saunter* means *to walk slowly, without any visible sense of direction or purpose* or *to meander.* Then, list a few connotations that each word has for you.

gut

family

princess

impeach

powder

An essential attribute of a content word is the **superordinate category** to which it belongs. *Superordinate* means "above" or "inclusive of the concept we are talking about"; thus, the superordinate category is the umbrella under which specific

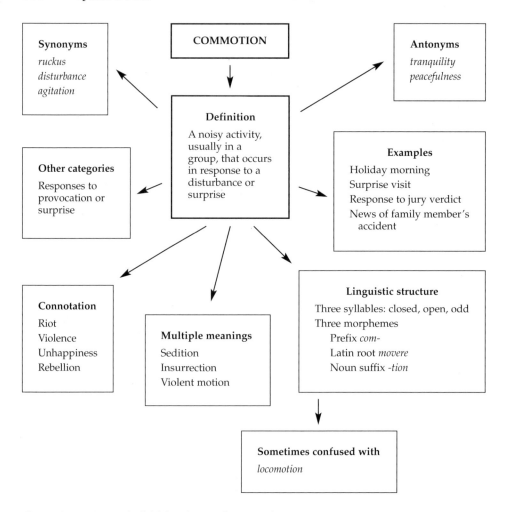

Figure 6.1. Semantic field for the word *commotion.*

words or concepts fit. The superordinate category *joints* includes *knees, elbows, ankles, knuckles,* and *shoulders* as category members or examples. Additional attributes differentiate each item from others in the same category. For example, the category *joints* can be further subdivided into *hinge joints* and *ball joints.* Within the **subordinate category** of hinge joints, the peripheral attributes of *knee* that differentiate it from *elbow* are the direction in which the joint moves, the location in the body, and the presence of a kneecap.

Meaning becomes refined and elaborated in our lexicons as more and more attributes are learned and associated with a word. As more refinements and distinctions between members of a category are understood, a **hierarchical** set of ideas evolves in our understanding, in which some ideas are superordinate and some are subordinate or subsumed within others.

In Exercise 6.2, what was the superordinate category, and what were the major subcategories? Were any words more difficult to classify than others? How deep and thorough does one's knowledge and experience with the subject matter have to be before this kind of exercise can be undertaken productively?

☆ EXERCISE 6.2

Arrange the following words into categories as quickly as you can. Do not add any words or leave out any words (time limit: 10 minutes).

paper	maple	rope	bark
softwood	beams	pine	axe
hardwood	mulch	oak	chain saw
paneling	birch	root	kindling
parts	branch	truck	needle
guitar	skidder	products	trees
spruce	mahogany	leaf	trunk

In the Landmark College program (in Putney, Vermont) for students with language learning difficulties, an exercise similar to Exercise 6.2 is used to assess how well incoming students can impose organization on material that belongs to a semantic network. The ability to manage the structure of meaning by identifying superordinate and subordinate categories to which words and concepts belong is a critical skill both for reading comprehension and for written composition. Success with outlining and categorization depends on background knowledge and experience with the content.

Content words (again, these are nouns, verbs, adverbs, and adjectives) have many attributes known as **semantic properties.** The better a word is known, the more of its properties or features are known. For example, you probably can state that *sumptuous* is an adjective that means "luxurious" or "opulent," that often is used to refer to feasts, and that usually connotes decadent overindulgence. Sacred celebrations in many tribal cultures often include *sumptuous* banquets that are prepared with great effort. The word *costly* shares some meaning with *sumptuous,* although it is not a synonym. The words *sumptuous* and *costly* are often used in the same context, that is, to describe lavish events, but the two words do not refer to exactly the same qualities. The meaning of the words *sumptuous* and *costly* overlap partially; they share some semantic properties but not enough for the words to be used interchangeably as synonyms.

Synonyms

Semantic properties of words may overlap to any degree, from a few shared elements of meaning to many, so the condition of **synonymy** (sameness of meaning) exists on a continuum. Some words are tentative or possible synonyms, whereas others are near-perfect substitutes for each other. *Car* and *automobile* are near-perfect synonyms; *van* and *truck* are further apart in meaning but are often used to refer to the same type of vehicle. *Picture* and *photograph* are partial synonyms; they are used interchangeably in some instances but not when the word *picture* refers to a framed painting. Absolutely perfect synonyms do not exist because each word has connotative and denotative meanings that distinguish that word from every other word. Even *couch* and *sofa* convey slight differences of formality and function within a house, depending on the speaker's frame of reference.

Class Membership

When words share semantic properties, they are said to be in a **semantic class** or network. *Tense, relaxed, explosive, laconic, hostile,* and *cautious* all are adjectives that belong to the class of words that have to do with temperament. *Bright, capable, brilliant, dull, average,* and *slow* all are terms that are used (some more kindly than others) to describe intellectual ability. *Multiply, divide, add, subtract, square,* and *factor* all are words in the semantic class having to do with mathematical operations. When we use words or hear words that we know, we mentally activate all of the words we have learned within that semantic network. A context that activates what we know will make it easier for us to recognize known or partially known words. If we are already thinking about math, for example, and we expect to read a word that belongs in our semantic field for math, we will recognize mathematical terms and read them a little bit faster than we would if there were no context.[2] This phenomenon is known as a *priming effect* in psychological experiments designed to unravel how we read words. The priming effect results from prior activation of a semantic network in memory.

☆ EXERCISE 6.3

What essential shared attribute or semantic feature of the following groups of words causes them to belong to a semantic network?

1. elephant, ostrich, giraffe, hippopotamus, rhinoceros

2. nephew, son, mother, daughter, cousin, aunt, grandfather

3. lamp, flashlight, candle, lantern

4. bob, crop, shave, plait, braid, curl

5. rice, barley, wheat, millet, oats

Formal Marking of Semantic Features

The process of identifying the meaning elements that words share or do not share is called **semantic feature analysis.** Semantic feature analysis is a way of objectifying, or describing formally, how meanings overlap and how they differ. By marking the presence or absence of a meaning element in a word with a plus (+) or minus (–), we can represent formally the ways in which words share meaning. *Home* and *house* are words that share a great deal of semantic overlap, to the point that they are often used as synonyms. We could represent some of their features as follows (a +/− symbol indicates that the feature is optional):

home   +dwelling   +human   +familial   +occupied   +/−structure
house   +dwelling   +human   +/−familial   +/−occupied   +structure

The featural overlap of common words in our vocabularies can be illustrated with a semantic feature chart that delineates the attributes shared by two or more words. For example, mark the semantic features of the words *wood* and *timber* with a plus or a minus sign. Your answers may be different from those of another person.

	trees	processed	grows	large	burns	rots	breathes
wood							
timber							

The difference between the terms is slight and is likely to be known better by people who work in construction, logging, milling, or hardware supply. Knowing a word well means knowing its shades of meaning, when to use it, and how it is different from other words with overlapping features. A major use of the word *timber* is its reference to the raw material in trees, standing and cut, before they have undergone milling or processing. Lumberjacks might use these terms more selectively than ordinary individuals because their knowledge of connotative meanings is much deeper than that of other people. The words *timber* and *wood* have several other meanings that overlap much less with each other. For example, *timber* also refers to a support beam in a house, an object that is not usually referred to as *wood*.

Other Kinds of Semantic Features

Words also have other properties or features that determine how they can be used in sentences and what words we combine with them or substitute for them. For example, nouns may be subdivided into those that are **countable** and those that are not. Countable nouns can take the quantifier adjectives *many* and *few*; **noncountable,** or mass, nouns can take the adjectives *much* and *less*. You can eat *too many carrots* but not *too much carrots*; or you can have *too much rice* but not *too many rice*. However, you can have *too few dollars* or *less money* than you'd like. The word *more* can modify either countable or noncountable nouns. Verbs may be subdivided into those that must take a direct object and those that can stand alone without an object. This is called the **transitive property** of verbs. For example, I can *subject* someone to something, but I can't *subject* (with no object). I can *reject* something, but I can't just *reject*. I can, however, *procrastinate* all by myself, without doing anything to anyone but me. Other intransitive verbs are *sleep, think*, and *hesitate. Sleep* and *think* can be followed by prepositional phrases (*I will sleep <u>until</u> 9:30; I thought <u>about</u> what you said*). But the word *hesitate* must be followed by an infinitive (*I hesitated <u>to call</u> you*). Content words have grammatical properties that most speakers of the language know just by hearing the words spoken often in context.

Types of Opposites

Antonyms are words of opposite meaning, but they fall into three subordinate categories—**gradable, complementary,** or **relational**—which differ in several ways. Gradable antonyms take meaning from the context in which they are used. Their meaning is relative and expresses the degree to which an attribute characterizes a person or an object. The attribute exists on a hypothetical scale, and the word conveys a point on that scale.

☆ EXERCISE 6.4

Consider these terms, and insert as many words as you can between the qualitative poles that each of these antonyms represents:

elated _____ depressed

scalding _____ freezing

expensive _____ cheap

Interpretation of a gradable antonym depends on one's frame of reference. For example, cheapness is a quality that exists primarily in relation to the resources of the buyer and the norm of the context. A cheap ring at Tiffany & Co. is an expensive one most everywhere else. Objects can also be affordable or inexpensive, two points between sets of gradable antonyms.

Within gradable antonym pairs, variable relationships exist. In some cases, one of the pair is **marked** and the other unmarked. The unmarked feature is the one that we use to ask questions about the attribute. For example, with *tall* and *short*, we ask, "How tall is the athlete?" even if someone tells us that he or she is short. If an object is described as *small*, we are likely to ask how big it is. *Tall* and *big* are the unmarked partners in the antonym pairs. If we are adjusting the volume on a stereo between *loud* and *soft*, we can ask if the music is loud enough or soft enough to please the listener. *Loud* and *soft* are members of a gradable antonym pair that are not marked.

Complementary pairs of opposites are dichotomous and do not represent points on a scale. The qualities exist in a complementary relationship; if one condition exists, the other cannot, and vice versa. There are no gradations between the opposite conditions. One can be married or single, dead or alive, male or female. The expression *to see things in black and white* means to think that if something is one thing it cannot be the other. A person who thinks this way thinks of all opposites as complementary when in fact some are gradable and fit into a continuum of qualities that has points referred to as "gray areas."

Antonym pairs may also be relational or symmetrical. Although they do not represent mutually exclusive qualities, relational antonyms represent qualities that exist in reciprocal relationship to one another, such as *coach–team, parent–child, supervisor–supervisee, doctor–patient, cause–effect*. That is, if you refer to one member of the relational pair, the existence of the other member of the pair is assumed.

A common way of forming antonyms in the language is to add prefixes, including *un-, in-, non-, mis-,* or *dis-,* to words as permitted: *happy/unhappy, hospitable/inhospitable, conformist/nonconformist, identify/misidentify,* and *allow/disallow*.

☆ EXERCISE 6.5

Determine whether these antonym pairs are gradable (g) or complementary (c):

light/heavy   introvert/extrovert
left/right   terrestrial/celestial
pretty/ugly   present/absent
awake/asleep   empty/full
open/shut   indoors/outdoors
buy/sell   civilized/barbaric

Multiple Meanings

Many English words, especially the oldest ones that derive from Anglo-Saxon, have more than one meaning. Some of our most common words can refer to dozens of different concepts or objects. Many of the words that children encounter early in their reading experience have multiple meanings. For example, think of the meanings of *run* that come to mind without looking them up in a dictionary. They would include the following and many more:

- Move the legs in a fast gait
- A fast gallop of a horse
- The first leg of a race
- A flaw in a stocking
- A path for skiers
- The path of a small creek
- The flow of sap in trees
- To print a story in a newspaper

☆ EXERCISE 6.6

List as many meanings as you know for the following words:

stand

cap

pot

jam

fit

Now, consult a dictionary to compare its listings with your meanings (an unabridged dictionary is best because it will show many meanings for each word). How many meanings did you know in comparison to how many are listed?

PHRASE AND SENTENCE MEANING

Phrase meaning depends on both individual word meanings and the structural combination of the words. Structural combination includes the order of the words and their grammatical role. For example, *reading to learn* means something different from *learning to read, I mean what I say* is different from *I say what I mean,* and so forth. A **paraphrase** preserves the meaning of a phrase but may change the order of the words or use different words that refer to the same ideas.

☆ EXERCISE 6.7

Paraphrase the following phrases:

lying over and over

a curious fantasy

stuff and nonsense

guests at the execution

ignore the petty details

blazing away brightly

mind the master's words

these melancholy little sighs

To write paraphrases or substitute words for each other with the intention of preserving meaning, children must be able to draw on a rather extensive vocabulary. Once again, a critical skill that we expect of children when they write depends on breadth and depth of word knowledge, including knowledge of the grammatical roles that words can play.

Phrasal meaning is organized around nouns and verbs, the two kinds of content words found in a kernel sentence (a minimal phrase containing a one-word noun plus a one-word verb that can stand as a complete sentence). The meaning of a **noun phrase** depends on how its adjectives, articles, and clauses are combined. In English, word order in the noun phrase influences meaning. For example, *tile floors* are different from *floor tiles.* The *head* of the phrase is the word after the preceding modifier. When a noun phrase includes a prepositional phrase, the preposition conveys the relationship between the head noun and the noun that follows the preposition, as *in the antique desk with the brass handles* or *the full moon over the mountain.*

The term **reference** is used to denote the relationship between a noun phrase and the object or idea to which it points. The object or idea to which a noun points is called a **referent.** When two or more terms refer to the same thing, they are **co-referents.** For example, the words, *White Fang* (proper noun), *wolf* (noun), *he* (pronoun), and *snarling brute* (noun phrase) all may refer to the same animal and therefore are co-referential. Reference is so embedded in our use of language that we may have little conscious awareness of our dependence on it for making sense of what we read. A good writer, however, is constantly aware of the need to make reference explicit and unambiguous to the reader.

☆ EXERCISE 6.8

With lines and arrows, mark the referential relationships that exist among the nouns, pronouns, and noun phrases in this passage from the Wizard of Oz (the first few are done for you):

"And I want him to send me back to Kansas," said Dorothy.

"Where is Kansas?" asked the man, with surprise.

"I don't know," replied Dorothy sorrowfully, "but it is my home, and

I'm sure it's somewhere."

"Very likely. Well, Oz can do anything; so I suppose he will find

Kansas for you. But first you must get to see him, and that will be a hard

task; for the Great Wizard does not like to see anyone, and he usually has

his own way. But what do YOU want?" he continued, speaking to Toto.

Toto only wagged his tail, for, strange to say, he could not speak.[3]

The interpretation of noun reference can be problematic for students who read slowly, who are inattentive, or who have trouble understanding the structure of written language. We must rely on linguistic cues while reading to a much greater extent than while conversing. Face-to-face communication supports messages in a number of ways that written communication does not. When we read, no other person is present who will, through gesture, phrasing, repetition, or emphasis, clarify what a word or phrase refers to. The reader must figure it out as he or she proceeds.

The **verb phrase** is the one grammatical entity that is a requirement in any written English sentence. Even one-word imperative sentences have a verb: *Halt!*

The verb has properties that affect both the subject and the object of a sentence. In formal linguistic descriptions, noun phrases are assigned thematic roles in relation to the verb. These include roles such as **agent, goal, theme, location, instrument,** and others that are beyond the scope of this book. Knowing a verb includes knowing how the verb must be used in relation to the noun phrases in the sentence. For example, as speakers of English, we know that the verb *to take* requires, at a minimum, an animate subject who will perform this action (agent) and a thing that will be the object of this action (theme). *The cheese takes* thus would not be a grammatical sentence.

Sentence meaning depends, of course, on the meaning of the constituent noun and verb phrases. The facts, events, or states of being to which the sentence refers may be true or false, depending on what we know about the world. *Mark McGwire hit 30 home runs in the 1998 baseball season* is a false sentence (he hit 70) even though it is made of meaningful words in a grammatical order because the factual reality of the world does not match the sense of the sentence.

Sentences that mean the same thing have the same **truth conditions.** The active and passive constructions *Princeton defeated North Carolina* and *North Carolina was defeated by Princeton* refer to the same conditions of truth. The statements *Roger is taller than Barrett* and *Barrett is shorter than Roger* also refer to the same truth or extension of meaning. The existence of truth conditions allows us to know when ideas expressed in different ways mean the same thing. In a sense, truth conditions are the referents for sentences, just as objects, events, and ideas are the referents for single words.

One sentence **entails** another if the truth of one sentence includes or implies the truth of another. For example, the sentence *Paula has lived with her husband for 20 years* entails the sentence *Paula is married.* The sentence *We buried the cat yesterday* entails the sentence *The cat died.* If the first sentence is true, then the entailed sentence must be true.

Nonsense

For various reasons, some sentences may make no sense. A grouping of words may sound like a sentence because word order follows the rules of syntax, but the sentence may include logical, lexical, and/or grammatical impossibilities. For example, the sentence *The Tower of Pisa leans straight up* contains a logical impossibility: towers that lean are not straight up. *Silent clanging wishes believe in magic* sounds poetic but makes no sense because the verb *believe* must have an animate subject (agent) and nothing can clang and be silent simultaneously. Poetic imagery, even in common children's rhymes, often exploits logical impossibilities to stir the imagination or please the ear, such as in this nursery rhyme:

> Hey! diddle, diddle,
> The cat and the fiddle,
> The cow jumped over the moon;
> The little dog laughed to see such a sport,
> And the dish ran away with the spoon.

The sentence *So frelled was she with her dumboggery that she zappled a shraveport right there* obeys the rules of word order and word structure. The words are even pronounceable and spelled according to standard syllable structure; they just have no referents. Therefore, they cannot be understood and are uninterpretable. Children's poems and stories, fortunately, often delight in nonsense, such as this New England lullaby:

Winky, Blinky, niddy, nod!
Father is fishing off Cape Cod.
Winky, Blinky, sleepy eyes,
Mother is making apple pies.
Winky, Blinky, cannot rise
What's the matter with baby's eyes?
Winky, Blinky, cre, cri, creep,
Baby has gone away to sleep.

Special Phrases: Idioms

All languages use word combinations or phrases that do not mean literally the sum of what their individual words mean. **Idioms** are phrases used as a unit to convey meanings and tend to resist any kind of evolutionary modification of form. Idioms must be known by the reader or interpreted from context just the way a new word meaning must be deciphered from context. Learning the meaning and use of idioms such as *get off your high horse, he took me to the cleaners,* and *my goose is cooked* is often a challenge for those who are learning a language because the whole idiomatic phrase has denotative and connotative meanings. Idiomatic usages must be learned separately from those of the individual words that compose them.

☆ EXERCISE 6.9

What does each of these idioms mean?

mark my words

hit me up

tread on his toes

blow the whistle

leave her high and dry

bite your tongue

'til the cows come home

get out of my hair

line your pockets

Many idiomatic expressions can, of course, be interpreted literally to mean something quite different from their figurative sense. When students misunderstand an idiom, they are usually hung up (so to speak) on its literal meaning. If one thinks that *emotional baggage* has something to do with suitcases, one might miss the point of a discussion about character dynamics. Likewise, if you tell someone, "Eat my hat," they should know you are not telling them to eat anything.

Metaphor

Metaphor is ubiquitous in written language, especially in descriptive or poetic text, and is probably the most common figure of speech. A metaphor is an implied or indirectly stated comparison between an idea and an unusual referent. A metaphor invokes the qualities of an unusual referent to describe or characterize the target word. For example, if someone is *blinded by love*, it means that the person's ability to make good decisions is impaired, that he or she has lost his way, and that he or she behaves like someone needing guidance—like a person who cannot see. The sense is clear although the meaning is figurative.

Metaphor is an efficient and pleasing way to convey sense. Expressions can be spare but rich in associations, as in this elegant poem about autumn by Emily Dickinson:

The morns are meeker than they were,
The berry's cheek is plumper,
The nuts are getting brown;
The rose is out of town.
The maple wears a gayer scarf
The field a scarlet gown.
Lest I should be old-fashioned
I'll put a trinket on.

PRAGMATICS: MAKING SENSE IN CONTEXT

Usually meaning is conveyed and understood within a **context.** Context, or the conditions that surround the use of language, may be either **situational** or **linguistic.** Situational context includes all of the real-life circumstances in which verbal communication takes place and the relationships among those who are communicating. *Linguistic context* comprises the words that precede and follow a given phrase or sentence—the discourse in which the language is embedded. *Discourse* consists of combinations of sentences that are woven together to convey complex ideas and may include a few sentences or 1,000 pages of a long novel.

Situational context includes what we know about the sensitivities and needs of our listener or the person who is reading what we write. We adjust how we say things according to what we think the listener (or reader) needs or wants to hear (or read). In conversation, we take turns; we give as much information as the listener wants; we attempt to inform clearly; we maintain a topic; we fill in gaps of silence when people are unfamiliar to us; we avoid asking intrusive questions and so forth, or other people view us as socially insensitive. Such pragmatic skills of verbal communication have parallels in the production of written language. Writers should be considerate of their readers' needs. For example, the author of a text-book provides more or less information about a topic depending on the anticipated background knowledge and interests of readers. Just as we would adjust our tone of voice and manner in saying, "Would you mind if I borrowed your car?" in accordance with who owned the car we wanted to borrow, so we adjust for our audience when we write. **Considerate text** is written so that the reader's need for clarity, topic maintenance, background, explicitness, and so forth is respected.

All of us speak a form of English that is a dialect, a regional or cultural variation of standard English. For some speakers, dialectical variation from standard English is minor; for others, home language patterns vary so extensively from the standard that "academic" language, the language of books, must be learned almost as a second language. Learning standard English does not require giving up a home dialect. It does, however, require awareness of which dialect to use in which situation. Individuals who shift easily between a home dialect and standard English engage in "code switching" on cue. For example, some members of the black community who use both AAEV and standard English often speak one dialect with community members in informal, home situations and another in formal, academic, or multicultural situations.[4] Most important, they know which situation calls for which linguistic behavior. Similarly, all of us use one tone of voice with children and another with elders; we use one choice of words with old friends and another with new acquaintances. The ability to interpret dialogue, understand an author's tone and intent, or compose a formal letter are pragmatic aspects of reading and writing.

REFERENCE IN DISCOURSE

Many topics in the domain of discourse analysis are beyond the scope of this book, but several are relevant to our discussion of meaning. Groups of sentences, arranged as paragraphs within larger organizational structures, are tied together thematically with a number of devices. **Anaphora** is the replacement of a whole noun phrase, thought unit, or sentence with a pronoun, as in *Teaching spelling with the new program is so effective that I make time for it every day.* In this sentence, the neutral pronoun it refers to more than spelling; the pronoun refers to *teaching spelling with the new program,* an elaborated noun phrase.

In written discourse it is not uncommon to find the anaphoric referent for a pronoun some distance away from the pronoun in the text. Obviously, the ability to hold the beginning of a sentence in phonological memory is important for making sense of anaphoric reference that is distant from its source, as in this passage from *Alice's Adventures in Wonderland:*

> There was a *table set out under a tree in front of the house,* and the March Hare and the Hatter were having tea at *it:* A *Dormouse* was sitting between them, fast asleep, and the other two were using *it* as a cushion, resting their elbows on *it,* and talking over *its* head. "Very uncomfortable for *the Dormouse,*" thought Alice, "only, as *it's* asleep, I suppose *it* doesn't mind."[5]

In contrast to anaphora, **deixis** is the relationship of a word to its referent that relies exclusively on situational context. The pronouns of the first and second person, including *I, you, we, yours, ours,* and *mine,* always depend on the specific context of the speaker and those whom the speaker addresses. The demonstrative articles *this* and *that* are always deictic; to know what they refer to, one must know the context in which they are used. Time expressions such as *yesterday, today,* and *tomorrow* are deictic; their referents change daily. *Here, there, this park, that mountain,* and similar terms of place are deictic; what they mean depends on where you are. These terms, along with anaphoric reference, present another challenge of language interpretation to young readers. If the referents are misunderstood, comprehension suffers.

TEACHING VOCABULARY AND OTHER ASPECTS OF MEANING

Reading researchers have known for many years that a substantial amount of the variance in reading comprehension is attributable to knowledge of the meanings of individual words. That is why the most valid and reliable reading tests usually include a direct measure of vocabulary knowledge. Good readers know more words and are better at deciphering the meanings of new words as they read. Likewise, they comprehend better because they know more words. Knowledge of a word, however, may be superficial or deep, sparse or elaborated, and abstract or deeply personal. Even if we knew little about the systematic comparison of methods in reading research, we might surmise from the earlier sections of this chapter that instruction should respect and complement the way in which semantic knowledge is organized in our verbal memories. In fact, research on vocabulary instruction has upheld teaching principles that are logical extensions of the language processes presented here.[6]

1. *Choose words for direct teaching that are central in a semantic field.* Of the 1,000–3,000 new words that fourth through eighth graders encounter in the texts they read each year, teachers have time to teach directly only a few per day. Even if 10–15 new word meanings were taught to a class each week, there would be time to teach fewer than 400 all year long. Many more words are learned from context, usually during reading. How should the words for instruction be chosen?

Words important to the theme of a passage read in the classroom are the most appropriate to study. Words presented in lists dissociated from a meaningful context are less desirable. Words are most likely to be learned thoroughly within a network of related ideas pertinent to a topic, theme, or text that is being studied. Words are learned more deeply when many aspects of their meaning have been explored, when they have been read and used in context, and when the entire knowledge structure to which they belong has been activated and developed.

2. *Teach word meanings in relation to other words that are known.* Vocabulary instruction should aim to teach students the relationships that exist among words so that they are learned as part of a network of ideas. The conceptual network should be presented as a structure that encompasses the superordinate, subordinate, and coordinate relationships between terms. Synonym and antonym relationships, analogies, and categorization should be staples of vocabulary development as well because they highlight the connections between ideas.

Graphic techniques for depicting semantic networks and word relationships are helpful to children. Semantic maps are visual depictions of the relationships among words and concepts. They are drawn as branches emanating from a central idea. When categories are labeled, examples of the categories and properties of category members are given. A map of the relationships among ideas in the semantic network *friends* might look like this:

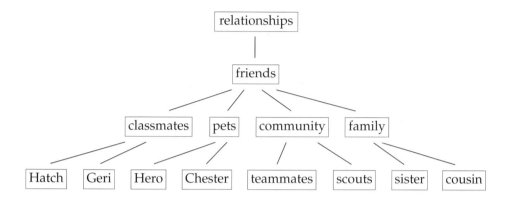

The web of interconnected ideas can be expanded as widely as one wishes. Traditional outlines are also extremely useful for depicting superordinate, subordinate, and coordinate relationships among concepts.

3. *Use linguistic and situational context to develop word knowledge.* The majority of words children learn are learned from reading itself.[7] Many more words are encountered in fiction and nonfiction text than are ever learned from television, conversation, or language spoken by adults.[8] We may have to read and hear words many times in context before we attempt to use or "own" a new word. There is no substitute for wide and varied reading to gain that exposure. Context supplies implicit information not only about word definition but also about the pragmatic constraints of appropriate word use. Reading itself also supplies a network of experiential associations to which a new word's meaning can be anchored.

4. *Teach both denotative and connotative meaning.* Students should be taught that complete definitions include a synonym and/or category to which the word belongs and some information about the word's distinguishing features. Connotative meaning should be discussed as well: When is this word used? What associations does it bring to mind? Connotative meaning will be learned when the word is encountered repeatedly in situational context.

5. *Teach multiple meanings for the same word.* Learning more than one meaning for a word deepens and broadens students' vocabulary knowledge and may facilitate both word recognition and comprehension. Even a simple word such as *lot* can be explored by young children from the early stages of reading instruction. With the discovery that words have multiple meanings, children may generalize an expectation for diversity and variation in language use. Children might then be less concerned with memorizing a "right" definition and more interested in learning and using several meanings for words.

6. *Teach idioms, metaphors, and other figures of speech.* Many students, such as those who are learning English as a second language, those who are concrete or literal in their interpretation of language, or those who simply have not been exposed to a wide range of uses of words and phrases, need to be taught to interpret and use idiomatic language. In lieu of memorizing meanings, students usually enjoy locating figurative uses of language in fables, poetry, songs, and tall tales. Use of

these terms in songs, poems, descriptions, and students' own stories should be encouraged.

7. *Identify the referents for nouns, pronouns, and phrases.* During discussions of text, awareness of anaphoric and deictic reference should be heightened through simple questioning techniques. Can the students say to whom or what a word, phrase, or pronoun refers? Can they draw arrows from one word to its referent or actually replace words with others? Can they rewrite sentences in which proper nouns are replaced by pronouns? Can they list all of the words in a passage that refer to the same person, place, or thing?

SUMMARY

Understanding what we read depends on the ability not only to decode the words in print but also to know the words' meanings in relation to real world truths and in relation to other words. Effective vocabulary instruction will target words most important in a semantic field and teach not only their individual meanings but also how they are connected to other words. Connections among words can be portrayed as synonyms, antonyms, overlapping meanings, thematic associations, analogies, class and example relationships, and figures of speech.

Meanings themselves are both definable and context dependent. Knowing a dictionary definition (denotative meaning) is important but is not sufficient for being able to use a word appropriately. We also must know how to use it, with whom, when, and for what shade of meaning. We must use it many times over to use it well. Thus, memorizing a dictionary of all of the words in a language would not enable someone to communicate with other speakers of that language. Deep, rich knowledge of words and varied experiences with their use are necessary for proficient reading and writing; paradoxically, children will learn words most readily from reading itself.

☆ SUPPLEMENTARY EXERCISES

1. On a separate sheet of paper, make an outline or **visual categorization** using the following words. Use all of the words and no others. Take about 10 minutes.

creep	adult	cockroaches	legs
burrow	body parts	blood	egg
homes	locusts	cocoon	antennae
invertebrates	algae	soil	larva
food	grasshoppers	wings	abdomen
ants	pupa	sac	mosquitoes
crawl	locomotion	thorax	
nest	web	species	
hop	head	leaves	
flies	microbes	phases	

2. Choose an important abstract word used in science teaching, such as *symmetry, evolution,* or *microscopic.* Make up several sentences that use the word. Then leave the word out of the sentences, and give the "cloze" sentences you have created to someone else. Did they identify the word? Now ask your subject if he or she could define the word on the basis of the contextual uses you gave. What are the advantages and limitations of context use in word definition?

3. In what way are the following groups of nouns the same and different?

    daughter, sister, niece   *versus*   nun, waitress, nurse

    rooster, bull, ram   *versus*   hen, ewe, cow

    table, chair, pencil   *versus*   water, cream, sand

    table, chair, pencil   *versus*   faith, hope, charity

    husband, brother, son   *versus*   clerk, preacher, judge

    grandfather, mother, niece   *versus*   brother, sister, cousin

4. Mark the antonym pairs as gradable (opposite ends of a continuous scale) or complementary (either/or).

	Gradable	*Complementary*
dead/alive		
hot/cold		
above/below		
fat/skinny		
married/single		
mild/spicy		
angry/delighted		
hideous/gorgeous		
straight/crooked		
introvert/extrovert		
winner/loser		

    Now take one of the *gradable* antonym pairs, and fill out the scale from one extreme to the other with words that show degrees of meaning.

5. Mark with a plus or a minus sign the semantic features that do or do not describe the following four objects:

	cup	*glass*	*mug*	*bowl*
handle				
ceramic				
round				
tall				
holds hot liquid				

holds cold liquid

paper

transparent

6. Use the following format to make a definition for each of these words: *web, tornado,* and *poem.*

    A/An _____ is a/an _____ (synonym)
    that _____ (is, does, has) _____ (critical feature).

7. Without using a dictionary, list on a separate sheet of paper all of the meanings you can think of for the following words: *walk, mouth, star,* and *book.*

8. List all of the descriptive words that come to mind when you think of the word *palace.*

    Compare notes with another person. How many of the same words or associations did the other person have?

ENDNOTES

1. From THE PHANTOM TOLLBOOTH by Norton Juster. Copyright © 1961 by Norton Juster. Copyright renewed 1989 by Norton Juster. Reprinted by permission of Harper-Collins Publishers Ltd.
2. Adams, 1990, 1998; Becker, 1985.
3. Baum, 1956, p. 84.
4. Perry & Delpit, 1998.
5. Carroll, 1865/1960.
6. Beck, McKeown, Hamilton, & Kucan, 1998; Beck, McKeown, & Omanson, 1990; Irvin, 1990; Nagy, 1988; Stahl & Shiel, 1992.
7. Cunningham & Stanovich, 1997, 1998; Nagy, Anderson, & Herman, 1987.
8. Hayes & Ahrens, 1988.

ADDITIONAL RESOURCE

Pinker, S. (1999). *Words and rules: The ingredients of language.* New York: Basic Books.

CHAPTER 7

Syntax

Every teacher of reading and writing seeks to improve students' ability to construct clear, concise, grammatical sentences. Understanding of sentence structure supports reading comprehension, and construction of sentences is elementary to written expression. Many teachers, however, are unsure how to enable students' growth in sentence comprehension or production. Some experts argue that mastery over complex sentence structure will accrue primarily when students read well-written text. The same experts often argue that students will learn to manipulate the parts of incomplete or awkward sentences primarily from having to write compositions and that explicit teaching about sentence structure is unnecessary and unproductive. Other experts argue that exercises such as diagramming, combining, or anagramming sentences will foster skill in sentence production beyond what will develop from writing practice itself. The purpose of this chapter is not to resolve pedagogical disputes about the role of direct instruction of syntax in reading or writing but to provide basic information about the operation of syntactic structures in language that may be useful in the classroom. With this conceptual base, teachers should have an easier time interpreting students' difficulties, demonstrating how sentences work, and selecting instructional strategies for students.

CORRECT OR INCORRECT SYNTAX?

To begin, the study of syntax, or sentence structure, in linguistics is not equivalent to the study of grammar in English classrooms. The term *syntax* refers to the underlying architecture of phrases and sentences produced by speakers of a language. It does not refer to the conventional rules of acceptable grammar that are formally taught in school and that are established to preserve standard usage. Syntactic processing is a level of language use that depends on recognition of permissible word sequences, interpretation of the meaning of word sequences, and generation of novel word sequences that conform to the structure of an underlying system. Linguists such as Noam Chomsky have devised theories of syntactic rule systems to explain and describe actual patterns of speaking (**descriptive grammar**) but are not concerned with upholding a particular standard of grammatical usage. The standards of correctness that are upheld by editors and writers of English and agreed on to promote consistent forms of expression are known as **prescriptive grammar.** Some countries even assign the role of prescriptive grammarian to an individual or committee; for example, it is the duty of designated royalty in England to guard the English language and the duty of an appointed committee in France to keep the language pure.

Whether we as speakers of English judge a sentence to be grammatically correct is a function of our education, home dialect, and current linguistic community. Even the most educated will judge to be acceptable sentences that violate rules of prescriptive grammar. Split infinitives, for example, are frowned on and discouraged by English teachers, but we can talk about *seeking to modify gradually* or *seeking to gradually modify* the way words are used, and our listeners are not likely to care which way we express the idea. The difference between *lie* and *lay* is being lost; although *to lay something down* pertains to putting an object down, it is common in American English to use the word *lay* for *lie,* as in *She went to lay down.* Acceptable grammatical usage is always in a state of change.

NATURAL KNOWLEDGE OF SYNTAX

Although it is beyond the scope of this book to explain syntactic structure in depth, to contemplate and become aware of some aspects of sentences is helpful. Consider the following sentences (an asterisk indicates a sentence that would not be spoken):

1a.   Addictions are overcome only with determination.
1b.   Only with determination are addictions overcome.
2a.   Flights are taken daily with instructors.
2b.   *Daily with instructors flights are taken.

In the case of sentences 1a and 1b, the meaning of the sentences is the same even though the order of the words is different. The word strings of the second set appear on the surface to be similar to those of 1a and 1b, respectively, but the change of word order that occurred between sentences 1a and 1b does not work to preserve the meaningful relationship between sentences 2a and 2b. Sentence 2b is awkward and would not be spoken. Something about it violates our natural sense of permissible syntax. Thus, we can recognize the relationship between word order and meaning and make judgments about sentences even though we may not be able to say why one sentence "sounds okay" and another does not. These examples, however, show that something beyond the surface arrangement of words is governing the structure of sentences. Meaning is not a simple function of the surface arrangement of words.

Other common linguistic phenomena must be explained by a theory of syntax. Consider this sentence:

3.   Flying hang gliders can be hazardous.

Sentence 3 can have two different meanings: The act of flying hang gliders can be dangerous to the person who does the flying, or the hang gliders themselves, when they are being flown, can be hazardous to anything else that happens to be in the air. In this case, one sentence can mean two different things. Such sentences are said to be ambiguous; the meaning is not clear without further clarification from context. Once again, something deeper than the surface order of the words governs our interpretation of meaning. We sense that there are two underlying meaning structures into which the same word sequence would fit.

There are, however, many instances in which meaning seems very dependent on word order. Consider these sentences:

4a.   These are the times that try men's souls.
4b.   These times that are men's try the souls.
4c.   *Try times men's are souls the these.

The first sentence (quoted from Thomas Paine) is grammatical and well known to those who have studied the American Revolution. The second contains the same words in a possible order; however, not only is the meaning different from the first sentence, but it also would be lost on most of us. The last example is such an obvious transgression of word order possibilities that it has no meaning to any English speaker. In these cases, word order makes a great deal of difference to meaning.

Our knowledge of syntax also involves a sense of how words must be used in relation to one another. Consider these sentences:

5a.   *The drunken man offended.
5b.   *Jerry laughed the joke.

Neither sentence is grammatical because the verbs are not behaving as they are designed to behave. The first sentence is incomplete. Someone who offends must offend someone or something. The verb *offend* itself has grammatical properties that require it to be used in a specific slot within a structure and that require the sentence to contain something else known as an *object* (in this case, the person or entity that is offended). A parallel but different condition exists in sentence 5b; the verb *laughed* cannot be followed by a noun phrase. We cannot laugh a joke, although we can tell a joke. Laughing is not something one does directly to someone or something else, although often the verb takes a prepositional phrase that tells at what, for what, when, or how the laughing occurred.

So, word order is related to meaning but in no simple way. Word order may change, but meaning may stay constant. Word order may be constant but may allow for different meanings. Changes in word order may affect meaning drastically. The properties of words themselves dictate some aspects of sentence structure, as they only seem to fit in certain slots. A language user's ability to know what is permitted and to understand the relationship between word order and meaning is part of that speaker's natural grammatical knowledge. It is learned from exposure to language and requires little formal instruction. In this context, then, the term *grammatical* refers to the collective judgments of a group of language users, not to formal, testable knowledge of what is "proper" English usage.

☆ EXERCISE 7.1

Which sentences are grammatical or acceptable according to your knowledge of the English syntactic rule system? Can you explain why a sentence is grammatical or ungrammatical?

Me and Harry went on a trip together.

I don't have no more gum to share.

If you breathe deep, you will be able to hold your breath longer.

Justina did real good on her exams.

My friend was stressing over all she had to do before vacation.

Due to overbooking, Bart was not able to get on the flight.

Can I take my dog with me in the car, Mom?

Do you have enough to go around?

Molly slept the baby all night.

GENERATIVE GRAMMAR

Clearly we do not learn to produce sentences by imitation or memorization because most of what we say is novel. The exact sequences of words in most of our sentences have not been spoken before. Other than stock phrases such as conversational niceties, routinized exchanges, or commands, we are much more likely to produce a sentence that has not been produced before than we are likely to repeat a sentence that is already familiar or in some way practiced. In the world of publishing, in fact, there is a prohibition against using the exact words of another writer without explicit attribution; novelty is expected.

If we are a native speaker of English or any other language, it is not necessary to have heard a sentence before to interpret its meaning or judge its grammaticality. Consider these sentences:

6a.   Paddington placed a purple azalea on the tiny tenderloin before serving it.
6b.   Roman gladiators levitated before suddenly dematerializing.

These sentences most likely are novel; they do not refer to actual events, but they can be interpreted. They may not jive with either fictional or nonfictional reality—they may have no truth value—but they are grammatical forms that follow the requirements of English.

Likewise, groupings of words may sound like sentences, but the words may not mean anything:

7a.   Tawley blepped the righton so sormedly that it deniliated.
7b.   If gyxes can squow the perfaction, then prinzes should remell the chobbi-fiddy.

Lewis Carroll's famous "Jabberwocky" poem from *Through the Looking Glass*[1] may be the best literary example of the delight that we can experience while reading syntactically correct nonsense. The existence of syntactically correct nonsense indicates that the syntactic rule structure exists apart from the meaning of the words it might contain. Sentences can have structure regardless of whether they mean anything true; conversely, truth can be expressed in sentences that are considered to be grammatically incorrect (*He weren't no good at caring for his family, no ways*). Syntax can be manipulated and analyzed in its own right, independent of meaning. We use the underlying forms to generate an infinite number of word combinations.

PHRASE STRUCTURE

The features of and truths about sentences already mentioned suggest that words are slotted into an underlying syntactic order when sentences are formed. Some words clearly go together or work together within the architecture of a sentence. When words seem glued together as a functional unit, they are part of a **phrase.** A standard **simple sentence** such as *The driver totaled the car* has a natural break between the **subject** (*The driver*) and the **predicate** (*totaled the car*). The natural division between these two essential parts of a sentence can be depicted in a tree diagram as follows:

The driver   totaled the car.

The recognition of these two basic phrases in the simple sentence requires syntactic knowledge of underlying, functional phrase structure. The subject is composed of a noun phrase plus any articles and/or modifiers that tell us more about the subject. Similarly, the verb phrase in the predicate is the action or state attributable to the subject plus any words that tell us more about that action or state of being. To elaborate our tree diagram of the simple sentence, we can label these parts NP (noun phrase) and VP (verb phrase), the two essential parts of a sentence (S). The symbols

$$S \longrightarrow NP + VP$$

mean that a sentence is composed of a noun phrase and a verb phrase. Note that this is quite different from defining a sentence as "a complete thought" or as a "group of words with the first word capitalized and punctuation at the end." In a tree diagram, the symbols NP and VP are always noted as the first branches of the sentence tree:

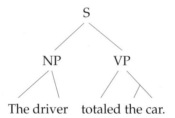

The phrase structure diagram now begins to look like an inverted tree that will grow as the sentence is elaborated. Each elaboration, however, will be subsumed within the basic hierarchy of sentence organization.

Elaboration works systematically within the subject and the predicate. For example, we can elaborate the subject and the predicate by adding adjectives (Adj.) before the nouns, by marking the article (Art.) and noun (N) within each noun phrase, and by marking the verb (V) and any noun phrase within the verb phrase:

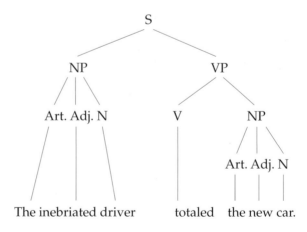

We can also elaborate the subject or the predicate by adding a prepositional phrase (PP), consisting of a preposition (Prep.) and a noun phrase, to either a noun or a verb phrase:

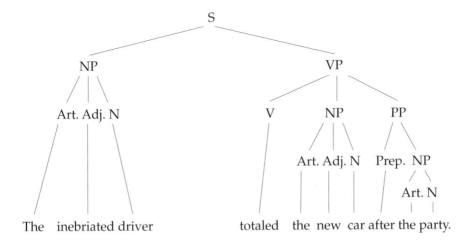

The phrase structure tree shows the words that naturally are grouped together. Prepositional phrases (PP) such as *after the party* have the structure of a preposition (Prep.) followed by a noun phrase (NP), which must have at least an article and a noun (Art. + N).

A similar array of words, however, could represent a different underlying phrase structure. If the sentence were *The inebriated driver totaled the new car with the sunroof*, the hierarchical structure of the sentence would be somewhat altered.

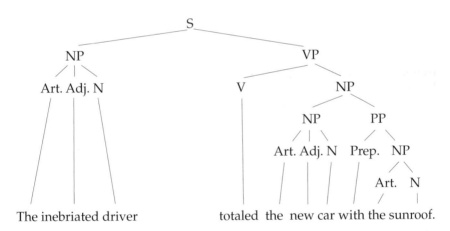

This phrase structure tree shows that the prepositional phrase is part of the verb phrase (predicate) but that it is nested under the noun phrase that contains the direct object (*the car*). In the previous sentence (*The inebriated driver totaled the new car after the party*), the prepositional phrase modified the verb: It told when the car was totaled, not what kind of a car it was.

Clearly, a sentence is more than a string of words. Sentence meaning is governed by underlying, hierarchical structures that allow us to interpret the clusters of words (phrases) that convey sense. Postulating underlying syntactic structures also helps to explain phrase ambiguity. A phrase such as *modern fashion designer* can have two possible meanings, as shown in the following diagrams:

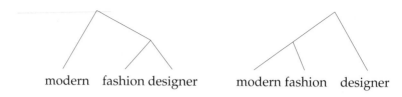

modern fashion designer   modern fashion designer

Either the designer creates modern fashions, or the fashion designer is modern, depending on what the context demands. Without a theory of underlying syntactic structure, linguists would not be able to explain why the phrase *modern fashion designer* is ambiguous at all. No other explanation at the level of word order or word meaning suffices to explain the fact that one simple phrase can have more than one sense.

Grammatical Categories

Many different words could be slotted into each of the phrase structures considered so far. There are endless phrases of the kind used in the sentences just diagrammed. Sentences whose words would fit exactly the same structure include the following:

8a. The conscientious teacher filed the summary reports after the meeting.
8b. A hungry shark circled the damaged boat during the storm.
8c. The soccer player kicked the muddy ball into the net.

Thus, a syntactic structure can hold an endless number of words if those words belong to the categories required for each slot in the syntactic scaffolding. All of the words that can be used in each specific slot in the sentence architecture belong to a **grammatical category.** For example, the category for *hungry, conscientious,* and *damaged* is one that supplies descriptive words immediately before nouns. These words, which we call *adjectives,* can also occur together in a sequence, as in *the hungry, tired, conscientious teacher.* Furthermore, the words in this category can be modified to show the degree to which the characteristic exists, as in *hungry, hungrier,* and *hungriest,* or *conscientious, more conscientious,* and *most conscientious.* The comparative and superlative forms of adjectives can be formed in two ways, but no words other than adjectives can be modified in such a manner.

Grammatical categories can be **lexical** or **phrasal.** Lexical categories contain words; phrasal categories may contain a single word or a group of words. Lexical categories are subsumed under phrasal categories. A phrase must contain a lexical item of the same type and function. For example, as stated previously, a noun phrase must contain a noun. A verb phrase must contain at least one verb, although it may also contain a direct object or a prepositional phrase. A prepositional phrase must contain a preposition, and it almost always contains a noun phrase. That is why ending a sentence with a preposition (*Do you know where she went to?*) is viewed as awkward or inappropriate—sort of.

The grammatical category for noun phrases, like others, serves more than one specific job within the sentence form. Noun phrases, which consist of at least a noun and often an article, adjective, or other modifying clause, may function as the subject of a sentence, the object of a verb, or part of a prepositional phrase. (Noun phrases may be as short as one word if that word serves as a noun.)

☆ EXERCISE 7.2

Identify noun phrases from among the following:

she	lovely peaceful silences
green and red	Montenegro
after running	were playing joyfully
many criminals	among the very best
the best swimming	

If a phrase can be combined with a verb phrase to make a complete sentence, it can be classified as a noun phrase. Thus, although the color words *green and red* are used most commonly as adjectives that modify a noun, they can also be a noun phrase, as in *Green and red are popular at Christmas*. Words may belong to more than one grammatical category, such as *object, contest,* and *market,* which can be nouns or verbs.

Linguists need to use grammatical categories to explain certain characteristics of words. Categories help explain why words behave differently from each other and why they can be used only in certain places in a sentence structure. The category of nouns makes sense because the words that belong to it can be plural, and no other words can be plural. It is convenient for linguists to list all of the forms that exist for plural nouns and assume that any noun will have one of those plural forms, as in the following words: *deer and sheep; wishes, lies,* and *dreams; criteria and data; alumni and alumnae;* and *crises and metamorphoses.* All are plurals, but the last three sets of words are formed with unusual patterns that are preserved directly from Latin and Greek. The characteristic of plurality then becomes a test for whether a word is a noun. The words *gracefuls, fasts, aboves,* and *thes* do not exist, so they must not be nouns. Some abstract nouns (*integrity, trustworthiness*) do not have common plural forms, however, so more than one test is needed to determine whether a word belongs to the noun category. It is also generally true that nouns can be preceded by articles *a, an,* and *the,* so even though *integrity* cannot be pluralized, we can say *The integrity of the leader was in question* and confirm that the word is a noun.

The grammatical categories we are exploring are usually presented in traditional grammar instruction as parts of speech. We are traditionally taught at least eight parts of speech in English classes: nouns, verbs (including auxiliary verbs), adjectives, adverbs, articles, conjunctions, pronouns, and prepositions. These terms or categories are convenient for instruction and linguistic description, but they do not pertain to any concrete, observable aspect of language that is transparent to the user. There is no reason why a student would be aware of these parts of speech unless identification, classification, and manipulation have been taught and practiced. Awareness of categories must be developed through exercises that foster metalinguistic reflection on the structure of sentences and the roles that words play.

Transformations

To explain further the structure of sentences, linguists must explain how statements are transformed into questions, imperatives (commands), and exclamations. It is not enough to classify sentences into these four basic types; in addition, certain rules seem to govern how a speaker gets from one sentence form to the other. Certainly students are constantly required to be able to transform questions into statements, such as on tests. One seventh-grade student showed a lack of skill in integrating the words of a question on a science test into the words of a lead statement: *Why ionic bonds are capable of conducting electricity is that ionic bonds . . .*

A **transformation** is an operation that moves phrases around within a given sentence structure. Our syntactic knowledge tells us that we can move some phrases and not others; that we can move phrases to certain positions but not others; and that to change a simple sentence from a positive statement to a negative statement, a passive voice statement, or an interrogative, certain rules must be followed or our meaning will not be understood by the listener. Consider these sentences:

9a. Becket murdered the prince in the castle.
9b. The prince was murdered by Becket in the castle.
9c. In the castle, Becket murdered the prince.
9d. Becket murdered the ruler of the nation.
9e. The ruler of the nation was murdered by Becket.
9f. *Of the nation, Becket murdered the ruler.

Sentences 9a and 9d appear on the surface to be very much alike. Simple diagrams, however, demonstrate that their underlying structures are different:

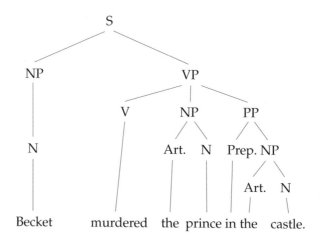

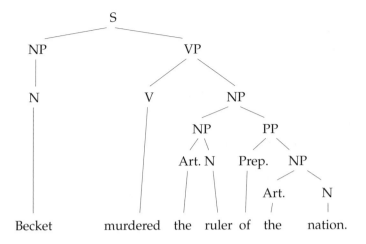

S
NP   VP
N   V   NP
                        NP   PP
                     Art. N   Prep.   NP
                                    Art.   N
Becket   murdered the ruler of the   nation.

The prepositional phrase in 9a acts differently from the prepositional phrase in 9d. In 9a, the prepositional phrase *in the castle* modifies the verb or is directly subsumed under the verb phrase. In 9d, the prepositional phrase *of the nation* modifies the noun in the noun phrase that makes up the object. These differences become important when a transformation from the active to the passive voice is constructed. In the passive voice (sentences 9b and 9e), the prepositional phrase occupies a different place; in sentence 9b, it stays with the verb phrase. In sentence 9e, it is moved with the noun phrase. Sentences 9c and 9f also show that the prepositional phrase behaves differently according to underlying syntactic structure. If the prepositional phrase *of the nation* is separated from the noun that it modifies (*ruler*), the sentence no longer has integrity (9f). When the phrase *in the castle,* however, is moved to precede *Becket murdered the prince* as in 9c, no meaning is lost and the sentence is permissible.

Differences in the underlying structure also determine what kind of interrogative transformations are allowed. Consider these sentences:

10a.   Becket murdered the prince in the castle.
10b.   Whom did Becket murder in the castle?
10c.   Becket murdered the ruler of the nation.
10d.   Whom did Becket murder?

The first question transformation (10b) uses the interrogative pronoun *whom* to replace the object noun phrase *the prince,* inserts the auxiliary *did,* and preserves the verb and prepositional phrase that modifies it. The second question transformation (10d) replaces the entire object noun phrase *the ruler of the nation* with *whom.* We could not transform 10c into *Whom did Becket murder of the nation?* again because the prepositional phrase is part of the noun phrase in that sentence structure.

SUMMARY

As speakers of a language system, we have syntactic knowledge that includes tacit awareness of phrases and grammatical categories for words, of the underlying phrase structures on which sentences are built, and of the ways in which various transformations can be produced. The "sentence sense" we would like to cultivate in students should be part of their natural linguistic capability. Many students, however, speak nonstandard dialects or have limited access to models of standard English usage. Others have limitations in language processing ability that interfere with comprehension and production. Subtle problems with syntax comprehension and production may be most obvious under the stringent demands of complex text reading and academic writing.

The theoretical constructs discussed in this chapter do not explain in detail what type of practice or instruction may improve students' ability to formulate, interpret, or manipulate the parts of sentences for comprehension or writing. Direct practice with sentence manipulation, however, can build students' facility with language analysis and production. The exercises that conclude this chapter represent a variety of strategies for sentence expansion, transformation, combination, and analysis that can be adapted for any age group.

☆ SUPPLEMENTARY EXERCISES

1. (To be done with a group) Each person should write a 6- to 12-word sentence on a strip of paper and then cut it apart into words. (Long sentences are not necessarily more difficult than short sentences.) Each group member gives his or her sentence anagram to another person as a puzzle—the object is to reconstruct the original sentence. Observe whether the person clusters words in phrases as he or she begins to work. As a group, discuss strategies that people used to solve the sentence puzzles.

2. Combine the following sets of simple sentences into elaborated single sentences that preserve the main idea of each simple sentence.

   Set #1

   The team won the game.

   They won in overtime.

   The team was determined.

   The game was for the championship of the league.

   Set #2

   The Coast Guard undertook a mission.

   They searched immediately after the plane crash.

   They searched for debris.

   They looked for survivors.

   They were not optimistic.

   Describe the operations you carried out on the simple sentences to combine each of the sentence sets into one complete, elaborated sentence.

3. Below are some kernel sentences. Elaborate each kernel sentence by first asking questions of the subject and predicate, such as "How many?" "What kind?" "Where?" "How?" "When?" or "How long?" and then adding these answers to the kernels.

Presidents lie.

Fans swoon.

Hawaii calls.

4. The following sentences are uninteresting because they are both unelaborated and formed with "1 dollar" words. Change the sentences to make them more interesting; use some "10 dollar" words that preserve the part of speech of the originals, and elaborate each sentence by adding phrases to the subject and predicate. Complex and compound sentences are allowed.

The fish swam around the boat.

The boy caught the fish.

He threw it back.

5. Given the following bit of charming nonsense by Lewis Carroll,[2] identify the subject and predicate of each sentence. Then identify the grammatical category (part of speech) that each of the italicized words is likely to be:

'Twas *brillig* and the *slithy toves* did *gyre* and *gimble* in the *wabe;*
All *mimsy* were the *borogoves* and the *mome raths outgrabe.*

6. In one nonstandard English dialect, speakers say, "I is going with you," and, "You is going with me"; the past tense becomes "I were going" and "He were going." In addition to observing that this is nonstandard grammar, can you find any reason that this verb form might be a systematic change in a grammatical category? Consider all of the forms of the verb *to be,* and speculate on the nature of the change to the verb in the nonstandard dialect:

I am	we are	I was	we were
you are	you are	you were	you were
he is	they are	he was	they were

7. The following phrases are ambiguous. Draw simple tree diagrams to show the phrase structures underlying the ambiguities of each phrase. Explain the different meanings of each.

negative film developer

older women's doctor

English language translator

white Audi driver

red maple cabinets

ENDNOTES

1. Carroll, 1865/1960.
2. Ibid., p. 134.

ADDITIONAL RESOURCES

Carlisle, J. (1998). *Models for writing.* Novato, CA: Academic Therapy Publications.
Englemann, S. *Reasoning and writing.* Chicago: SRA/McGraw-Hill.
Greene, J.F. (1995). *LANGUAGE!: A reading, writing, and spelling curriculum for at-risk and ESL students* (Level 2). Longmont, CO: Sopris West.
Greene, T., & Enfield, M.L. (1993). *Framing your thoughts.* Bloomington, MN: Language Circle Enterprises.
Harris, K.R., & Graham, S. (1994). *Helping young writers master the craft: Strategy instruction and self-regulation in the writing process.* Cambridge, MA: Brookline Books.
King, D.H. (1989). *Writing skills for the adolescent.* Cambridge, MA: Educators Publishing Service.
Strong, W. (1983). *Sentence combining: A composing book.* New York: Random House.
Warriner, J.E. (1988). *English composition and grammar: Complete course.* Orlando, FL: Harcourt Brace & Co.

CHAPTER 8

Language and Instruction

Many disputes that preoccupy professionals in reading education might be resolved with reference to known stages of reading and writing development and the learning required at each stage. Readiness for learning to use language is less a function of general maturation than it is a function of linguistic knowledge and linguistic awareness. Knowledge of each layer of language organization proceeds in stage-like progressions in the domains of phonological awareness, concepts of print, word recognition, and spelling. The development of proficiency in reading and writing, even in domains such as syntax and discourse processing, which are not as well-defined, follows the principles of other language-learning processes. Language learning involves the perception and assimilation of the structural patterns and rules of the language, development of the ability to discern when those patterns and rules apply, and memory for specific linguistic units and linguistic forms, which are then used in language production. Instruction is most likely to be successful when the content being taught matches what the child is ready (conceptually) to learn.

THE EMERGENT READER

The child who comes to reading and writing with some exposure to books and stories may or may not understand the **alphabetic principle,** that alphabet letters are

Table 8.1. Emergent reader characteristics and needs (ages 4–5)

Child knows	Child needs to learn	Teaching strategies
A few alphabet letters	All alphabet letters	Teach alphabet matching, naming and ordering.
Rhyming, clapping syllables	Phoneme segmentation and blending	Use Sound Boxes, Say-It-and-Move-It,[a] and Say It Fast.
How to write letters of own name	Writing all letters	Provide multisensory practice with arrows to show direction of letter strokes.
Concepts of print	Letter–sound connections	Teach keyword association, feeling the sound, sorting words by sound, and building words with letter cards.
A few icons or signs; can read own name	30–50 known words in print	Have child trace and say whole words and match words to pictures, people, or objects.
How a story goes	Retelling, describing, connecting story to own experience	Use wordless books, created books, and shared reading and writing.

[a]Instructions and materials for this activity can be found in Blachman, Ball, Black, & Tangel (2000).

used to represent the segments of speech. Gaining this understanding is critical for early reading success. As intervention studies have shown over and over, children who do not grasp how the alphabet works are likely to need help developing phoneme awareness as well as knowledge of letter names and the sounds they represent.[1] These are the most critical skills to teach in kindergarten if reading failure is to be prevented.

The stimulation of language comprehension and language use in kindergarten will set the stage for later reading comprehension. Exposure to language in books is particularly helpful. Children expand their vocabularies when they are read to and engaged in talking about their reading experiences.[2] Vocabulary is learned from books more than from normal conversation with adults or children or from television exposure. Children who are less familiar with books may need to be taught what to expect from print. Table 8.1 aligns the child's level of literacy with appropriate instruction goals and strategies.

Phoneme Awareness

Several validated instructional approaches for kindergarten phoneme awareness development are now available.[3] Typically children enjoy these programs, which take about 15–20 minutes of class time per day over a period of 15–20 weeks during the last half of kindergarten. Well-designed programs follow the sequence of phoneme awareness development typical of most young learners (see Table 8.2) and give children ample practice with each activity over several days. There is a gradual progression from global auditory awareness and focusing activities to manipulation of the speech sounds in words. A number of research studies[4] have suggested that powerful phoneme awareness development programs have the following characteristics:

- A gradual, systematic progression through a developmentally and linguistically appropriate sequence of activities
- Brief, fun, active manipulation of oral language
- Minimal or carefully chosen use of print in beginning lessons
- Gradual introduction of print as children become aware of sounds
- Instruction in how to blend sounds together as well as how to take them apart or substitute them for one another
- Use of modeling, demonstration, and application rather than lengthy explanations
- Use of active responses from children, such as moving counters into boxes, showing syllables or sounds with blocks, matching objects, moving cards in a pocket chart, clapping, speaking, and singing (worksheets are seldom effective during lessons)

Early Alphabetic (Early Decoding) Stage

The cornerstone for early reading success is the ability to decode the words fluently using letter–sound correspondences (see Table 8.3 for more on early alphabetic reader characteristics and needs). Decoding proficiency permits and fosters a child's automatic recognition of whole words as fluency is acquired.[5] Some words, such as *said*, must be memorized as **"memory" words** from the beginning because

Table 8.2.   Progression of phoneme awareness development

Age typically mastered by (in years)	Skill
3	Recitation of rhymes Rhyming by pattern alliteration
4	Syllable counting (50% of all 4-year-olds can count syllables)
5	Syllable counting (90% of all 5-year-olds can count syllables) Phoneme counting (fewer than 50% of all 5-year-olds can count phonemes
6	Initial consonant matching Blending two to three phonemes Phoneme counting (70% of all 6-year-olds can count phonemes) Rhyme identification Onset–rime division
7	Blending three phonemes Segmentation of three to four phonemes (blends) Phonetic spelling Phoneme deletion
8	Consonant cluster segmentation Deletion within clusters

Note: Based on a synthesis of many studies; formerly published in the California Reading Leadership materials, Sacramento County Office of Education, 1997.

Table 8.3. Early alphabetic reader characteristics and needs (ages 5–6)

Child knows	Child needs to learn	Teaching strategies
50 sight words	100–150 sight words	Build a file box for words.
Blending/segmenting three and four sounds orally	Blending letter sounds through a new word	Teach recognition and spelling of letter–sound correspondences in one-syllable words.
Consonant sounds in beginning of words	Consonants, short vowels, silent *e*, consonant digraphs, blends	Provide practice reading *decodable* text.
How to spell sounds in words using inventive strategies	Conventional spelling vocabulary	Have child sort words by spelling pattern, spell by sounding out during dictation, and use in sentences.
How to attempt to write sentences under pictures	How to write complete sentences Question/statement exchanges	Use child-created books, sentence frames, and elaboration of subject and predicate, and make questions.
How to write letters slowly	How to write letters fluently	Offer practice writing whole alphabet.
How to retell events/stories	Classification and ordering of ideas Elaborated verbal reporting	Use story frames, group composition. Ask child to retell, reenact, summarize, and predict.

they are both irregular and frequent in written text. Phoneme awareness training should continue in first-grade reading instruction as a component of reading lessons, with an emphasis on transferring blending skills to reading print. Many students need to read text that provides practice in the letter–sound associations they have been taught.

Decodable text provides concentrated practice with specific sound–symbol associations and a few learned **sight words**. Reading decodable text provides a bridge between phonics instruction and the reading of trade books. One strategy for making decodable text more appealing in content and story line than is usually achieved with a limited vocabulary is to intersperse text for an adult to read with lines that the beginning reader can read. Robert Slavin has used this technique extensively in his Success For All program.[6]

Even though the focus of beginning reading instruction must be learning how to read, daily lessons must also include vocabulary development, exposure to information and ideas in books, and familiarity with language patterns in written text. Language instruction at these levels may occur in conjunction with reading aloud to children or helping them memorize repetitious language patterns in books designed for shared reading.

At the first-grade level, the teacher must ensure that the student can employ a strategy of sound–symbol association and sound blending so that independent reading of unknown words is possible (see Table 8.4 for more first-grade reader characteristics and needs). During this stage, rapid recognition of whole words develops in tandem with phonic word recognition; one supports the other. Most of the regular one-syllable correspondence patterns should be introduced for word recognition, although the introduction of these patterns for spelling should be more slowly paced.

PRINCIPLES FOR TEACHING DECODING WELL

One of the reasons that instruction in decoding has not been executed effectively at times is that it is a complex and technical undertaking. If the principles below are followed, however, it can be efficient and successful.

Follow a Logical Organization

The most common approaches to teaching sound–symbol correspondence are based on the alphabet sequence and the sounds of 26 letters. If beginning instruction in decoding is limited to the alphabet letter sounds, however, the identities of consonants /ʍ/, /θ/ (voiceless), /ð/ (voiced), /š/, /č/, /ŋ/, and /ž/ and vowels /ɔj/, /æw/, /ɔ/, /ʊ/, and /ə/ (schwa) are obscured because no single letters of the alphabet represent these phonemes. Twelve phonemes of approximately forty remain "hidden" when the alphabet is the organizing basis of instruction. A few letters also have no defined job. The letter *c* is redundant for /k/ and /s/. The letter *q* is redundant for the sound of /k/, and the letter *x* is redundant for the combination /ks/ or the phoneme /z/.

The alphabet–sound approach in phonics instruction also overlooks the fact that some letter names bear little relationship to the sounds that the letters repre-

Table 8.4. Beginning to middle first-grade level reader characteristics and needs

Child knows	Child needs to learn	Teaching strategies
Short vowel patterns, silent *e*, digraphs, blends	Vowel teams, diphthongs, *r*-controlled forms, basic syllable patterns	Ask child to sort words, build with letter cards, read words with a partner, decode nonsense words, and practice in decodable text.
How to read word by word	Reading fluency of 60–70 words per minute in graded text	Offer partner reading, rereading easy books, and audiotaped reading at easy level.
More than 100 sight words	Recognition vocabulary of more than 200 words	Provide computer practice, cloze exercises, word games, and multisensory techniques.
Primer-level reading	Second primer level	Offer guided reading of literature in small groups.
How to enjoy being read to	Independent reading	Provide take-home books and graphs of books read.
How to write with no plan	Plan and organize ideas for writing	Use graphic organizers for sequencing ideas, and use writer's chair for audience connection.

sent and are much harder to learn than the sounds themselves. If a child learns letter names without a clear conceptual and associative emphasis on the sounds the
letters symbolize, confusions in reading and spelling will occur. Consider Table 8.5,
which shows the letters that typically are confused in reading and in spelling.

Children who confuse *will* and *yell* need more practice differentiating letter
sounds from letter names. Teachers must deliberately use the labels "name" and
"sound" during teaching when referring to letters and phonemes, respectively.
Some experts argue that teaching letter names is unnecessary,[7] but letter names are
so much a part of daily classroom life that clarity and practice are probably the most
important factors in helping children learn them.

Well-designed instruction will provide children with good key-word associations to help them remember letter sounds. Key words should be carefully chosen.
Commercially prepared alphabets often have confusing and inaccurate information, so they should be used cautiously. For example, the letter *e* should not have
the word *eye* associated with it. The "word wall" idea that has proliferated in
primary classrooms must be used with care as to how sounds are represented.
Alphabet letters often are posted along a colorful bulletin board; under each are
high-frequency words for which children are to develop automatic recognition.
The resulting array typically includes confusing lists of words under the vowel letters, such as the following:

Aa	Ee	Ii	Oo	Uu
apple	egg	it	orange	under
and	eight	is	of	use
away	eat	in	on	us
all	end	I'm	once	united
are			open	
			off	
			out	

If children are shown that words starting with the letter *o* begin with as many
as six different sounds, including the /w/ in *once*, they may surmise that letters are
irrelevant to sound and must be learned by some magical memory process. Sight
words do need to be learned, gradually and cumulatively, but they should not be
used to teach the regular correspondences. At the first-grade level, word walls
organized by initial letter only are less appropriate than word walls that convey
some consistent information about sound–symbol correspondences (see Tables 8.6
and 8.7 for traditional and alternative ways of teaching consonant spellings).

Teaching children each sound, then anchoring the sound to a grapheme (letter, letter group, or letter sequence) with a key-word mnemonic mimics the way
alphabetic writing was invented. The sound /s/ is associated first with "snake" and
the letter *s* and later with *ce, ci,* and *cy* combinations (*city, race, bicycle*). With an
instructional goal of teaching 80–120 spellings for the approximately 40 phonemes
and then moving to syllables and morphemes, teachers can teach the whole system
in a comprehensive, clear, logical sequence over several years. Instruction can
begin with high-utility, low-complexity consonant and vowel units and move
gradually to less common, conditional, and more complex graphemes. Spelling
units of several letters (*-tch, -igh, -mb, ce-, -ough*) are treated as the blocks from

Table 8.5. Letters often confused in reading and spelling

Letter	Name	Sound	Typical reading errors	Typical spelling errors
y	/waj/	/y/	*will = yell*	YL for *will*, BOU for *boy*
u	/yu/	/u/	*use = us*	UESTRDA for *yesterday*
w	/dʌbl yu/	/w/	*then = when*	UEN for *when*
x	/ɛks/	/ks/ or /gz/		ECKSAM for *exam*
h	/eč/	/h/		WOH for *watch*

which words are built, rather than as mysterious combinations of "sounded" and "unsounded" letters.

With the sound-to-spelling approach, children are taught that spelling units (graphemes) represent the approximately 40 sounds and often are more than one letter. For example, *eight* has two phonemes and two graphemes—the vowel /e/ spelled *eigh* (also in *weigh, weight, sleigh*) and the consonant /t/. Teachers are less likely to try to "blend" /t/ and /h/ to make /θ/ or /s/ and /h/ to make /š/ if the letter combinations are understood as operating as digraph units. In addition, words that begin with [s] will not be grouped with those that begin with [š].

From the beginning of a decoding program, children are also shown that there is often more than one way to spell a phoneme. Illustrating this fact has been called *establishing a set for diversity,* or helping students expect that there will be variation in the representational system.

Teach Pattern Recognition, Not Rule Memorization

Most individuals learn to decode words in print because they accumulate explicit and tacit knowledge of linguistic patterns—phonological, orthographic, and morphological. Any audience of literate adults can be cajoled into displaying their unconscious knowledge of orthographic constraints. Ask a group to spell [θrɔjǰ]. The majority will use *oi* instead of *oy*, although many will have trouble explaining that *oi* is used internally for /ɔj/ and that *oy* is used at the ends of words. Most will also use *ge* instead of *dge*, because a diphthong is never followed by *dge*.[8] If a group is asked to read a nonword such as *pertollic,* the middle syllable will be stressed and the vowel written as *o* will be pronounced lax. Readers of English know intrinsically that in the Latin layer of the language, the root, not the prefix or suffix, is usually stressed and a doubled consonant following a vowel causes the root to be short.

Awareness and use of such organizational patterns, not memorization of rules, facilitates learning; the goal of gaining insight is to read more fluently, not to recite orthographic trivia. Some critics of phonics instruction lament that there are too many rules to teach, that the rules don't always apply, or that the rules are too complicated to be taught. This criticism is most apt when the correspondence system is represented in long lists of statements about orthographic patterns without using the speech sound system as the reference point, such as the following:

If a vowel letter is at the end of the word, the letter usually stands for the long sound.

The letter *w* is sometimes a vowel and follows the vowel digraph rule.

The letter *a* has the same sound when followed by *l, w,* and *u.*

Table 8.6. Typical sequence for teaching consonant spellings in traditional basal reading series

Categories	Examples
Single consonants (one sound)	*b, d, f, h, j, k, l, m, n, p, r, t, v, w*
Variant or odd consonants	*c, g, s, qu, x, z*
Digraphs	*th, sh, ch, wh, ph, gh, ng*
Blends	*cr, dr, br, fr, tr, gr, pr, sc, sw, sk, sl, sn, tw, fl, cl, pl, gl, sl, spr, spl, squ, str, scr, shr, thr, chr, -nd, -nk, -nt, -lt, st, sk, sp*
Silent consonants	*wr, kn, ps, mn, gn, -mb, -ck, -lk*

These observations, among many others, obscure what is at work in speech–print correspondence, and children should not be asked to learn them. To demonstrate the language patterns embodied in these "rules," we should show children groups of words that share a single-letter, long-vowel spelling: *me, he, she, we, be; go, so, no,* and *yo-yo.* We should explain that the letter *w* never represents a vowel alone, although it is used in vowel digraphs to show the feature of lip rounding on the back vowels *aw, ow, ew.* Finally, we should demonstrate that *aw* and *au* are two spellings for /ɔ/; *au* is used internally in a syllable (*applaud, laundry, taut*), and *aw* is used in word-final position and before word-final *n* and *l* (*saw, thaw; brawn, brawl; drawn, drawl*). Part of teaching decoding well is to select what is useful, understandable, and applicable and to represent it as directly and logically as possible.

What does worthwhile practice entail, beyond phoneme awareness, initial sound–symbol linkage, and sound blending? Many teaching strategies apply. Words can be analyzed in a student–teacher dialogue so that students discover their structures and then generalize them to new words; patterns may be sorted so that groups of words are compared and classified;[9] phonic concepts may be applied to reading "foreign" words, names, low-frequency words, or nonwords; and cloze exercises can require students to make fine discriminations of words that look or sound alike in text reading. Writing words after reading them reinforces pattern knowledge. Some children with significant reading impairments need to be taught every phoneme–grapheme association explicitly, but others will begin to generalize independently if they have a solid basis from which to proceed.[10] Thus, we teach the major spellings for /k/ as a beginning decoding skill (*c, k, ck*) but wait to highlight the Greek *ch* and the French *-que* until entries from those languages are considered as an etymological group (*chorus, orchestra, school, chloroform, pachyderm; antique, pique, mystique*).

Use Active, Constructive Exploration

Workbooks are great for independent practice when concepts have been taught well. They are not categorically despicable but just are often misused as a substitute for teaching. Concepts, however, should be developed in the context of student–teacher interaction and activities designed to encourage reflection about language form. The brain responds to novelty and to tasks that ask us to respond actively and strategically,[11] which is why we usually learn better by doing than by listening. Some powerful approaches to phonological awareness, for example, emphasize mouth position and the ability to compare how words feel when they are spoken.[12] Some decoding programs ask children to stand at the chalkboard and write words as the words are analyzed, sounded out, and explained. Other programs use manipulative letters and trays. Still others give children small lap slates to write words as they are dictated and illustrated on an overhead projector. Letter cards can be manipulated in personal pocket charts that are made with manila folders. Hand gestures are employed for sweeping through sounds and blending them into words. All of these active techniques require the learner to select, classify, and consciously manipulate sounds and letters so that more thorough word learning occurs.

Spelling–Decoding Continuum for Elementary Instruction

As Marcia Henry suggested, every layer of language organization merits attention in the elementary curriculum.[13] A coherent progression for reading and spelling begins with phoneme awareness training and concludes with study of the Greek combining forms that are so prevalent in math and science vocabulary. Grade by grade, a typical emphasis would be as follows:

K   Phoneme awareness, letter names, and letter sounds
1   Anglo-Saxon consonant and vowel sound–spelling correspondences
2   More complex Anglo-Saxon spelling patterns
3   Syllabication, compounds, and word endings (inflections)
4   Latin-based prefixes, roots, and suffixes
5–6   More complex Latin-based forms
7–8   Greek combining forms

Table 8.7.   Nontraditional, alternative presentation of consonant spellings (sound–symbol organization)

/p/	/b/	/t/	/d/	/k/	/g/
pot	bat	tent	dime	cup	go
		walked	stayed	kettle	ghost
				deck	fatigue
				school	
				oblique	
/f/	/v/	/θ/, /ð/	/s/	/z/	/š/
fish	very	thin	see	zoo	shop
phone		then	fuss	jazz	sure
stiff			city	Xerox	Chicago
tough			science	rose	-tion, -sion
/č/	/ǰ/	/m/	/n/	/ŋ/	/h/
cheer	judge	man	net	king	hair
batch	wage	tomb	knight	lanky	who
	gent	autumn	sign		
	gym				
	gist				
/l/	/r/	/j/	/w/	/ʍ/	
lake	run	yes	want	whistle	
tell	wrist	use	one		

Table 8.8. Orthographic stage reader characteristics and needs (approximately second grade)

Child knows	Child needs to learn	Teaching strategies
How to read with some fluency (60–80 words per minute)	Fluency of more than 80 words per minute	Have child reread familiar books, alternate oral reading with partner, or audiotape reading.
How to write more than one sentence but uses no logical structure	Use of connecting words and paragraph sequence	Supply connecting words to unlinked sentences.
Most one-syllable word patterns	Recognition of closed, open, r-controlled, vowel team, consonant-le, and silent-e syllables in longer words	Provide practice in syllable identification and classification, syllable combining, and syllable division.
Spelling of regular, one-syllable words and 50–100 basic sight words	Spellings of compounds, words with endings, vowel team words, and more variant patterns	Ask child to sort words, test-study-test in organized program, and use in writing and proofreading.
Common vocabulary (overuses it)	More variety in speaking, writing, and reading	Teach antonyms, synonyms, classification, definition, and context use.
Only period and question mark; is unfamiliar with other punctuation	Use of comma, capitals, and exclamation and quotation marks	Offer dictations, proofreading, and group composition.
How to write about own experiences in "train of thought" style	More control over flow of ideas, and use a plan	Encourage and model individually stages of writing process.
How to retell without summarizing or extracting main idea	Paraphrasing, summarizing, questioning, and connecting	Provide guided discussion, reader response, and modeling of strategies.

Decoding Beyond Second Grade

Understanding word structure for reading, vocabulary, and spelling necessitates knowledge of syllable patterns and morphology. Good readers will learn to break longer words into segments if necessary, supply accent, and relate familiar word parts to meaning when possible. Each level of orthography—sounds, syllables, and morphemes—has its own organization, and each of those levels differs according to the language from which a word is derived.

At each level of word knowledge, there is an order of difficulty inherent in the material itself and a general progression by which children master the domain. For example, children learn the past tense -ed for speaking, reading, and spelling over several years. At first, children become aware that the past-tense form means that the event happened already. Then they read and spell -ed as a phonetic element, as in WAKT for walked. As they develop a category for word endings, children may confuse -ed with other endings, such as -ing and -s. Next, children overgeneralize the spelling -ed to any base word that has a /t/ or /d/ on the end (MOSTED). Finally, they learn when and why to use the spelling -ed and notice the presence of the construction in print. All of this takes 3 or 4 years.

Instruction that follows a systematic progression to help children learn the past tense might proceed like this. First, children would focus on the concept of past-tense actions in spoken language. Next, they might be asked to notice the presence of the ending on written words and identify the sounds the endings make (/t/, /d/, /əd/). In second grade they might begin to spell some words with -ed but would not necessarily have to learn the rules for dropping e and changing y when an ending is added (see Table 8.8 for more on second-grade reader characteristics and needs). At about second grade, children would be expected to read accurately all of the major inflections (-ed, -ing -est, -er, -es, -s). Not until third grade would they delve into rules for changing spellings when -ed is added. An advanced skill (fourth grade, perhaps) would involve the discovery of the pattern that determines how to pronounce -ed and the realization that it is not pronounced as a separate syllable in words such as *attached, raced,* or *used.*[14]

SUMMARY: THE POWER OF INSTRUCTION

Word recognition, reading fluency, knowledge of word meanings, and familiarity with complex syntax enhance reading comprehension; likewise, exposure to text enhances familiarity with words and linguistic structures. Achieving balance in reading instruction does not mean dabbling superficially in a variety of skill domains but means teaching each component thoroughly, systematically, and well. Maintaining a balance also means covering a range of components daily and weekly, along with a steady supply of great literature and purposeful writing projects. Considerable expertise is required to teach everyone to read, but well-informed classroom teachers using valid instructional programs are up to the job. There is no more important task for educators to undertake.

ENDNOTES

1. Ball & Blachman, 1991; Blachman, Tangel, Ball, Black, & McGraw, 1999; Brady, 1997; Foorman et al., 1998.
2. Hart & Risley, 1995; Scarborough & Dobrich, 1994.
3. Adams, Foorman, Lundberg, & Beeler, 1998; Blachman et al., 1999.
4. Brady et al., 1994; Cunningham, 1990; Felton, 1993.
5. Ehri, 1997.
6. Slavin, Madden, Karweit, Livermon, & Dolan, 1990. Decodable text and its role in reading instruction is discussed in Learning First Alliance, 1998.
7. McGuinness, 1997.
8. Hanna et al., 1966.
9. Bear et al., 2000.
10. Share & Stanovich, 1995.
11. Bransford, Brown, & Cocking, 1999.
12. Lindamood & Lindamood, 1998.
13. Henry, 1997.
14. The pronunciation of the past-tense ending in English is governed by the speech sound that precedes it. If the preceding sound is a voiced consonant or vowel, the past-tense ending is pronounced /d/. If the preceding sound is a voiceless consonant, the past-tense ending is pronounced /t/. If the word ends in a /d/ or a /t/, the full syllable /əd/ is used.

References

Adams, M.J. (1990). *Beginning to read: Thinking and learning about print.* Cambridge, MA: MIT Press.

Adams, M.J., Foorman, B.R., Lundberg, I., & Beeler, T. (1998). *Phonemic awareness in young children: A classroom curriculum.* Baltimore: Paul H. Brookes Publishing Co.

Adams, M.J., Treiman, R., & Pressley, M. (1998). Reading, writing, and literacy. In I.E. Sigel & K.A. Renninger (Eds.), *Handbook of child psychology: Vol. 4. Child psychology in practice* (5th ed., pp. 275–355). New York: John Wiley & Sons.

Akmajian, A., Demers, R.A., Farmer, A.K., & Harnish, R.M. (1998). *Linguistics: An introduction to linguistics and communication* (6th ed.). Cambridge, MA: MIT Press.

Bailet, L.L. (1990). Spelling rule usage among students with learning disabilities and normally achieving students. *Journal of Learning Disabilities, 18,* 162–165.

Ball, E.W., & Blachman, B.A. (1991). Does phoneme awareness training in kindergarten make a difference in early word recognition and developmental spelling? *Reading Research Quarterly, 26,* 49–66.

Balmuth, M. (1992). *The roots of phonics.* Timonium, MD: York Press.

Baum, L.F. (1956). *The wizard of Oz.* New York: Grosset & Dunlap.

Bear, D., Invernizzi, M., Templeton, S., & Johnston, K. (2000). *Words their way* (2nd ed.). Upper Saddle River, NJ: Prentice-Hall.

Beck, I.L., McKeown, M.G., Hamilton, R.L., & Kucan, L. (1998). Getting at the meaning: How to help students unpack difficult text. *American Educator, 22,* 66–71, 85.

Beck, I., McKeown, M.G., & Omanson, R.C. (1990). The effects and uses of diverse vocabulary instructional techniques. In M.G. McKeown & M.E. Curtis (Eds.), *The nature of vocabulary acquisition* (pp. 462–481). Mahwah, NJ: Lawrence Erlbaum Associates.

Becker, C.A. (1985). What do we really know about semantic context effects during reading? In D. Besner, T. Waller, & G. MacKinnon (Eds.), *Reading research: Advances in theory and practice* (Vol. 5, pp. 125–166). New York: Academic Press.

Berko, J. (1958). The child's learning of English morphology. *Word, 14,* 150–177.

Blachman, B. (Ed.). (1997). *Foundations of reading acquisition and dyslexia: Implications for early intervention.* Mahwah, NJ: Lawrence Erlbaum Associates.

Blachman, B.A., Ball, E.W., Black, R., & Tangel, D.M. (2000). *Road to the code: A phonological awareness program for young children.* Baltimore: Paul H. Brookes Publishing Co.

Blachman, B.A., Tangel, D.M., Ball, E.W., Black, R., & McGraw, C.K. (1999). Developing phonological awareness and word recognition skills: A two-year intervention with low-income, inner-city children. *Reading and Writing: An Interdisciplinary Journal, 11,* 239–273.

Bolinger, D.L., & Sears, D.A. (1981). *Aspects of language* (3rd ed.). Orlando, FL: Harcourt Brace & Co.

Brady, S. (1997). Ability to encode phonological representations: An underlying difficulty of poor readers. In B. Blachman (Ed.), *Foundations of reading acquisition and dyslexia: Implications for early intervention* (pp. 21–47). Mahwah, NJ: Lawrence Erlbaum Associates.

Brady, S., Fowler, A., Stone, B., & Winbury, N. (1994). Training phonological awareness: A study with inner-city kindergarten children. *Annals of Dyslexia, 44,* 26–102.

Brady, S., & Moats, L.C. (1997). *Informed instruction for reading success: Foundations for teacher preparation* (A position paper of the International Dyslexia Association). Baltimore: International Dyslexia Association.

Bransford, J., Brown, A., & Cocking, R. (Eds.). (1999). *How people learn: Brain, mind, and experience in school.* Washington, DC: National Academy Press.

Brown, I.S., & Felton, R.H. (1990). Effects of instruction on beginning reading skills in children at risk for reading disability. *Reading and Writing: An Interdisciplinary Journal, 2,* 223–241.

Brown, R. (1973). *A first language: The early stages.* Cambridge, MA: Harvard University Press.

Carlisle, J.F. (1987). The use of morphological knowledge in spelling derived forms by learning disabled and normal students. *Annals of Dyslexia, 37,* 90–108.

Carlisle, J.F. (1988). Knowledge of derivational morphology and spelling ability in fourth, sixth, and eighth graders. *Applied Psycholinguistics, 9,* 247–266.

Carlisle, J.F., & Nomanbhoy, D.M. (1993). Phonological and morphological awareness in first graders. *Applied Psycholinguistics, 14,* 177–195.

Carroll, L. (1960). *Alice's adventures in wonderland and through the looking glass: A Signet classic.* New York: The New American Library, Inc. (Original work published 1865)

Chall, J. (1983). *Stages of reading development.* New York: McGraw-Hill.

Chomsky, C. (1970). Reading, spelling, and phonology. *Harvard Educational Review, 40,* 287–309.

Chomsky, N., & Halle, M. (1968). *The sound pattern of English.* New York: HarperCollins.

Cramer, S.C., & Ellis, W. (Eds.). (1996). *Learning disabilities: Lifelong issues.* Baltimore: Paul H. Brookes Publishing Co.

Cunningham, A.E. (1990). Explicit versus implicit instruction in phonemic awareness. *Journal of Experimental Child Psychology, 50,* 429–444.

Cunningham, A.E., & Stanovich, K.E. (1997). Early reading acquisition and its relation to reading experience and ability 10 years later. *Developmental Psychology, 33*(6), 934–945.

Cunningham, A., & Stanovich, K. (1998). What reading does for the mind. *American Educator, 22*(1/2), 8–15.

Derwing, B., & Baker, W. (1979). Recent research on the acquisition of English morphology. In P. Fletcher & M. Garman (Eds.), *Language acquisition* (pp. 209–223). Cambridge, England: Cambridge University Press.

Derwing, B.L., Smith, M.L., & Wiebe, G.E. (1995). On the role of spelling in morpheme recognition: Experimental studies with children and adults. In L.B. Feldman (Ed.), *Morphological aspects of language processing* (pp. 3–27). Mahwah, NJ: Lawrence Erlbaum Associates.

deVilliers, J., & deVilliers, P. (1973). A cross-sectional study of the acquisition of grammatical morphemes. *Journal of Psycholinguistic Research, 2,* 267–278.

Edwards, H.T. (1992). *Applied phonetics: The sounds of American English.* San Diego: Singular Publishing Group.

Ehri, L. (1994). Development of the ability to read words: Update. In R. Ruddell, M. Ruddell, & H. Singer (Eds.), *Theoretical models and processes of reading* (pp. 323–358). Newark, DE: International Reading Association.

Ehri, L.C. (1997). Sight word learning in normal and dyslexic readers. In B. Blachman (Ed.), *Foundations of reading acquisition and dyslexia: Implications for early intervention* (pp. 163–189). Mahwah, NJ: Lawrence Erlbaum Associates.

Felton, R. (1993). Effects of instruction on the decoding skills of children with phonological processing problems. *Journal of Learning Disabilities, 26,* 583–589.

Fischer, F.W., Shankweiler, D., & Liberman, I.Y. (1985). Spelling proficiency and sensitivity to word structure. *Journal of Memory and Language, 24,* 423–441.

Fletcher, J.M., & Lyon, G.R. (1998). Reading: A research-based approach. In W. Evers (Ed.), *What's gone wrong in America's classrooms?* (pp. 49–90). Stanford, CA: Hoover Institution Press.

Foorman, B.R., Francis, D.J., Fletcher, J.M., Schatschneider, C., & Mehta, P. (1998). The role of instruction in learning to read: Preventing reading failure in at-risk children. *Journal of Educational Psychology, 90,* 1–15.

Foorman, B.R., Francis, D.J., Shaywitz, S.E., Shaywitz, B.A., & Fletcher, J.M. (1997). The case for early reading intervention. In B. Blachman (Ed.), *Foundations of reading acquisition and dyslexia: Implications for early intervention* (pp. 243–264). Mahwah, NJ: Lawrence Erlbaum Associates.

Fowler, A., & Liberman, I.Y. (1995). The role of phonology and orthography in morphological awareness. In L.B. Feldman (Ed.), *Morphological aspects of language processing* (pp. 157–188). Mahwah, NJ: Lawrence Erlbaum Associates.

Francis, D.J., Shaywitz, S.E., Stuebing, K.K., Shaywitz, B.A., & Fletcher, J.M. (1996). Developmental lag versus deficit models of reading disability: A longitudinal, individual growth curves analysis. *Journal of Educational Psychology, 88,* 3–17.

Freyd, P., & Baron, J. (1982). Individual differences in acquisition of derivational morphology. *Journal of Verbal Learning and Verbal Behavior, 21,* 282–295.

Fromkin, V., & Rodman, R. (1993). *An introduction to language* (4th ed.). Orlando, FL: Harcourt Brace & Co.

Fromkin, V., & Rodman, R. (1998). *An introduction to language* (6th ed.). Orlando, FL: Harcourt Brace & Co.

Ganske, K. (2000). *Word journeys.* New York: Guilford Press.

Gaskins, I.W., Ehri, L.C., Cress, C., O'Hara, C., & Donnelly, K. (1996). Procedures for word learning: Making discoveries about words. *The Reading Teacher, 50,* 312–327.

Gillingham, A., & Stillman, B.W. (1997). *The Gillingham manual: Remedial training for children with specific disability in reading, spelling, and penmanship* (8th ed.). Cambridge, MA: Educators Publishing Service.

Hanna, P.R., Hanna, J.S., Hodges, R.E., & Rudorf, E.H., Jr. (1966). *Phoneme–grapheme correspondences as cues to spelling improvement* (USDOE Publication No. 32008). Washington, DC: U.S. Government Printing Office.

Hart, B., & Risley, T.R. (1995). *Meaningful differences in the everyday experience of young American children.* Baltimore: Paul H. Brookes Publishing Co.

Hayes, D.P., & Ahrens, M.G. (1988). Vocabulary simplification for children: A special case of "motherese"? *Journal of Child Language, 15,* 395–410.

Henderson, E. (1990). *Teaching spelling.* Boston: Houghton Mifflin.

Henry, M. (1988). Beyond phonics: Integrated decoding and spelling instruction based on word origin and structure. *Annals of Dyslexia, 38,* 259–275.

Henry, M. (1997). The decoding/spelling curriculum: Integrated decoding and spelling instruction from pre-school to early secondary school. *Dyslexia, 3,* 178–189.

Henry, M. (1999). A short history of the English language. In J.R. Birsh (Ed.), *Multisensory teaching of basic language skills* (pp. 119–143). Baltimore: Paul H. Brookes Publishing Co.

Henry, M., & Redding, N. (1996). *Patterns for reading and spelling.* Austin, TX: PRO-ED.

Hillerich, R.L. (1985). *Teaching children to write, K–8.* Upper Saddle River, NJ: Prentice-Hall.

Holmes, V.M., & Brown, N.F. (1998, April 18). *Effective strategies in skilled spellers.* Paper presented at the Society for the Scientific Study of Reading, San Diego.

Irvin, J. (1990). *Vocabulary instruction: Guidelines for instruction.* Washington, DC: National Education Association.

Juel, C. (1988). Learning to read and write: A longitudinal study of 54 children from first through fourth grades. *Journal of Educational Psychology, 80,* 437–447.

Juster, N. (1989). *The phantom tollbooth.* New York: Alfred A. Knopf. (Original work published 1961)

Kibel, M., & Miles, T.R. (1994). Phonological errors in the spelling of taught dyslexic children. In C. Hulme & M. Snowling (Eds.), *Reading development and dyslexia* (pp. 105–127). London: Whurr.

Labov, W. (1995). Can reading failure be reversed?: A linguistic approach to the question. In V. Gadsden & D. Wagner (Eds.), *Literacy among African-American youth: Issues in learning, teaching and schooling* (pp. 39–68). Cresskill, NJ: Hampton Press.

Learning First Alliance. (1998). *Every child reading: An action plan of the Learning First Alliance.* Washington, DC: Author.

Leong, C.K. (1989). Productive knowledge of derivational rules in poor readers. *Annals of Dyslexia, 39,* 94–115.

Liberman, I.Y., Rubin, H., Duques, S., & Carlisle, J. (1985). Linguistic abilities and spelling proficiency in kindergartners and adult poor spellers. In D. Gray & J. Kavanaugh (Eds.), *Biobehavioral measures of dyslexia* (pp. 163–175). Timonium, MD: York Press.

Lindamood, P., & Lindamood, P. (1998). The Lindamood sequencing program for reading, spelling, and speech: Teacher's manual for the classroom and clinic. Austin, TX: PRO-ED.

MacKay, D.G. (1978). Derivational rules and the internal lexicon. *Journal of Verbal Learning and Verbal Behavior, 17,* 61–71.

McGuinness, D. (1997). *Why our children can't read and what we can do about it.* New York: Free Press.

Moats, L.C. (1994). The missing foundation in teacher education: Knowledge of the structure of spoken and written language. *Annals of Dyslexia, 44,* 88–102.

Moats, L.C. (1995). The missing foundation in teacher preparation. *American Educator, 19, 9,* 43–51.

Moats, L.C. (1996). Phonological spelling errors in the writing of dyslexic adolescents. *Reading and Writing: An Interdisciplinary Journal, 8,* 105–119.

Moats, L.C. (1998). Teaching decoding. *American Educator, 22*(1 & 2), 42–49, 95.

Moats, L.C., & Lyon, G.R. (1996). Wanted: Teachers with knowledge of language. *Topics in Language Disorders, 16,* 73–81.

Moats, L.C., & Smith, C. (1992). Derivational morphology: Why it should be included in language assessment and instruction. *Language, Speech and Hearing Services in Schools, 23,* 312–319.

Morrow, L.M. (1992). The impact of a literature-based program on literacy achievement, use of literature, and attitudes of children from minority backgrounds. *Reading Research Quarterly, 27,* 253.

Nagy, W.E. (1988). *Teaching vocabulary to improve reading comprehension.* Urbana, IL: National Council of Teachers of English.

Nagy, W.E., & Anderson, R.C. (1984). How many words are there in printed English? *Reading Research Quarterly, 24,* 262–282.

Nagy, W.E., Anderson, R.C., & Herman, P.A. (1987). Learning word meanings from context during normal reading. *American Educational Research Journal, 24,* 237–270.

Nagy, W.E., Anderson, R.C., Schommer, M., Scott, J.A., & Stallman, A.C. (1989). Morphological families in the internal lexicon. *Reading Research Quarterly, 24,* 262–282.

National Assessment of Educational Progress. (1995). *1994 NAEP—Reading: A First Look.* Washington, DC: National Center for Education Statistics.

National Institute for Literacy. (1998). *The state of literacy in America.* Washington, DC: Author.

Nicholson, T. (1997). Closing the gap on reading failure: Social background, phonemic awareness, and learning to read. In B. Blachman (Ed.), *Foundations of reading acquisition and dyslexia: Implications for early intervention* (pp. 381–407). Mahwah, NJ: Lawrence Erlbaum Associates.

Owens, R. (1992). *Language development: An introduction.* New York: Merrill.

Paulsen, G. (1988). *Hatchet.* New York: Viking Penguin.

Perry, T., & Delpit, L. (Eds.). (1998). *The real Ebonics debate: Power, language, and the education of African American children.* Boston: Beacon Press.

Pressley, M. (1998). *Reading instruction that works: The case for balanced teaching.* New York: Guilford Press.

Rack, J.P., Snowling, M.J., & Olson, R.K. (1992). The nonword reading deficit in developmental dyslexia: A review. *Reading Research Quarterly, 27,* 29–53.

Rayner, K. (1997). Understanding eye movements in reading. *Scientific Studies of Reading, 1,* 317–339.

Rubin, H. (1988). Morphological knowledge and early writing ability. *Language and Speech, 31,* 337–355.

Rubin, H., Patterson, P.A., & Kantor, M. (1991). Morphological development and writing ability in children and adults. *Language, Speech and Hearing Services in the Schools, 22,* 228–235.

Sacramento County Office of Education. (1997). *Learning to read.* Sacramento: California Reading Initiative Center, Author.

Scanlon, D., & Vellutino, F.R. (1996). Prerequisite skills, early instruction and success in first grade reading: Selected results from a longitudinal study. *Mental Retardation and Developmental Disabilities Research Reviews, 2,* 54–63.

Scarborough, H.D., & Dobrich, W. (1994). On the efficacy of reading to preschoolers. *Developmental Review, 14,* 245–302.

Scarborough, H.S., Ehri, L.C., Olson, R.K., & Fowler, A.E. (1998). The fate of phonemic awareness beyond the elementary school years. *Scientific Studies of Reading, 2,* 115–142.

Schreuder, R., & Baayen, R.H. (1995). Modeling morphological processing. In L. Feldman (Ed.), *Morphological aspects of language processing* (pp. 131–154). Mahwah, NJ: Lawrence Erlbaum Associates.

Seymour, P.H.K. (1992). Cognitive theories of spelling and implications for education. In C. Sterling & C. Robson (Eds.), *Psychology, spelling, and education* (p. 53). Clevedon, England: Multilingual Matters, Ltd.

Shankweiler, D., Lundquist, E., Dreyer, L., & Dickinson, C. (1996). Reading and spelling difficulties in high school students: Causes and consequences. *Reading and Writing: An Interdisciplinary Journal, 8,* 267–294.

Share, D.L., & Stanovich, K.E. (1995). Cognitive processes in early reading development: Accommodating individual differences into a model of acquisition. *Educational Psychology (special issue): Issues in Education, 1,* 1–57.

Shaywitz, S.E., Escobar, M.D., Shaywitz, B.A., Fletcher, J.M., & Makuch, R.W. (1992). Evidence that dyslexia may represent the lower tail of a normal distribution of reading ability. *New England Journal of Medicine, 326,* 145–150.

Slavin, R.E., Madden, N.A., Karweit, N.L., Livermon, B.J., & Dolan, L. (1990). Success for all: First year outcomes of a comprehensive plan for reforming urban education. *American Educational Research Journal, 27,* 255–278.

Snow, C.E. (1990). The development of definitional skill. *Journal of Child Language, 17,* 697–710.

Snow, C.E., Burns, M.S., & Griffin, P. (Eds.). (1998). *Preventing reading difficulties in young children.* Washington, DC: National Academy Press.

Stahl, S.A., & Shiel, T.G. 1992. Teaching meaning vocabulary: Productive approaches for poor readers. *Reading and Writing Quarterly (special issue): Overcoming Learning Difficulties, 8,* 223–241.

Stanovich, K.E. (1994). Romance and reality. *The Reading Teacher, 47,* 280–291.

Stanovich, K.E., & Siegel, L.S. (1994). The phenotypic profile of reading-disabled children: A regression-based test of the phonological-core variable difference model. *Journal of Educational Psychology, 86,* 24–53.

Stolz, J.A., & Feldman, L.B. (1995). The role of orthographic and semantic transparency of the base morpheme in morphological processing. In L.B. Feldman (Ed.), *Morphological aspects of language processing* (pp. 109–130). Mahwah, NJ: Lawrence Erlbaum Associates.

Tangel, D., & Blachman, B. (1995). Effect of phoneme awareness instruction on the invented spelling of first grade children: A one-year followup. *Journal of Reading Behavior, 27,* 153–185.

Templeton, S. (1989). Tacit and explicit knowledge of derivational morphology: foundations for a unified approach to spelling and vocabulary development in the intermediate grades and beyond. *Reading Psychology: An International Quarterly, 10,* 233–253.

Templeton, S., & Bear, D.R. (Eds.). (1992). *Development of orthographic knowledge and the foundations of literacy: A memorial Festschrift for Edmund H. Henderson.* Mahwah, NJ: Lawrence Erlbaum Associates.

Templeton, S., & Scarborough-Franks, L. (1985). The spelling's the thing: Knowledge of derivational morphology in orthography and phonology among older students. *Applied Psycholinguistics, 6,* 371–390.

Torgesen, J.K., Wagner, R., & Rashotte, C. (1997). Approaches to the prevention and remediation of phonologically based reading disabilities. In B. Blachman (Ed.), *Foundations of reading acquisition and dyslexia: Implications for early intervention* (pp. 287–304). Mahwah, NJ: Lawrence Erlbaum Associates.

Treiman, R. (1997). Spelling in normal children and dyslexics. In B. Blachman (Ed.), *Foundations of reading acquisition and dyslexia: Implications for early intervention* (pp. 191–218). Mahwah, NJ: Lawrence Erlbaum Associates.

Tunmer, W.E., & Hoover, W.A. (1993). Phonological recoding skill and beginning reading. *Reading and Writing: An Interdisciplinary Journal, 5,* 161–179.

Tyler, A., & Nagy, W. (1989). The acquisition of English derivational morphology. *Journal of Memory and Language, 28,* 649–667.

U.S. Department of Education, National Center for Education Statistics, National Assessment Governing Board. (1994). *1994 National Assessment of Educational Progress.* Washington, DC: U.S. Government Printing Office.

U.S. Office of Technology Assessment. (1993). *Adult literacy and new technologies.* Washington, DC: U.S. Government Printing Office.

Venezky, R. (1967). English orthography: Its graphical structure and its relation to sound. *Reading Research Quarterly, 2,* 75–105.

Wechsler, D. (1992). *Wechsler Individual Achievement Test.* San Antonio, TX: The Psychological Corporation.

White, T.G., Power, M.A., & White, S. (1989). Morphological analysis: Implications for teaching and understanding vocabulary growth. *Reading Research Quarterly, 24,* 283–304.

Woodcock, R.W., & Johnson, M.B. (1989). *Woodcock–Johnson Psychoeducational Battery–Revised.* Allen, TX: DLM.

Wysocki, K., & Jenkins, J.R. (1987). Deriving word meanings through morphological generalization. *Reading Research Quarterly, 22,* 66–81.

Yule, G. (1996). *The study of language* (2nd ed.). Cambridge, England: Cambridge University Press.

Case Studies

The following case studies are provided to support discussions among student teachers and to illustrate linguistic phenomena in children's work.

JEREMY

This spontaneous journal entry was written during the first week of November by a first grader, Jeremy, who had just experienced an introductory lesson on the /č/ phoneme and its spelling with *ch*. His spelling shows good knowledge of basic sound–symbol correspondences and orthographic patterns. He is beginning to spell morphemically, keeping the parts of *coming* intact (*come* + *ing*) and spelling *learned* as *lurn* + *ed*. Jeremy is ready to study the spelling of words with inflections and should be encouraged to write personal narratives, descriptions, and paragraphs that explain observations about the real world.

ROBBIE

Robbie is in the same first-grade class as Jeremy, and his journal entry was produced on the same day. After the lesson on spelling /č/ with *ch*, Robbie writes *Chuck*

Journal entry by Jeremy, a first grader.

Journal entry by Robbie, a first grader in Jeremy's class.

likes to eat some chili and some chocolate. He demonstrates confusion of the voiced and voiceless consonant pair /ǰ/ and /č/ when he uses the letter *j* as the initial letter of the words *chili* and *chocolate.* He does not spell morphemically: He spells the speech sounds in *likes* with a sound-by-sound approach. He inserts a nasal after a vowel where it does not belong in *eat.* These may be the initial signs of a problem with phoneme identity that merit focused practice with minimal pairs of words that contrast the target sounds. Robbie may have a mild problem with phoneme awareness that needs additional screening and assessment.

BRUCE

Bruce, a first grader in a class taught with a reading program that included systematic phoneme awareness and phonics instruction, wrote this journal entry after 2 months in the first grade. Bruce's teacher has written correct spellings underneath the misspelled words. Note the omission of the nasals /n/ and /m/ in the child's spelling of *haunted* and *gramp,* respectively. The omission of nasals occurs

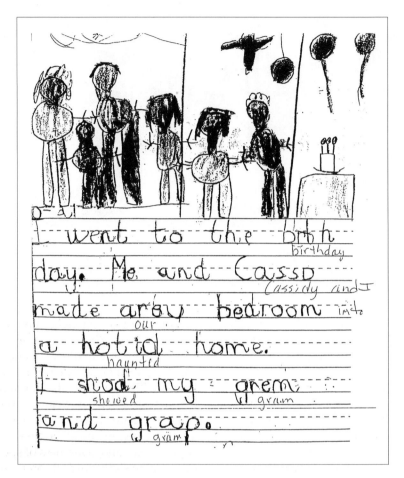

Journal entry by Bruce, a first grader in a class taught with a reading program that included systematic phoneme awareness and phonics instruction
(teacher corrections beneath writing).

only when the nasal consonant comes between a vowel and a following consonant
within a syllable. Bruce has learned the words *went* and *and* as wholes by this time,
along with other sight words such as *my* and *the*. The unknown vowel /ɔ/ in *haunted*
is spelled with the vowel that is closest in articulation: /ɑ/ ("short *o*"). Syllabic [r] in
birthday is spelled logically with one letter, as there is no separate vowel segment
in that syllable. Sentence structure is developing well for this first grader. Bruce is
ready to learn words with nasal blends at the end (*-mp, -nd, -nt*) and the spellings
for some *r*-controlled vowels.

JANET

This second grader has fallen behind in reading and has scored below grade level
in spelling accuracy. Janet's spelling, however, is phonetically accurate. The speech
sounds are represented faithfully, although Janet's knowledge of the actual symbols used in conventional spelling is limited. The spellings are generated with let-

goo	go
ann	and
yel	will
hme	him
coc	cook
lot	light
jrs	dress
reh	reach
ntr	enter

Spellings given by Janet, a second grader (actual spellings on right).

ter names and sequential spelling strategies typical of later phonetic spelling but are immature for a child in second grade. Note the use of the letter name "h" to spell /č/ in *reach,* the representation of affrication of the initial /d/ in *dress* (spelled with a *j*), the choice of the mid low vowel /ɑ/ for /aj/ in *light,* and the use of the letter name "y" to spell /w/ in *will.* The syllabic spellings of *enter,* the doubling of the /n/ in *and* in place of the final /d/, and the doubling of /o/ in *go* all are typical for phonetic spellers. Janet seems to assume that all words have three letters. Her phoneme awareness is quite well developed; instruction must emphasize remembering the graphemes used to represent phonemes and awareness of spelling patterns. Writing regular words to dictation, practicing sight words through multisensory tracing techniques, learning graphemes for phonemes, and sorting words by spelling pattern would be appropriate for her.

HARRY

Harry, a second grader, wrote these sentences on the Test of Achievement in the Woodcock-Johnson Psychoeducational Test Battery–Revised (Woodcock & Johnson, 1989). The spelling is typical of late phonetic and early orthographic stages (see Chapters 1 and 8, respectively, for descriptions of these stages). Note that the words *egg* (item 8) and *leg* (item 15) are spelled as they sound, with the /ɛ/ raised up to an /e/ when the tongue anticipates rising in the back of the throat to make the velar consonant /g/. Note the confusion of the nasal consonants in *animal* (item 9). In *girl* (item 10), the inseparable combination /ɚ/ is spelled with the logical letter choice, *r,* and the *i* is inserted as an afterthought because it is unnecessary for portraying the sounds in the word. In *throwing* (item 13) and *light* (item 14), the long vowels are spelled with single letters that contain the vowel sounds in their names. Orthographic awareness is evident when the child spells the diphthong /ɔj/ in *boy* (item 15) with a vowel letter combination *ou.* Harry seems to understand that the vowel is a diphthong but is unsure of the correct spelling.

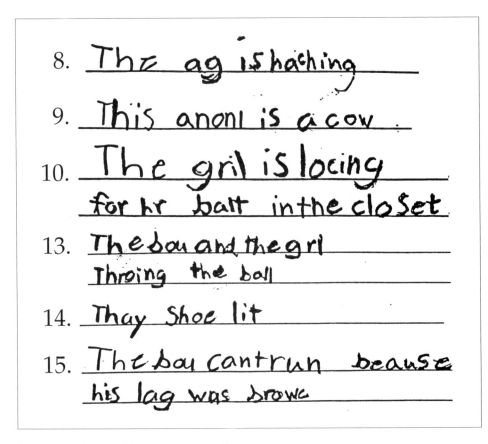

8. The ag is haching

9. This anoni is a cow .

10. The gril is locing for hr balt in the closet.

13. The boi and the grl Throing the ball

14. Thay shoe lit

15. The boi cantrun beause his lag was browe

Sentences written by Harry, a second grader.

CYNTHIA

Cynthia is a 9-year-old third grader with an above-average verbal IQ score. Following is her written expression subtest of the Wechsler Individual Achievement Test (Wechsler, 1992), on which she was asked to describe her ideal place to live. She has rather prominent difficulties identifying and transcribing the speech sounds in words in spite of her high verbal reasoning ability. She did poorly on diagnostic tests of phonological awareness.

Cynthia's spelling of the word *items* contains an alveolar nasal /n/ in place of a stop consonant /t/. Her spellings of the words *bay* and *bathrooms* begin with a reversed *b* (*d*) that is clearly an orthographic substitution. In addition to orthographic errors, however, Cynthia's writing contains phonologically based errors. Her spelling of the word *garage* ends with a voiceless sound /č/ in place of the voiced /ž/ or /ǰ/. She seems to use the letter *a* as a default vowel in words such as *with, slide, real,* and *dining.* Her spelling of the word *kitchen* includes a nasal after the vowel that does not belong there, and her spellings of the words *point, basement,* and *front* in the last three lines all are missing a nasal after a vowel and before a consonant. Diffuse problems with placement of /r/ and /l/ within a syllable are evident in *apple, tree,* and *garage.* The substitution of /w/ for /r/ in *real* is common in children with lin-

(items)

r.   in mis,   (garage)
                (two)
          tow aay goach.
                  (b) a
) five dathroom's.
              Six room's
                          slid?
          in door Pooll wath   a   Salad
                    with
                        real   far
that   you   Can   go   wall fate
on.   Dan ing room   thet   has
     connects   Kitchen
a   catn   to   the   Kenckin.
                         dish
the kenckin   has   a   bash—
washer.   that   has
                 tree   point
it's in a lpple teer poat.
              u-Turn
no Pasmet.   u tuner   in
  front
font of my hose.

Description of an ideal place to live, by Cynthia, a 9-year-old (corrections above writing).

gering phonological production problems. The *p* at the beginning of *basement* is evidence of a voicing confusion. The many phonological confusions suggest that Cynthia's fundamental problem with phoneme awareness must be addressed directly if she is to improve. Instruction for her should emphasize phoneme identification, phoneme contrasts, and phoneme sequencing during the decoding and spelling components of lessons.

Cynthia uses a listing strategy for her ideas, and there are no capital letters. Her vocabulary and descriptive detail are good for her age, but she cannot simultaneously generate complete sentences and transcribe her thoughts. Her verbal ability as measured by IQ tests appears to be considerably higher than the level of her written language output. She needs a structured approach to sentence expansion and sentence construction as well as emphasis on planning her writing before she makes a draft.

BRITT

Britt, a third grader, has fallen behind grade level in reading. She has scored about one standard deviation below her expected level on a test of word recognition and

> Der Emily wont to
> go to the alpin slid
> with me on Sunday
> if you can cam coll
> me on satrday ner
> Long time and
> then. we can mack
> the plas ofve the
> telufon. and it will
> be a slep ofer so
> bring or sleping bag
> and wom clows becas
> we rae going to camp
> out.
>   from
>   B

Letter from Britt, a third grader, to her friend Emily (corrections above writing).

relies heavily on context to decode new words. She attempts to spell phonetically, although she uses a letter name strategy typical of much younger children: spelling long vowels with one letter as in words such as *slide*, *alpine*, and *near*. She omits the liquid /r/ in *warm* but spells the middle syllable of *Saturday* with a syllabic /r/. She substitutes voiceless for voiced consonants in *over* (/f/ for /v/) and *lunch* (/ǰ/ for /č/). She omits the nasal consonant after the vowel and before the final consonant in *plans*. On another spelling test given at the same time, she made several other voicing substitutions, including UNGL for *uncle*, HOSPIDAL for *hospital*, and EFRY for *every*. She also has little mastery over sentence structure, as the composition contains one long, run-on sentence: *Dear Emily, Want to go to the Alpine Slide with me on Sunday? If you can come, call me on Saturday near lunch time and then we can make the plans over the telephone and it will be a sleepover so bring your sleeping bag and warm clothes because we are going to camp out. From B.*

Britt's inability to keep up with her classmates in reading and spelling appears to have its origin in a phonological processing weakness, evident in persistent confusions of consonant phonemes that share some features but not others. Her reading and spelling lessons should begin with phoneme awareness exercises designed to contrast the speech sounds she confuses. As part of a comprehensive language arts program, Britt's writing instruction should build sentence-level writing skills, including sentence combining, sentence expansion, and transformations from one type of sentence to another.

APPENDIX B

Sample Lesson Plans

Contributed by Mike Minsky of the Greenwood Institute, Putney, Vermont

LESSON 1: INTRODUCING THE
LETTER–SOUND CORRESPONDENCE /ɪ/ TO A NOVICE READER

The student already knows that the letter *a* represents the "short *a*" sound as in *lamb* and knows the sound–symbol correspondences for consonants *d, f, g, n, p, s,* and *t*. The student's reading is restricted to consonant-vowel-consonant words involving those letters and a few sight words. The goal of the lesson is to introduce the "short *i*" sound as in *itch*.

The lesson begins with the teacher writing a list of one-syllable words with short *i* on the board. These may have some letters and combinations the student does not know, so the teacher reads the list first. (What the teacher might say is in quotation marks.)

"I am going to write some words on the board and read them aloud." The teacher writes and reads the list.

bit   mitt
sit   sip

fit   flip
knit   grip
lit   ship
nip

"What sound do you hear in the middle of all of these words?" If the student can't say the sound, the teacher explains that the first sound of *itch, in,* and *if* is the sound in the middle of all of the words.

"Say the sound /ɪ/ by itself. Is it an open sound or a closed sound? If it is an open sound, it is a vowel. What kind of sound is /ɪ/?"

The teacher points to the list of words. "What is the letter (shape) in the middle of these words?"

"Can you think of any other words that have /ɪ/?" Note that vowels followed by /n/ and /m/ are nasalized and may be problematic for some children to identify; examples containing these patterns are to be avoided initially. Words with /ɪg/ are also to be avoided, because the vowel before /g/ sounds like "long *e.*" The teacher gives the student sentences that will cue recall of a target word:

Another word for lie is (fib).

The small sail on the front of the sailboat is a (jib).

A word for a child is a (kid).

The witch has wart on her (lip).

My brother takes his fishing pole to the river to catch (fish).

Tag. You are (it).

Sometimes you just have to scratch an (itch).

"The letter we use to show this sound is *i.* This letter is called 'i.'" When we spell a word with /ɪ/, we use the letter *i* to show the sound." The teacher writes the letter *i* on the chalkboard. "This letter is *i.* The key word is *it.* The sound it makes is /ɪ/. Now copy the letter *i* while you look at the example. Make it big so that you can feel your arm move. Start at the top, go down to the line, and dot the *i.* Name the letter. Say the key word. Say the sound." The teacher repeats several times if necessary.

"When we see the letter *i* at the beginning or inside of a word, it can tell us to make the /ɪ/ sound with our mouths. The /ɪ/ sound is a vowel, an open sound, like the one you already know, /æ/. For which vowel is your jaw lower, /ɪ/ or /æ/?" The teacher shows the chart that shows vowel spellings by mouth position (see Figure 5.5) and locates the two vowels in their positions.

"Now I'll say a word. You say the vowel you hear in the word, /ɪ/ or /æ/."

bit	last	ranch
bat	blast	branch
kit	mist	crisp
rat	pinch	
spit	crash	

"Now we'll use letter cards to read some words and make new words." The teacher gives letter cards for *g, t, p, n, f, s, d, a,* and *i.* "This word says 'tip.'

"What word do I get if I take away /t/ and put /s/ in its place? What happens if I take the /s/ and make it a /d/?

Spell it with your cards. Good, you changed *sip* to *dip.* Now change *dip* to *nip.* Now, I will write some letters. Give me the sound for each letter I write." As each letter is written, the teacher points to the letter, waits for the student to make the sound, and then sweeps under the sounds to indicate that the student is to blend them.

The teacher guides the student to use the letter cards to build as many words as possible. Sentence cues and other meaningful cues can help a student identify what word is to be spelled. The teacher always has the student say the word aloud and repeat the sound sequence. Words can be built by changing one sound at a time in a chain of words, such as *pat, pit, pin, pan, Dan, din, fin, fit, fat,* and *fan.*

"I am first going to tell you a word: *pit.* Repeat it after me: *pit.* Say the sounds. Spell it aloud as you write it. Read the word you have written." The teacher then gives phrases for dictation that use the most common sight words already studied, such as *the, is, a, not,* and *has.*

sit on a pin	Dan sat on a pin.
sat on a pit	The man has a fan.
dip in the pit	Dad is not fat.
has a fan	Dan has a pit.
is not fat	Did Dad dip in the pit?

The teacher discusses how *pit* has several meanings.

LESSON 2: WORKING WITH SUFFIXES

This lesson introduces a group of suffixes. Students have previously studied the concept of a suffix and the spelling and meanings of suffixes such as *-ed, -ing, -less, -ness,* and *-ly.* Similar to the previous lesson, this lesson is essentially a dialogue between teacher and students moving from previously learned to new material.

"The word *happiness* has a suffix. Can anyone tell me what a suffix is?" The teacher waits for a response. "Yes, a suffix is a part of a word that is added to the end of another word and that changes the meaning in some way. Can you give me an example of some suffixes?" The teacher waits for responses.

"Good. Now we are going to learn a new one. I'll give you a root and then say a sentence that needs a new word made out of the root and a suffix. Tell me what word I need to add to finish the sentence." After the students say each word, the teacher writes it on the board:

Play. My puppy likes to play. He is very _____.
Care. You have to take a lot of care when crossing a street. You have
   to be _____.
Thank. My cousin thanked me a lot when I cleaned his garage.
   He was _____.
Fear. I was full of fear in the deserted building. I was _____.

"What does the suffix *-ful* mean? Yes, it means full of. A cheerful person is full of cheer. A joyful person is full of joy. But be careful when you spell the suffix—it has only one *l*. It is not spelled like the word *full*." The teacher makes new words by putting a card with the suffix *-ful* next to roots. Then the teacher reviews these words to see how many of those words can take the additional suffix *-ly*. Students are asked to write new words with the two suffixes: *carefully, thankfully, joyfully, playfully, fearfully,* and so forth.

The teacher makes a word web with all of the forms of the word *help* that can be created by adding the suffixes and prefixes the students have studied: *helpful, unhelpful, unhelpfully, helping, helped, helps, helpless, helplessness, helpers, helplessly,* and so forth. The teacher picks several words to use in creating written sentences with the students and emphasizes the construction of strong, detailed sentences with elaborated ideas. Sentences should tell enough about who is doing what, as in this sentence: *The cheerful boy ran up the stairs excited that he had won a puppy.*

LESSON 3: ORAL READING FOR FLUENCY

This lesson follows a sequence called Standard Oral Reading Procedure (SORP) in the Orton-Gillingham approach (Gillingham & Stillman, 1997). The teacher supports students to achieve fluency and accuracy in text reading. Daily practice with both oral and silent reading in text at the students' independent reading level or at the instructional reading level is recommended for developing readers.

"We are going to read some passages aloud from Chapter 8 in *Hatchet* by Gary Paulsen (1988). First let's go over the words that might be new but that you can probably read. Look at these words." The teacher prints the words on the chalkboard, cards, or chart paper:

nostril	accomplish	terrified
porcupine	gesture	raspberries

"First, divide the words into syllables before trying to pronounce them. In the word *gesture,* pay attention to the letter that comes after the *g*. The two last words have suffixes, and a final *y* has been changed to an *i*. So, you might want to cover the suffix with a card and read the root word first." The students read the words. If necessary the teacher corrects syllable division and has the students read the individual syllables correctly before they are blended into a word.

"Here are two more words that I am going to divide into syllables and read for you." The teacher writes *me/di/um* and *in/i/tial* on the chalkboard, cards, or chart paper.

"Now can you read these words? We will be studying words like *medium* and *initial* next week. I want you to skim pages 79–81 first and underline any words you think you might need help with." After the students have browsed the selection, the teacher says, "Are there any words you want me to go over with you? Spell them aloud for me from the book, and I will write them on the board for you to divide into syllables and figure out." The teacher keeps track of these words for later review. As much as possible, the teacher enables students to analyze the words, to read them by making analogies to known words, or to use the sentence context as an aid to figure them out.

"Now we'll start reading aloud from page 79. Who would like to begin? Remember to read the outlaw (sight) words correctly." The teacher can vary the strategies for oral reading. Exchanging paragraphs, reading simultaneously, or having students raise a hand when they are ready to take over are effective. Students who are afraid to read aloud should never be forced into an embarrassing confrontation and can read aloud for the teacher in private. The teacher keeps a running record of errors on a list and selects some for later instruction in word analysis and phrase reading. New vocabulary can also be placed into sentence anagrams—sentences broken apart and written word by word on cards for rebuilding. Every oral reading lesson should include comprehension activities such as summarizing the main points, predicting what is coming next, interpreting passages that entail both literal and figurative meanings, explaining the use of words in context, and questioning what the author intended.

APPENDIX C

Additional Examples of
Orthographic Patterns in English

CONSONANT GENERALIZATIONS

/č/ *ch, -tch* The letters *tch* are used after stressed, short vowels (*batch, ketch, ditch, blotch, butcher*), but the letters *ch* are used after tense vowels or after consonants (*poach, pouch, punch*).

/ǰ/ *-dge, -ge* At the ends of words, /ǰ/ is spelled *-dge* after stressed, short vowels (*badge, edge, ridge, lodge, budge*).

/kw/ *qu* This sound combination in the beginnings of words or syllables is spelled *qu. Qu* is the only two-letter spelling unit that works together to spell two unique sounds. When *qu* comes at the beginning of a syllable, *the* letter *u* stands for the consonant /w/, as in *assuage.*

/k/ *k, c, ch* The sound /k/ is spelled with *k* before the vowels *i* and *e;* with *c* before *a, o,* and *u;* with *ch* in Greek-derived words; and with *ck* after accented short vowels.

The letter *y* The letter *y* has four jobs in English orthography. It represents three vowels and one consonant. The consonant is the glide /j/, as in *yellow* and *yes*. The vowels are /i/ as in *baby* and *lady*; /ɪ/, as in *gym* and *chloro-phyll*; and /aj/ as in *cry, by, sly,* and *try*.

/ŋ/   There are two spellings for this sound, *ng* and *n*. The *n* spelling is used before the speech sounds /k/ and /g/, as in *lanky* and *language*.

VOWEL SPELLING GENERALIZATIONS

Vowel phoneme	Graphemes				Sample words
	Open syllable, ends with vowel	Middle of syllable, vowel team, or vowel-consonant-*e*	End of word	Less common spellings	
/i/	*e*	*ee, ea*	*y*	*ei, ie, ey, e-*consonant-*e*	*fever, see, sea, baby, piece, deceive, key, Pete*
/e/	*a*	*a*-consonant-*e, ai*	*ay*	*ei, eigh, ey, ea*	*savor, date, bail, pay, vein, eight, they, great*
/aj/	*i*	*i*-consonant-*e, igh*	*y*	*ie, y-*consonant-*e, i*	*bicycle, rice, fight, cry, pie, byte, find, wild*
/o/	*o*	*o*-consonant-*e, oa*	*ow*	*oe, o, ough*	*potion, stoke, boat, flow, toe, bold, most, though*
/u/	*u*	*u*-consonant-*e*	*ew*	*ue, ui, eu*	*ruby, music, flute, cute, chew, few, blue, suit, euphonic*
/ɔ/	—	*au (aw* before *n* and *l*)	*aw*	*a, alk, all, augh*	*applaud, paw, pawn, crawl, water, talk, tall, caught*
/ɔj/	—	*oi*	*oy*	—	*boisterous, boil, coy, toy*
/æw/	—	*ou (ow* before *n, l,* and sometimes *d*)	*ow*	—	*shout, ground, crown, crowd, owl*

APPENDIX D

Syllable Review
and Self~Evaluation

SIX TYPES OF SYLLABLES IN ENGLISH ORTHOGRAPHY

Syllable type	Examples	Definition
Closed	_dapple_ _hostel_ _beverage_	A syllable with a short vowel, ending in a consonant
Open	_program_ _table_ _recent_	A syllable that ends with a long vowel sound that is spelled with a single vowel letter
Consonant-_le_	_bible_ _beagle_ _little_	An unaccented final syllable containing a consonant before /l/ followed by silent _e_
Vowel team and diphthong	_awesome_ _trainer_ _congeal_ _spoilage_	Syllables with long or short vowel spellings that use a vowel combination (diphthongs /æw/ and /ɔj/ are included in this category)
R-controlled	_spurious_ _consort_ _charter_	Any syllable in which the vowel is followed by an /r/ (vowel pronunciation often changes before /r/)
Vowel- consonant-_e_	_compete_ _despite_ _conflate_	Syllable with a long vowel sound that is spelled with a vowel, a consonant, and silent _e_

Note: Some unstressed and odd syllables do not fit into these categories, such as _-age_ in _verbiage,_ _-ture_ in _sculpture,_ and _-ion_ in adoration.

WORD LISTS FOR CERTAIN SYLLABLE TYPES[1]

Two Closed Syllables

absent	custom	kingdom	ransom
album	dentist	midget	subject
basket	distant	pretzel	tennis
contact	helmet	publish	velvet
contest	husband	pumpkin	victim

Closed and Consonant-_le_ Syllables

apple	cackle	huddle	puzzle
babble	castle	little	scramble
bottle	cattle	mumble	squabble
brittle	crumble	pebble	tremble
bundle	drizzle	puddle	wiggle

[1]Much more extensive word lists of this type can be found in Ganske (2000).

Closed and *R*-Controlled Syllables

altar	cluster	jogger	sculptor
anchor	dollar	manner	splendor
beggar	fender	nectar	splinter
blister	filter	plaster	tractor
cancer	hangar	plumber	tremor

Stressed *R*-Controlled Syllables

[ɑr]	[er]	[er]	[er]
barber	airplane	cherish	berry
charcoal	chairperson	Gerald	derrick
garlic	dairy	herald	error
jargon	fairway	imperative	herring
marshal	hairbrush	merit	merriment
stardom	prairie	peril	terrace
target	stairway	sheriff	terrible

[ajr]	[ir]	[ir]	[ir]
admire	appear	career	adhere
entire	dreary	cheerful	austere
fireman	earache	jeering	cashmere
inspire	nearby	killdeer	hereby
perspire	rearing	leerily	merely
require	spearmint	peering	revere
tiresome	tearful	sheered	severe
	yearling	veneer	sincere

[ɔr]	[ɔr]	[ɔr]	[ɔr]
adorn	adore	aboard	courtship
border	before	coarsely	fourteen
chorus	boredom	hoarding	fourth
dormant	explore	hoarseness	mourned
floral	galore	soared	pouring
forty	horehound		resource
glory	ignore		
northwest	restore		
porthole	scoreless		
snorkel	shoreline		
torture	storefront		

[ʌr]	[ʌr]	[ʌr]	[ʌr]
birthday	certain	dearth	burdened
circus	certify	earliest	curtain
dirty	dervish	earned	duration
flirtatious	herbal	earthling	endurance
girded	hermit	pearly	further
rebirth	merchant	rehearse	murmur
skirmish	nerdy	relearn	nurture
thirsty	perfect	search	purchase
unstirred	sterling	searchlight	return
virtue	thermos	unearthed	surly
whirlwind	vertical	yearning	turkey

Stressed Open Syllables

[e]	[i]	[aj]	[o]	[ju]
baby	cedar	biceps	cobalt	butane
cradle	decent	cider	donor	duty
data	depot	diver	frozen	future
favor	female	hijack	grocery	guru
gracious	prefix	migraine	locate	human
lady	recent	pliers	motor	music
major	regal	rival	odor	pupil
nature	secret	spiral	Prozac	stupid
saber	sequence	tiger	social	tumor

Vowel-Consonant-*e* Syllable

debate	compete	invite	xylophone	exude
inflate	complete	recite	alone	protrude
degrade	phoneme	imbibe	devote	exhume
invade	supreme	sublime	dethrone	presume
unmade	recede	iodine	expose	intrude
rebate	impede	Caroline	remote	pollute
captivate	delete	refine	hopeless	amuse
insulate	replete	finely	boneless	conclude
regulate	convene	ninety	notebook	jukebox
female	stampede	sidewalk	lonesome	tubeless
shameful	extreme	widespread	suppose	yuletide

Unstressed Syllables: Cannot Be Spelled Simply by Sounding Out

button	angel	audit	bodice	alley
captain	anvil	banquet	cornice	chimney
deafen	bridal	credit	crevice	jersey
human	fertile	digit	justice	
kitten	fossil	faucet	notice	monkey
pardon	kernel	jacket	practice	cookie
raisin	rascal	merit	furnace	goalie
urban	sterile	pamphlet		rookie
			menace	prairie
			necklace	
			palace	angry
			surface	clergy
			terrace	empty
				guilty

☆ SYLLABLE SELF-EVALUATION

1. How many syllables are in each of these words?

   revolutionary _____   chewier _____

   scissors _____   geothermal _____

   idealistic _____   microorganism _____

   segue _____

2. Every syllable must have which of the following?

   stress   at least one consonant   a vowel sound   a letter

3. Which are closed syllables?

   sheer   it   chew   toast

4. Which are complex syllables with a consonant cluster?

   knight   brought   thing   bird

5. Which words have two open syllables?

   re/do   a/head   re/lease   ser/ene

6. All of the following words have an *r*-controlled vowel sound pronounced like the /er/ in *bird* except:

   earthen   prefer   purring   mournful

7. Which statements are untrue about accent (syllable stress)?

   a) One-syllable words are accented.
   b) The second word in a compound is usually accented.
   c) The root of a Latin-based word is more often accented than the prefix or suffix.
   d) With words such as *conduct* and *object*, accent can determine which form of the word is a noun and which form is a verb.
   e) When the vowel sound in the last syllable of a word is spelled with a vowel team, that syllable is most often accented.
   f) Accent often is placed on inflected endings, including the plural and past tense.
   g) In most multisyllabic words ending in -*tion*, the primary accent falls on the syllable preceding -*tion*.
   h) When there is a doubled consonant within a word, the accent usually falls on the syllable that ends with that consonant.

100 Words
Commonly Used in Writing

Following are 100 words commonly used by children in writing, ordered by descending frequency and categorized as pattern-based (standard font) or odd (italicized). The oddities must be memorized as exceptions to sound–symbol correspondence principles.

I	for	*are*	came	down
and	but	just	time	did
the	have	*because*	back	*mother*
a	up	*what*	will	our
to	had	if	can	don't
was	*there*	day	*people*	school
in	with	*his*	from	little
it	*one*	this	saw	into
of	be	not	now	*who*
my	so	very	or	after
he	all	go	*know*	no
is	*said*	*do*	*your*	am
you	*were*	about	home	well
that	then	*some*	house	*two*
we	like	her	an	put
when	went	him	around	man
they	them	*as*	see	didn't
on	she	*could*	think	us
would	out	get	by	things
me	at	got	over	*too*

"FAMILIES" FOR SOME OF THE ODDITIES

there	one	two	we
here	once	twelve	he
where	only	twenty	she
	alone		me
to	their	would	is
do	heir	could	his
too	heirloom	should	was
			has
			as
who	because	know	what
whom	pause	knew	was
whose	clause	known	want
whole	applause	knee	water

From Hillerich, R.L. (1978). *A writing vocabulary of elementary children.* Springfield, IL: Charles C Thomas; adapted by permission.

Developmental
Spelling Inventories

A qualitative inventory of spelling development is an efficient and valid way of determining at what point children might be in their acquisition of word knowledge. The first versions of this kind of tool were validated by Edmund Henderson and his graduate students at the University of Virginia during the 1980s and 1990s (Henderson, 1990; see also Templeton & Bear, 1992). Two levels of inventory follow, contributed by Dr. Francine Johnston, a co-author of *Words Their Way* (Bear, Templeton, Invernizzi, & Johnston, 1996). A few minor changes in Johnston's scoring system have been made for this book.

DIRECTIONS FOR ADMINISTERING THE SPELLING INVENTORIES

The two tests that follow are designed to assess the orthographic knowledge that elementary school students bring to the tasks of reading and spelling. Students are not to study these words before testing. Doing so would invalidate the purpose of the inventory, which is to find out what students truly know. You can administer this same list of words to measure children's progress three times: in September, January, and May.

These words are ordered in terms of their relative difficulty for children in kindergarten to fifth grade. For this reason you need only to call out the words with features that your children are likely to master during the year. Do call out enough words, however, to get a sense of the range of ability in your class. For most kindergartners you may only need to call out the first five to eight words on the Primary Spelling Inventory. For first graders, call out at least 15 words. For second and third graders, use the entire primary list. Use the entire Elementary Spelling Inventory for fourth and fifth graders and for any third graders who are able to spell more than 20 of the words on the primary list. You should also call out additional words for any kindergartners or first graders who are spelling most of the words correctly.

Testing

Call out the words as you would for any spelling test. Use each word in a sentence to be sure your children know the exact word. Assure your students that this is not for a grade but to help you plan better for their needs. Seat the children to minimize copying, or test the children in small groups (especially in kindergarten and early first grade).

Scoring the Test

Copy an individual score sheet for each child and simply add a point for each correct grapheme or spelling feature of each word. Some of the features are single graphemes that correspond to single phonemes; others are grapheme combinations that spell linguistic units such as onsets, rimes, inflections, or affixes. Add an additional point in the "Correct" column if the entire word is spelled correctly. Note that some words are scored for some features and not others and that the number of possible points varies for each word. For example, in the primary list, you are not asked to look at whether children spell the final consonants correctly in the words *shine* and *blade* or whether the children spell the initial consonant in *talked* correctly.

Assigning Points and Analyzing the Results

Staple each child's spelling test to the individual score sheet. Total the number of points under each feature and across each word. Add the feature and word totals to find the total point score. This number can be compared over time, but the most useful information will be the feature analysis. Look down each feature column to determine the needs of the child. Transfer these numbers to a class composite sheet to get a sense of your group as a whole and to form groups for instruction. Highlight children who are making two or more errors on a particular feature. For example, a child who gets six of seven short vowels correct on the primary list can be considered in pretty good shape, although some review work might be in order. A child who gets only two or three of the seven short vowels, however, needs a lot of work on that feature. Because the total possible number will vary depending on how many words you call out, the criteria for mastery will vary. You can generally think like this: If x is the number of possible correct responses, then a score of x or $x - 1$ indicates good control of the feature, whereas a score of $x - 2$ or more indicates a need for instruction. If a child did not get any points for a feature, it is beyond his or her ability and earlier features need to be addressed first.

Primary Spelling Inventory—Individual Score Sheet

Child _____ Grade _____ Date _____

Teacher _____ Total Points _____

Test words	Initial consonant	Final consonant	Digraph	Blend	Short vowel	Vowel-consonant-e	Vowel team/diphthong	R-controlled vowel	Inflection	Correct? Add 1 point	Word totals
1. fan	f	n			a						
2. pet	p	t			e						
3. dig	d	g			i						
4. mop	m	p			o						
5. rope	r	p				o-consonant-e					
6. wait	w	t					ai				
7. chunk			ch	nk	u						
8. sled				sl	e						
9. stick		-ck		st	i						
10. shine			sh			i-consonant-e					
11. dream				dr			ea				

WORDS THEIR WAY: WORD STUDY FOR PHONICS, VOCABULARY . . . 2/E by Bear/Invernizzi et al., ©1996. Adapted by permission of Prentice-Hall, Inc., Upper Saddle River, NJ.

				a-consonant-e						
12. blade		bl								
13. coach	-ch				oa					
14. fright		fr			igh					
15. snowing		sn			ow			-ing		
16. talked					-a			-ed		
17. camping		-mp						-ing		
18. thorn	th					or				
19. shouted	sh				ou			-ed		
20. spoil		sp			oi					
21. growl		gr			ow					
22. chirp	ch					ir				
23. clapped		cl						-pped		
24. tries		tr						-ies		
25. hiking								-king		
Feature totals										Total points:

WORDS THEIR WAY: WORD STUDY FOR PHONICS, VOCABULARY . . . 2/E by Bear/Invernizzi et al., ©1996. Adapted by permission of Prentice-Hall, Inc., Upper Saddle River, NJ.

Child _____ Grade _____ Date _____

Teacher _____ Total Points _____

Elementary Spelling Inventory—Individual Score Sheet

Test words	Short vowel	Blend/ digraph	Long vowel pattern	Other vowel	Rule-based variant consonant	Inflection with rule spelling	Syllable juncture	Unaccented syllable	Suffix	Correct? Add 1 point	Word totals
1. speck	e	sp			ck						
2. switch	i	sw			tch						
3. throat			oa								
4. nurse				ur							
5. scrape			a-cononant-e								
6. charge		ch		ar	ge						
7. phone		ph	o-consonant-e								
8. smudge	u	sm			dge						
9. point		nt		oi							
10. squirt		squ		ir							
11. drawing		dr		aw		-ing					

WORDS THEIR WAY: WORD STUDY FOR PHONICS, VOCABULARY . . . 2/E by Bear/Invernizzi et al., ©1996. Adapted by permission of Prentice-Hall, Inc., Upper Saddle River, NJ.

12.	trapped	tr			-pped								
13.	waving				-ving								
14.	powerful		ow				-er	-ful					
15.	battle					tt	-tle						
16.	fever					v	-er						
17.	lesson					ss	-on						
18.	pennies				-ies	nn							
19.	fraction							-tion					
20.	sailor					l		-or					
21.	distance					st		-ance					
22.	confusion							-sion					
23.	discovery						dis-	-ery					
24.	resident						si	-dent					
25.	visible							-ible					
	Feature totals												

Total points:

WORDS THEIR WAY: WORD STUDY FOR PHONICS, VOCABULARY . . . 2/E by Bear/Invernizzi et al., ©1996. Adapted by permission of Prentice-Hall, Inc., Upper Saddle River, NJ.

Answer Key

Answers appear in italics, with the exception of phonetic symbols.

☆ BRIEF SURVEY: PHONEME COUNTING

Count the number of speech sounds or phonemes that you perceive in each of the following spoken words. Remember, the speech sounds may not be equivalent to the letters. For example, the word *spoke* has four phonemes: /s/, /p/, /o/, and /k/. Write the number of phonemes in the blank to the right of each word.

thrill _4_	ring _3_	shook _3_
does _3_	fix _4_	wrinkle _5_
sawed _3_	quack _4_	know _2_

☆ BRIEF SURVEY: SYLLABLE COUNTING

Count the number of syllables that you perceive in each of the following words. For example, the word *higher* has two syllables, the word *threat* has one, and the word *physician* has three.

cats __1__   capital __3__   shirt __1__

spoil _1 or 2_   decidedly __4__   banana __3__

recreational __5__   lawyer __2__   walked __1__

☆ BRIEF SURVEY: PHONEME MATCHING

Read the first word in each line and note the sound that is represented by the underlined letter or letter cluster. Then select the word or words on the line that contain the same sound. Underline the words you select.

1. **pu̲sh**   although   _sugar_   duty   pump
2. **w̲eigh**   pie   height   _raid_   friend
3. **doe̲s**   miss   _nose_   votes   rice
4. **in̲tend**   this   whistle   _baked_   batch
5. **ri̲ng**   _sink_   handle   signal   pinpoint

☆ BRIEF SURVEY: RECOGNITION OF SOUND–SYMBOL CORRESPONDENCE

Find the letters and letter combinations in the following words that correspond to each speech sound in the word. For example, the word _stress_ has five phonemes, each of which is represented by a letter or letter group: s / t / r / e / ss. Now try these:

_b / e / s / t_   _f / r / e / sh_   _s / c / r / a / tch_

th / ough   _l / au / gh / ed_   _m / i / dd / le_

_ch / ir / p_   _q / u / ai / n / t_

☆ BRIEF SURVEY: DEFINITIONS AND CONCEPTS

Write a definition or explanation of the following:

1. Vowel sound (vowel phoneme)   _A vowel sound is an open speech sound that is the nucleus of a syllable._
2. Consonant digraph   _A consonant digraph is a letter combination corresponding to one unique sound._
3. Prefix   _A prefix is a Latin bound morpheme (meaningful part), added before a root, that changes the meaning of the whole word._
4. Inflectional (grammatical) morpheme   _An inflectional morpheme is a grammatical ending added to a verb, adjective, or noun that changes the number, degree, or tense of the word but does not change the meaning of the word._
5. Why is phoneme awareness important?   _It is one (but not the only) necessary skill in learning to read an alphabetic writing system._

6. How is decoding skill related to reading fluency and comprehension? *The ability to decode words accurately will not of itself support good reading. In addition to decoding, one needs to read words fluently so that attention can be relegated to comprehension.*

☆ COMPREHENSIVE SURVEY OF LANGUAGE KNOWLEDGE

1. From the list below, find an example of each of the following (answer will be a word or part of a word):

   Inflected verb ___*slowed*___

   Compound noun ___*sandpaper*___

   Bound root ___*cred (Latin), cyc (Latin/Greek), psych (Greek)*___

   Derivational suffix ___*ful, ible*___

   Greek combining form ___*neuro + psych + ology*___

2. For each word on the left, determine the number of syllables and the number of morphemes:

	Syllables	Morphemes
bookworm	2	2
unicorn	3	2
elephant	3	1
believed	2	3
incredible	4	3
finger	2	1
hogs	1	2
telegram	3	2

3. A closed syllable is one that *contains a short vowel and ends in a consonant.* An open syllable is one that *contains a long vowel sound spelled with one vowel letter that ends the syllable.*

4. How many speech sounds are in the following words?

sigh _2_	thrown _4_	scratch _5_
ice _2_	sung _3_	poison _5_
mix _4_	shrink _5_	know _2_

5. What is the third speech sound in each of the following words? (*Both international phonetic alphabet and phonic symbols are shown, respectively.*)

joyful _/f/_	should _/ʊ/ or /o͝o/_	talk _/ɔ/ or /aw/_
tinker _/ŋ/ or /ng/_	rouge _/ž/ or /zh/_	shower _/w/_
square _/w/_	start _/ɑ/ or /ŏ/_	
protect _/o/_	patchwork _/č/ or /ch/_	

6. Underline the schwa vowels:
    tel<u>e</u>phone   addend<u>a</u>   <u>a</u>long   prec<u>iou</u>s   imp<u>o</u>siti<u>o</u>n   <u>u</u>nless
7. Underline the consonant blends:
    knight   <u>cl</u>imb   wreck   napkin   <u>s</u>qu<u>i</u>shed   <u>sp</u>ringy   fir<u>st</u>
8. Underline the consonant digraphs:
    <u>s</u>pherical   <u>ch</u>ur<u>ch</u>   numb   <u>sh</u>rink   <u>th</u>ought   <u>wh</u>e<u>th</u>er
9. When is ck used in spelling?   *The spelling ck is used when a /k/ sound follows a stressed, short (lax) vowel.*
10. What letters signal that a c is pronounced /s/?   *e, i, or y following the c*
11. List all of the ways you know to spell "long o":   *o, oa, ow, oe, o-consonant-e, ough*
12. List all of the ways you know to spell the consonant sound /f/:   *f, ff, gh, ph*
13. When adding a suffix to a word ending with silent *e*, what is the spelling rule?   *Drop the e if the suffix begins with a vowel; keep the e if the suffix begins with a consonant.*
14. How can you recognize an English word that came from Greek?   *It might have ph for /f/, ch for /k/, or y for /ɪ/ or /ī/ spelling; it is likely to be constructed from two or more combining forms; and it is likely to be a mythological (myth), a scientific (chlorophyll), or a mathematical (dyscalculia) term.*

☆ EXERCISE 2.1

Count the number of phonemes in the following words:

ice __2__	choose __3__	mix __4__	soothe __3__
sigh __2__	sing __3__	pitched __4__	her __2__
day __2__	thorn __3 or 4__	straight __5__	boy __2__
aide __2__	quake __4__	measure __4__	shout __3__

☆ EXERCISE 2.2

Identify the third phoneme in the following words:

choose __[z]__	pneumonia __[m]__	kitchen [č] *or* [ch]
writhe [ð] *or* [th]	vision [ž] *or* [zh]	square __[w]__
sink [ŋ] *or* [ng]	folk __[k]__	

☆ EXERCISE 2.4

Write the symbol for first and last consonants in each word. Pay attention to how the words sound, not how they are spelled.

some __[s], [m]__   judge __[ĭ], [ĭ]__   wide __[w], [d]__
knight __[n], [t]__   nose __[n], [z]__   thing __[θ], [ŋ]__
clear __[k], [r]__   shoal __[š], [l]__   rhyme __[r], [m]__
write __[r], [t]__   which __[ʍ], [č]__   phone __[f], [n]__
once __[w], [s]__   choose __[č], [z]__   yawn __[y], [n]__
thatch __[θ], [č]__   comb __[k], [m]__   hymn __[h], [m]__
guest __[g], [t]__   quest __[k], [t]__   gem __[ĭ], [m]__
gym __[ĭ], [m]__   whole __[ʍ], [l]__   rouge __[r], [ž]__
pave __[p], [v]__   there __[ð], [r]__   thief __[θ], [f]__

☆ EXERCISE 2.6

2. Now write the full phonetic transcription for these words:

put __[pʊt]__   putt __[pʌt]__   puke __[pjuk]__
coin __[kɔjn]__   shower __[šæwɚ]__   sigh __[saj]__
should __[šʊd]__   thesis __[θisɪs]__   chain __[čen]__
sacks __[sæks]__   sax __[sæks]__   preppy __[prɛpi]__
critter __[crɪrɚ]__   ceiling __[silɪŋ]__   cymbal __[sɪmbəl]__
whether __[ʍɛðɚ]__   question __[kwɛsčən]__   measure __[mɛžɚ]__

3. Translate these words into standard English spelling:

ɔlðo ðə prabləm ʌv dɪslɛksiə ɪz nat ə kəndɪšən ʍerɪn pipl si θɪŋz
bækwɚd ðə sɪmtəm ʌv rivɚsəlz hæz bɪn ovɚpled baj ðə prɛs

*Although the problem of dyslexia is not a condition wherein people see
things backward, the symptom of reversals has been overplayed by the press.*

☆ CHAPTER 2 SUPPLEMENTARY EXERCISES

1. Determine what these groups of speech sounds have in common:
    a) [t], [d], [n], [s], [z]   *All are alveolar consonants.*
    b) [m], [n], [ŋ]   *All are nasal consonants.*
    c) [r], [l], [y], [w], [h], [m], [n], [ŋ]   *All are sonorant consonants.*
    d) [k], [g], [ŋ]   *All are velar consonants.*
    e) [t], [g], [d], [k], [p], [b]   *All are voiced or voiceless stop consonants.*
    f) [u], [ʊ], [o], [ɔ]   *All are back rounded vowels.*
2. Write an example of the following type of speech sound:
    a) Rounded back high vowel __[u]__
    b) Mid front lax vowel __[ɛ]__
    c) Voiced velar nasal __[ŋ]__
    d) Unvoiced interdental fricative __[θ]__

    e)   Voiced affricate ____[ǰ]____

    f)   Lateral liquid ____[l]____

    g)   Diphthong that begins with lip rounding ____[ɔj]____

3.   Contrast the sounds in the following minimal pairs of words. How do the sounds differ from one another, and how are they alike?

    a)   tee*th*, tee*the*   *They differ in voicing. Both are interdental fricatives.*

    b)   c*o*ne, c*o*n   *The first is tense; the second is lax. Both are mid back vowels.*

    c)   ri*ch*, ri*dge*   *They differ in voicing. Both are affricates.*

    d)   lea*f*, lea*ve*   *They differ in voicing. Both are labiodental fricatives.*

    e)   *p*ap, *m*ap   *The first is oral; the second is nasal. Both are bilabial stops.*

4.   Write the phonetic symbol for the last phoneme in the following words. (Avoid being fooled by the spelling!)

cheese ____[z]____	laugh ____[f]____	enjoy ____[ɔj]____
attached ____[t]____	baby ____[i]____	collage ____[ž]____
Xerox ____[s]____	aglow ____[o]____	
you ____[u]____	wealth ____[θ]____	

5.   On a separate sheet of paper, write the following poem (from "The World Is Too Much with Us" by William Wordsworth) in phonetic transcription. Brackets are optional in this exercise.

The world is too much with us; late and soon,
Getting and spending, we lay waste our powers:
Little we see in Nature that is ours;
We have given our hearts away, a sordid boon!
This Sea that bares her bosom to the moon;
The winds that will be howling at all hours,
And are up-gathered now like sleeping flowers;
For this, for everything, we are out of tune;
It moves us not.

ðə wɚld ɪz tu mʌč wɪθ ʌs let ænd sun
getɪŋ ænd spɛndɪŋ wi le west æwɚ pæwɚz
lɪɾl wi si ɪn nečɚ ðæt ɪz æwɚz
wi hæv gɪvən æwɚ harts əwe ə sɑrdɪd bun
ðɪs si ðæt berz hɚ buzəm tu ðə mun
ðə wɪndz ðæt wɪl bi hæwlɪŋ æt ɑl æwɚz
ænd ar ʌpgæðɚd næw lajk slipɪŋ flæwɚz
for ðɪs for ɛvriθɪŋ wi ar æwt ʌv tun
ɪt muvz ʌs nɑt

6.   On a separate sheet of paper, translate the following poem (author unknown) from phonetic symbols to standard English spelling:

aj tek ɪt ju ɔlrɛdi no
ʌv tʌf ænd bæw ænd kɔf ænd do
sʌm me stʌmbəl bʌt nat ju
ɑn hɪkəp θʌro slæw ænd θru
so næw ju ar rɛdi pɛrhæps

tu lɛrn ʌv lɛs fəmɪljɚ træps
biwɛr ʌv hɚd ə drɛdful wɚd
ðæt lʊks lajk bird ænd sæwndz lajk bɚd
ænd dɛd ɪts sɛd lajk bɛd nat bid
for gʊdnɛs sek dont kɔl ɪt did

I take it you already know
Of tough *and* bough *and* cough *and* dough.
Some may stumble but not you
On hiccough, thorough, slough, *and* through.
So now you are ready perhaps
Beware of heard, *a dreadful word*
That looks like beard *and sounds like* bird.
And dead? *It's said like* bed, *not* bead;
For goodness sake, don't call it deed.

7. Here are some spelling errors (followed by correct spellings) made
    by sixth-grade students. Match the spelling errors to the type of error
    they represent:
    a) Nasal omission or deletion ___*WOSUT/wasn't*___
    b) Liquid confusion ___*CLORER/color*___
    c) Voiced/voiceless stop substitution ___*SGARY/scary*___
    d) Fricative substitution ___*STASUN/station*___
    e) Flap for a medial stop ___*LEDR/letter*___
    f) Back vowel substitution ___*FOWD/food*___
    g) Front vowel substitution ___*INGLISH/English*___
    h) Oral (nonnasal) for a nasal ___*SINGIG/singing*___

☆ EXERCISE 3.1

Find the unaccented vowels that have lost their distinctiveness in pronunciation (schwas). Write other forms of the words, if any, in which the
vowels recover an identity. Your perceptions may be different from
someone else's.

imitate	*(none)*	expository	*exposition*
blossom	*(none)*	argumentative	*argumentation*
about	*(none)*	orthographic	*orthography*
application	*apply*	competent	*compete*
complexity	*cómplex*	deleterious	*delete*
narrative	*narrate*	beautiful	*beautician*

☆ EXERCISE 3.2

Write these words phonetically, using the aspiration sign [ʰ] for aspirated
voiceless stops, the schwa [ə] for unaccented vowels, and the tilde [˜]
above nasalized vowels that precede nasal consonants.

kitchen	[kʰɪčẽn]	steam	[stĩm]
purchase	[pʰɚčəs]	challenge	[čælẽnǰ]
tender	[tʰẽndɚ]	approve	[əpruv]
problem	[pʰrɔblə̃m]	snap	[snæp]
skate	[sket]	threat	[θrɛt]
spirit	[spirit]	solution	[səlušə̃n]

☆ EXERCISE 3.3

What phonological principle is shown in children's spelling of each set of words below (invented spelling in capital letters before the target word)?

1. LAG/leg ENK/ink EGLU/igloo   *A lax vowel before a velar consonant is raised.*

2. CHRIK/trick GRAK/drink CHRA/tray   *A /d/ or /t/ before /r/ is affricated.*

3. SWEDR/sweater PUDING/putting PEDE/pretty   *The /t/ is pronounced as a tongue flap.*

☆ EXERCISE 3.4

Find at least 10 more examples of words that demonstrate the homorganic nasal rule. Sort them into those that have /m/, /n/, or /ŋ/ after a vowel, and look at the consonant that follows each nasal sound. Does the principle of sound sequencing hold?

Bilabials after /m/	*Alveolars after /n/*	*Velars after /ŋ/*
simple	tender	language
symbol	tentative	finger
chimpanzee .	consonant	ingot
amputate	pantomime	thinking
empathize	underpants	English

☆ CHAPTER 3 SUPPLEMENTARY EXERCISES

1. Reverse the sequence of speech sounds in each of these words, or say them backward. Think of the sounds, not the letters.

   teach [čit]

   sigh [ajs]

   cuts [stʌk]

   pitch [čɪp]

   lip [pʰɪl]

   easy [izi]

judge   [ǰʌǰ]

speak   [kips]

palm   [mɔp]

cash   [šæk]

snitch   [čĭns]

face   [sef]

3. In each of the following minimal pairs of spoken words, two phonemes contrast to form different words. Identify by number, from the right-hand column, the primary feature by which each contrasting phoneme pair differs:

tick, chick __5__		a.	voicing
seek, sick __4__		b.	nasalization
rich, ridge __1__		c.	front/back placement
keel, cool __3__		d.	tenseness/laxness
whet, when __2__		e.	affrication

4. Automatic aspiration of /p/, /t/, and /k/ in the beginning of words is the result of an unconscious phonological rule in action. When does aspiration occur? What difference might aspiration, or lack of it, make to the ease with which students learn to decode and spell these phonemes?   *Aspiration of a voiceless stop consonant occurs when a consonant precedes a vowel or is the first consonant in a beginning blend. Aspiration is a feature that increases the likelihood of a consonant's being identified or perceived within the string of phonemes in a word. When voiceless stop consonants are unaspirated, they are more likely to be misperceived or confused with their voiced equivalents.*

5. Write concise definitions for the following terms:

Phonology   *Phonology is the system of rules by which we combine, sequence, and produce speech sounds in a language.*

Phonetics   *Phonetics is the study of the inventory of speech sounds that are used in a phonological system.*

Phoneme   *A phoneme is a speech sound in a language system that is distinguished by a set of articulatory features and that is used in combination with others to make words. It is the smallest unit of sound that distinguishes one word from another.*

Allophone (phone)   *An allophone is one of two or more variants of a phoneme that is produced by phonological rule or regional/dialect variation.*

6. Think of minimally contrasting pairs of words that differ only in the target sounds in initial, medial, and final position.

	Initial	Medial	Final
/k/, /g/	coat, goat	ankle, angle	dock, dog
/ǰ/, /č/	jug, chug	ledger, lecher	rich, ridge
/t/, /n/	tape, nape	kettle, kennel	rate, rain

	Initial	Medial	Final
/s/, /š/	show, sew	fashion, fasten	crash, crass
/f/, /v/	fairy, very	rifle, rival	strife, strive
/ŋ/, /n/	——	singer, sinner	rung, run

7. Given these four phonemes, how many possible words (real and nonsense) can you make with the set that conform to the order rules of English phonology? (Words should be pronounceable.) Which words have complex syllable structures?

/r/, /s/, /k/, /a/

[skar]	[rask]	[srak]	[sakr]
[kars]	[askr]	[arks]	[aksr]

They all have complex syllables, with the exception of [sakr] because /r/ is used as a syllable.

8. a) Some consonant sounds in English never begin a word. List them.   */ž/, /ŋ/*

   b) List the consonants in English that must always be followed by a vowel if they are in the beginning of a syllable. These consonants would never be followed by another consonant to make a blend. (Look back at the consonant inventories in Tables 2.1 and 2.2.)   *Nasals (/m/, /n/, /ŋ/), glides (/w/, /j/, /h/), liquids (/l/, /r/), and affricates (/č/, /ǰ/) are never followed by a consonant before a vowel within a syllable.*

9. Here are some phonological rules that affect word production in English. Find a spoken word that is an example of each of these rules:

   a) Automatic nasalization of a vowel before a nasal consonant
   sample, chunk, bend

   b) Reduction of an alveolar stop to a voiced flap when preceded by a stressed vowel and followed by an unstressed vowel
   better, little, write

   c) Elongation of a tense vowel before a voiced final consonant and shortening of a tense vowel before a voiceless final consonant
   bead, beet

   d) Raising of a lax vowel before a voiced velar consonant   *egg, igloo, ink*

10. What do the three words in each of these sets of spelling errors have in common? What phonological processing weaknesses might they represent?

    a) JELE for *chili*, GARASH for *garage*, SBENT for *spend*
    These errors show voicing substitution.

    b) POIT for *point*, KINCHEN for *kitchen*, FRUT for *front*
    These errors show deletion or misplacement of nasal after a vowel and before consonant.

    c) SPEAS for *spears*, COLOL for *color*, TEE for *tree*
    These errors show deletion or substitution for liquid. /r/.

☆ EXERCISE 4.1

1. Underline the base word (free morpheme) from which each longer word is constructed:

    <u>tear</u>ful   <u>warm</u>ly

    <u>humor</u>ous   <u>king</u>dom

    <u>fortun</u>ate   antidise<u>stabl</u>ishmentarianism

    un<u>like</u>   <u>knight</u>hood

    re<u>turn</u>   mis<u>spell</u>

    (establish, *which seems to be the base in antidisestablishmentarianism, can be divided further into* e + stabl + ish)

2. Identify all of the morphemes in these words:

    watch + dog   tele + market + ing   co(m) + tract

    mistletoe   odo + meter   in + ject + ion

    pip(e) + ed   pre + vari + cate   bio + de + grad + able

    dodg(e) + er + s   i(n) + legal   power

☆ EXERCISE 4.2

Identify the number of morphemes in these words:

softer __2__   delirious __3__   felt __2__

teacher __2__   higher __2__   serious __1__

water __1__   fire __1__

butter __1__   melt __1__

☆ EXERCISE 4.3

Create some possible and some impossible words from the following menu by mixing and matching word parts:

Prefix	Root	Suffix	Word	Impossible word
inter	spir(e)	(a)tion	*interruptible*	*noncredarian*
dis	cred	icate	*discredited*	*presecticate*
non	sect	(i)able	*nonsectarian*	*disspiration*
pre	var	arian	*prevaricate*	*nonrupted*
in	rupt	ed	*inspiration*	*intervarable*

☆ EXERCISE 4.4

Place the number 1, 2, 3, or 4 next to the word pairs that follow, according to the degree of relatedness or similarity you perceive. Words with 1 are definitely related in meaning, words with 2 are related but somewhat less closely, words with 3 seem to have a more distant connection, and words with 4 do not have a meaningful connection.   *Each person's answers to this exercise may vary, but most people agree that* joy/join, amnesty/amniotic, catch/ketchup, *and* cap/capture *are unrelated pairs.*

☆ EXERCISE 4.5

The meaning of a compound is not always the same as the sum of its parts. Define the following words and think about how the meanings of the compounds and their parts compare:

redcoat   *British soldier during the American Revolution*

laughing gas   *chemical that when inhaled affects the voice quality of the user*

looking glass   *mirror*

blackboard   *chalkboard of any color*

turncoat   *traitor*

bigwig   *important person*

rubbernecking   *slowing down while driving on the highway to look at an incident or accident*

☆ EXERCISE 4.6

Identify the part of speech of each word in these pairs (noun = n, verb = v, and adjective = a). Some words may serve more than one grammatical role.

preside _v_   president _n_

legislate _v_   legislature _n_

compete _v_   competition _n_

invent _v_   inventor _n_

sign _v/n_   signify _v_

peril _n_   perilous _a_

disturb _v_   disturbance _n_

active _a_   activity _n_

type _v/n_   typify _v_

face _v/n_   facial _n/a_

☆ EXERCISE 4.7

First, identify the parts of speech of the words on the left (noun = n, verb = v, and adjective = a); then, add suffixes to create derived forms that serve the grammatical functions indicated. You may need to alter the spellings of the original words when adding the suffixes.

generous __a__   noun ___*generosity*___

decide __v__   adjective ___*decisive*___

successive __a__   noun ___*succession*___

extent __n__   verb ___*extend*___

depend __v__   adjective *dependable, dependent*

occur __v__   noun ___*occurrence*___

teach __v__   noun __*teacher, teaching*__

pretense __n__   verb ___*pretend*___

revise __v__   noun ___*revision*___

intend __v__   adverb ___*intentionally*___

☆ EXERCISE 4.8

Underline all of the inflections, and notice where they occur:

inducement<u>s</u>	*factor<u>s</u>*	*misunderstood (none if adjective; stood is abstract past tense if verb)*
legal<u>izing</u>	*sing<u>ing</u>*	
production<u>s</u>	*tardi<u>est</u>*	
high<u>er</u>	*sho<u>ed</u>*	*lost (abstract past tense)*
disentangl<u>ed</u>	*unhappi<u>est</u>*	

☆ EXERCISE 4.9

Give yourself 3 minutes to generate as many words as you can on a separate sheet of paper that use any one of these Greek-derived morphemes:

chrom   *chromatic, chromosome, monochrome, and so forth*

cycle   *bicycle, cyclical, recycle, and so forth*

therm   *thermometer, thermonuclear, isotherm, thermal, and so forth*

☆ EXERCISE 4.10

1. From the derived form of the word given, write the base word, and underline any part of the word that is pronounced or written differently in the derived form.

   reference   *ref<u>e</u>r*

   precision   *preci<u>se</u>*

   dramatic   *dram<u>a</u>*

   theatrical   *the<u>a</u>tre*

   possession   *pose<u>ss</u>*

sanity *sane*

originality *original*

ridiculous *ridicule*

sociology *social*

political *politic*

ritual *rite*

2. Decide what kind of change has occurred between the base form and the base in the derived form of these words (1 = no change, 2 = orthographic [spelling] change only, 3 = phonological [sound] change only, 4 = both phonological and orthographic changes).

bat/batty *2*

human/humanity *3*

wide/width *4*

differ/difference *4* (*depends whether* difference *is pronounced* [dɪfɚˈɔ̄ns] *or* [dɪfrɔ̄ns])

sun/sunny *2*

athlete/athletic *4*

personal/personality *3*

propel/propeller *2*

combine/combination *4*

idiot/idiotic *3*

usual/usually *1*

extend/extension *4*

nature/natural *4*

define/definition *4*

assist/assistance *1*

☆ CHAPTER 4 SUPPLEMENTARY EXERCISES

1. Divide these words into morphemes. Use a dictionary if necessary.

mis + spell

sens + (a)ble

in + oper + able

psych + ology

pre + fer + (r)ing

morph + em(e) + ic

stimul + ate

a(d) + tach + ed

beaut(y) + ful + ly

ex + cite + ment

in + spir(e) + (a)tion

pac + ify

in + sane + ly

forget(t) + able

con + tinu + ity

dis + miss

re + co(n) + mend

tele + vis + ion

3. Divide these words twice, once to show the syllables and again to show the morphemes. The two are not always in agreement because different language structures are involved at each layer of language organization:

	Syllables	Morphemes
competition	com/pe/ti/tion	com+pet(e)+(i)+tion
precision	pre/ci/sion	pre+cis(e)+ion
scaling	sca/ling	scal(e)+ing
tractor	trac/tor	tract+or
invasive	in/va/sive	in+vas+ive
gentle	gen/tle	gent+le

4. Words like *remain, finger,* and *hamburger* look as though they might have separate morphemes but do not in modern English usage. They cannot be divided into meaningful parts. Think of three more words that look on the surface as though they could be made of separate morphemes but (at least in modern use) are not.

diminish	*delight*	*respond*	*battery*
bison	*hammer*	*ceiling*	*infant*

5. Make up five new words, composed of common prefixes, roots, and suffixes, that could be real words but that are not established words in English, such as *unpudgable.* Possibilities include exorbaceous, pre-tractation, subneurometrics, unfractable, *and* discredurious.

6. Below is list of correct and incorrect spellings of words. English spelling often retains the spellings of meaningful parts even when pronunciation changes, so the correct spellings of the words listed can be affirmed by knowing the pronunciation and spelling of another form of the word. Determine the correct spellings. Then, to the right of these lists, write a form of each word that can help you remember the correct spelling.

		Other word
compitition	*competition*	*compete*
persperation	*perspiration*	*perspire*
physician	physision	*physical*
restiration	*restoration*	*restore*
pleasure	plesure	*please*
resign	resine	*resignation*
publisity	*publicity*	*public*
electrisity	*electricity*	*electric*
demacratic	*democratic*	*democracy*
president	presedent	*preside*
comprable	*comparable*	*compare*
history	histry	*historical*
janiter	*janitor*	*janitorial*
managor	*manager*	*managerial*
majer	*major*	*majority*
industry	indistry	*industrious*

7. Match the terms in column B to one of the words in column A:

A

incredible *5*

credits *3*

accredit *1*

cred *4*

creditor *2*

B

1. Assimilated prefix (changed to match root's beginning)

2. Derivational noun suffix

3. Inflectional suffix

4. Bound root morpheme

5. Derivational adjective suffix

☆ EXERCISE 5.1

Identify whether the following words are likely to be Anglo-Saxon (AS), Latin (L), Greek (G), or other (O) without looking them up in a dictionary. You may want to refer to Table 5.1.

hemisphere *G*

inducement *L*

groundhog *AS*

gnocchi *O*

arms *AS*

kaput *O*

dealt *AS*

stadium *L*

etymology *G*

suffix *L*

knight *AS*

wanted *AS*

☆ EXERCISE 5.2

Identify the letters or letter combinations (graphemes) that correspond to the phonemes in the following words. Each grapheme should correspond to a phoneme. For example, the graphemes in *shriek* are *sh / r / ie / k*.

s / ow	sh / o / ve	p / r / ai / se
b/ a / tch	J / e / ll / o	p / eo / p / le
eigh / t	q / u / i / e / t	

☆ EXERCISE 5.3

Explain the spellings for /k/.
Pattern: When a word begins with /k/, the letter c is used before the vowels a, u, and o, and the letter k is used before the vowels i and e. The qu combination is used at the beginnings of almost all words that start with the /kw/ combination. When a word ends with /k/, ck is used after a stressed lax vowel.

☆ EXERCISE 5.4

Classify the underlined syllables in these words by syllable type, and also record syllables that don't fit. List the syllables according to these seven types. The first six are done for you.

Closed	Open	Consonant-*le*	Vowel team	R-controlled	Vowel-consonant-*e*
-sent	hu-	-gle	ail-	-surd	-eme
-spect	mi-	-ble	few	-ger	-pale
ab-	ta-		boast-	-mark	-pete
-mong	vi-			hair-	-bine
-tion				fur-	

Other: _-ive_

☆ EXERCISE 5.5

Fill in the blanks.

pat + _ed_ = patted	begin + ing = _beginning_
run + er = runner	sad + ness = _sadness_
step + _ed_ = stepped	beg + er = _beggar_
skip + ing = skipping	bad + ly = _badly_

☆ EXERCISE 5.6

Why is the consonant doubled or not doubled in these words?

occur	occurrence	occurred	occurring
commit	commitment	committee	committed
excel	excellent	propelled	propeller
legal	legality	legalization	legalese

The words occur, commit, propel, *and* excel *are accented on the second sylla-ble and end in one consonant preceded by one vowel. Therefore, the consonant is doubled when a suffix with a vowel is added. The word* legal *is accented on the first syllable, so the doubling rule does not apply.*

☆ EXERCISE 5.7

Fill in the blanks.

Base word + suffix = affixed word
Example: fame + ous = *famous*

wise + ly = _____*wisely*_____
flake + y = _____*flaky*_____
close + ness = _____*closeness*_____
blame + ful = _____*blameful*_____
ice + y = _____*icy*_____
joke + ing = _____*joking*_____
late + est = _____*latest*_____
state + ment = _____*statement*_____
grade + ed = _____*graded*_____

☆ EXERCISE 5.8

Take the following words apart into the base word and the suffix, and explain what happened to make these spellings:

studious = *study + ous*	sillier = *silly + er*	buying = *buy + ing*
keyed = *key + ed*	praying = *pray + ing*	studying = *study + ing*
uglier = *ugly + er*	stories = *story + es*	happiness = *happy + ness*
beautiful = *beauty + ful*	sorriest = *sorry + est*	partying = *party + ing*

Pattern: The letter y *changed to* i *if an added suffix began with a vowel other than* i*. There was no change if the* y *was part of a vowel team as in* ay, uy, *and* ey.

☆ EXERCISE 5.9

Write the sound of the ending ([d], [t], or [əd]), then count the number of syllables in the word. Remember, a syllable is a spoken unit organized around a vowel sound.

Word	[d], [t], [əd]	Number of syllables
instituted	[əd]	4
spelled	[d]	1
opened	[d]	2
popped	[t]	1
offended	[əd]	3
exhumed	[d]	2
breathed	[d]	1
approached	[t]	2
enraged	[d]	2
prevented	[əd]	3

Now, list together all of the words that share a common pronunciation of -ed, and determine why some words have a voiced [d] at the end, some have an unvoiced [t], and some have a syllabic [əd].   *When a verb ends in a voiced consonant, the past tense will be pronounced /d/. When a verb ends in a voiceless consonant, the past tense will be pronounced /t/. When a word ends in a /d/ or a /t/, the past tense will be pronounced /əd/.*

☆ EXERCISE 5.10

1. Separate the prefixes from the roots of these words, and identify the form of the prefix before it was assimilated. You may want to look back at Table 4.1.

   irregular = ___*in + regular*___   attract = ___*ad + tract*___

   colleague = ___*com + league*___   accommodate = ___*ad + commodate*___

   support = ___*sub + port*___   apprehend = ___*ab + prehend*___

   immigrate = ___*in + migrate*___   surrogate = ___*sub + rogate*___

   different = ___*dis + ferent*___

2. Now, fix these spelling errors, which were created by using the original prefix prior to assimilation:

   inlegal ___*illegal*___   comrelated ___*correlated*___

   adsertion ___*assertion*___   adpendix ___*appendix*___

   inmeasurable ___*immeasurable*___   subpress ___*suppress*___

   adgression ___*aggression*___   inluminate ___*illuminate*___

☆ CHAPTER 5 SUPPLEMENTARY EXERCISES

1. Find the grapheme that corresponds to each phoneme in the words below. Note that the number of graphemes should equal the number of phonemes.

s / ea	*wr / e / tch*	*ch / r / o / me*
s / l / i / ng	*wh / o*	*r / a / n / k*
v / i / ll / a / ge	*b / ea / r / d*	*ps / y / ch / o / l / o / g / y*

2. Underline the consonant blends (not every word has a blend):

dumb

known

fir*st*

mu*sk*rat

*squ*awk

*sc*otch

*shr*i*nk*

3. Underline the consonant digraphs (not every word has a digraph):

whether

church

shepherd

wrack

daughter

physic

4. Group the following syllables according to syllable type.

Closed	Open	Consonant-*le*	Vowel team	R-controlled	Vowel-consonant-*e*
com	*se*	*gle*	*ploit*	*fer*	*pete*
ment	*po*	*ble*	*rain*	*tor*	*ate*

5. Sort the following words into groups by the sound of the letter *c*. Explain when the letter *c* has a "soft" /s/ sound and when it has a "hard" /k/ sound:

	/s/	/k/
caught		x
cereal	x	
receive	x	
pecan		x
sauce	x	
incidence	x	
coagulate		x
cuff		x
civilization	x	

Pattern: The letter c is pronounced /s/ when it precedes e, i, or y; otherwise, it is pronounced /k/.

6. Explain what happens to "silent *e*" when suffixes are added to base words such as the following:

careless	lately	driving	invitation
basement	useless	rising	using
homely	ninety	cloned	simply

(Some exceptions include *advantageous, noticeable, awful,* and *judgment;* you need not explain these exceptions).

Pattern: If a word ends in a silent e and a suffix with a vowel is added, drop the e and add the suffix. If the suffix begins with a consonant, keep the e.

7. What are the two phonemes represented by the letter *n* in the following words?

    English   bank   ingot   trunk   /ŋ/

    Ecklund   band   input   trundle   /n/

8. Are the vowel sounds in these word pairs the same or different?

    few   feud   build   gild

    grief   sheaf   cruise   crucial

    meadow   better   boil   boy

    All of the pairs have the same vowel sound.

9. Make observations about the structure of these words that you could point out while teaching the words to children:

    messy   *The word* messy *has two syllables; there is a base word and an adjective suffix; the base word follows the f, l, s doubling rule (the /s/ is spelled with a doubled s because it's a one-syllable word with a short vowel).*

    incredulous   *The word* incredulous *has four syllables; it has a prefix, root, and suffix; the root is* cred *(to believe); accent falls on the root; the d in* cred *is affricated (pronounced like [ǰ]) because of the glide in the following u [ju].*

    solemn   *The n is silent; in a related word form, the n is pronounced (*solemnity*); stress is on the first syllable, which is closed even though there is only one consonant between the two syllables.*

☆ EXERCISE 6.2

Arrange the following words into categories as quickly as you can. Do not add any words or leave out any words (time limit: 10 minutes).

		TREES		
Softwood	*Hardwood*	*Products*	*Parts*	*Tools*
pine	maple	paper	bark	axe
spruce	oak	rope	trunk	chain saw
	birch	paneling	root	skidder
	mahogany	mulch	needle	truck
		beams	branch	
		kindling	leaf	
		guitar		

☆ EXERCISE 6.3

What essential shared attribute or semantic feature of the following groups of words causes them to belong to a semantic network?

1. elephant, ostrich, giraffe, hippopotamus, rhinoceros
    All of these are wild African animals that are also found in zoos.
2. nephew, son, mother, daughter, cousin, aunt, grandfather
    All of these are blood relatives of family.
3. lamp, flashlight, candle, lantern
    All of these are manmade sources of light.
4. bob, crop, shave, plait, braid, curl
    All of these are ways to style hair.
5. rice, barley, wheat, millet, oats
    All of these are grains.

☆ EXERCISE 6.4

Consider these terms, and insert as many words as you can between the qualitative poles that each of these antonyms represents:

elated *overjoyed delighted happy indifferent sad forlorn* **depressed**

scalding *boiling hot warm tepid cool cold frosty frigid* **freezing**

expensive *outrageous expensive costly dear affordable a bargain* **cheap**

☆ EXERCISE 6.5

Determine whether these antonym pairs are gradable (g) or complementary (c):

light/heavy *g*	introvert/extrovert *g*
left/right *c*	terrestrial/celestial *c*
pretty/ugly *g*	present/absent *c*
awake/asleep *c*	empty/full *g*
open/shut *c*	indoors/outdoors *c*
buy/sell *c*	civilized/barbaric *g*

☆ EXERCISE 6.7

Paraphrase the following phrases:

lying over and over   *dissembling repeatedly*

a curious fantasy   *an odd flight of imagination*

stuff and nonsense   *bric-a-brac*

guests at the execution   *invited onlookers at the planned killing*

ignore the petty details   *overlook the unimportant bits*

blazing away brightly   *burning luminously*

mind the master's words   *obey the chief's orders*

these melancholy little sighs   *these forlorn expirations*

☆ EXERCISE 6.8

With lines and arrows, mark the referential relationships that exist among the nouns, pronouns, and noun phrases in this passage from the Wizard of Oz (the first few are done for you):

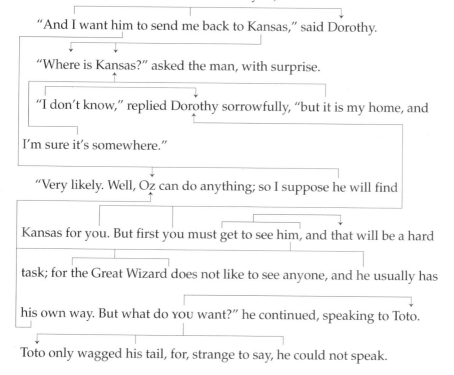

"And I want him to send me back to Kansas," said Dorothy.

"Where is Kansas?" asked the man, with surprise.

"I don't know," replied Dorothy sorrowfully, "but it is my home, and

I'm sure it's somewhere."

"Very likely. Well, Oz can do anything; so I suppose he will find

Kansas for you. But first you must get to see him, and that will be a hard

task; for the Great Wizard does not like to see anyone, and he usually has

his own way. But what do you want?" he continued, speaking to Toto.

Toto only wagged his tail, for, strange to say, he could not speak.

☆ EXERCISE 6.9

What does each of these idioms mean?

mark my words   *I'll be right about the future*

hit me up   *asked me for*

tread on his toes   *invaded his territory or took his prerogative*

blow the whistle   *stop, tell the authorities about wrongdoing*

leave her high and dry   *abandon*

bite your tongue   *restrain your verbal impulses*

'til the cows come home   *forever*

get out of my hair   *leave me alone*

line your pockets   *obtain money or goods*

☆ CHAPTER 6 SUPPLEMENTARY EXERCISES

1. On a separate sheet of paper, make an outline or **visual categorization** using the following words. Use all of the words and no others. Take about 10 minutes.

INVERTEBRATES

Species	*Body parts*	*Homes*
mosquitoes	*wings*	*web*
locusts	*abdomen*	*nest*
cockroaches	*antennae*	*soil*
flies	*legs*	*cocoon*
ants	*head*	*burrow*
grasshoppers	*thorax*	

Phases	*Locomotion*	*Food*
sac	*hop*	*blood*
egg	*crawl*	*microbes*
larva	*creep*	*algae*
pupa		*leaves*
adult		

2. Choose an important abstract word used in science teaching, such as *symmetry, evolution,* or *microscopic.* Make up several sentences that use the word. Then leave the word out of the sentences, and give the "cloze" sentences you have created to someone else. Did they identify the word? Now ask your subject if he or she could define the word on the basis of the contextual uses you gave. What are the advantages and limitations of context use in word definition?   *An advantage is that context shows the connotative and pragmatic uses of a word; a disadvantage is that several exposures to examples may be necessary before the meaning is clear.*

3. In what way are the following groups of nouns the same and different?

    daughter, sister, niece   *versus*   nun, waitress, nurse

    They are all females (family members versus professions).

rooster, bull, ram   *versus*   hen, ewe, cow
They are all domesticated animals (male versus female).

table, chair, pencil   *versus*   water, cream, sand
They are all nouns (solid versus liquid).

table, chair, pencil   *versus*   faith, hope, charity
They are all nouns (concrete versus abstract).

husband, brother, son   *versus*   clerk, preacher, judge
They are all people (family members versus professions).

grandfather, mother, niece   *versus*   brother, sister, cousin
They are all family members (vertical versus lateral generations).

4. Mark the antonym pairs as gradable (opposite ends of a continuous scale) or complementary (either/or).

	Gradable	*Complementary*
dead/alive		x
hot/cold	x	
above/below		x
fat/skinny	x	
married/single		x
mild/spicy	x	
angry/delighted	x	
hideous/gorgeous	x	
straight/crooked		x
introvert/extrovert	x	
winner/loser		x

Now take one of the *gradable* antonym pairs, and fill out the scale from one extreme to the other with words that show degrees of meaning.

furious *angry irritated irked indifferent pleased delighted* **thrilled**

5. Mark with a plus or minus sign the semantic features that do or do not describe the following four objects:

	cup	*glass*	*mug*	*bowl*
handle	+	−	+	−
ceramic	+	−	+	+
round	+	+	+	+
tall	−	+	−	−
holds hot liquid	−	+	+	+
holds cold liquid	+	+	−	+
paper	+	−	−	−
transparent	−	+	−	−

6. Use the following format to make a definition for each of these words: *web, tornado,* and *poem.*

    A/An _____ is a/an _____ (synonym)
    that _____ (is, does, has) _____ (critical feature).

    A web is a matrix of threads that spiders spin to catch insects for food.

    A tornado is a violent wind storm that spins in a circular pattern and has a calm "eye" in the middle.

    A poem is language arranged in a pattern designed to evoke images and emotions.

☆ EXERCISE 7.2

Identify noun phrases from among the following:

she	*lovely peaceful silences*
green and red	*Montenegro*
after running	were playing joyfully
many criminals	among *the very best*
the best swimming	

☆ CHAPTER 7 SUPPLEMENTARY EXERCISES

2. Combine the following sets of simple sentences into elaborated single sentences that preserve the main idea of each simple sentence.

    Set #1
    The team won the game.
    They won in overtime.
    The team was determined.
    The game was for the championship of the league.
    The determined team won the league championship game in overtime.

    Set #2
    The Coast Guard undertook a mission.
    They searched immediately after the plane crash.
    They searched for debris.
    They looked for survivors.
    They were not optimistic.
    Immediately after the plane crash, the Coast Guard pessimistically undertook a mission to search for debris and survivors.

Describe the operations you carried out on the simple sentences to combine each of the sentence sets into one complete, elaborated sentence.

These operations required prepositional phrase construction, insertion of adjectives to modify nouns, and joining of nouns in a prepositional phrase.

3. Below are some kernel sentences. Elaborate each kernel sentence by first asking questions of the subject and predicate, such as "How many?" "What kind?" "Where?" "How?" "When?" or "How long?" and then adding these answers to the kernels.

    Presidents lie.

    Fans swoon.

    Hawaii calls.

    Before the impeachment trial, journalists in Washington alleged that the president had lied.

    Many screaming fans in the stadium swooned when the rock band came on stage.

    Hawaii calls again, she thought, remembering its beaches, waterfalls, and volcanoes that she saw on her last trip there.

5. Given the following bit of charming nonsense by Lewis Carroll, identify the subject and predicate of each sentence. Then identify the grammatical category (part of speech) that each of the italicized words is likely to be:

    'Twas *brillig (adj.)* and the *slithy (adj.) toves (n.)* did *gyre (v.)* and *gimble (v.)* in the *wabe (n.)*;
    All *mimsy (adj.)* were the *borogoves (n.)* and the *mome raths (n.)* outgrabe *(adj.)*.

6. In one nonstandard English dialect, speakers say, "I is going with you," and, "You is going with me"; the past tense becomes "I were going" and "He were going." In addition to observing that this is nonstandard grammar, can you find any reason that this verb form might be a systematic change in a grammatical category? Consider all of the forms of the verb *to be*, and speculate on the nature of the change to the verb in the nonstandard dialect:
    In both the present tense and past tense of the verb to be *in nonstandard dialect, the changes from standard represent a regularization of an irregular form. The speaker is using the same form for all voices. Regularization of irregular forms is a logical adaptation of a language pattern.*

7. The following phrases are ambiguous. Draw simple tree diagrams to show the phrase structures underlying the ambiguities of each phrase. Explain the different meanings of each.

negative film developer

a film developer who has a negative attitude

negative film developer

someone who develops film negatives

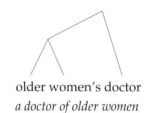

older women's doctor

a doctor of older women

older women's doctor

an older doctor whose patients are women

English language translator

a translator of English

English language translator

a translator from England

white Audi driver

a Caucasian driver

white Audi driver

a driver of a white Audi

red maple cabinets

cabinets painted red

red maple cabinets

cabinets made from red maple

☆ APPENDIX D: SYLLABLE SELF-EVALUATION

1. How many syllables are in each of these words?

    revolutionary __6__   chewier __3__

    scissors __2__   geothermal __4__

    idealistic *4 or 5*   microorganism __6__

    segue __2__

2. Every syllable must have which of the following?

     stress   at least one consonant   *a vowel sound*   a letter

3. Which are closed syllables?

     sheer   *it*   chew   toast

4. Which are complex syllables with a consonant cluster?

     knight   *brought*   thing   bird

5. Which words have two open syllables?

     re/do   a/head   re/lease   ser/ene

6. All of the following words have an *r*-controlled vowel sound pronounced like the /ɚ/ in *bird* except:

     earthen   prefer   purring   *mournful*

7. Which statements are untrue about accent (syllable stress)?

a) One-syllable words are accented.

b) The second word in a compound is usually accented.

c) The root of a Latin-based word is more often accented than the prefix or suffix.

d) With words such as *conduct* and *object*, accent can determine which form of the word is a noun and which form is a verb.

e) When the vowel sound in the last syllable of a word is spelled with a vowel team, that syllable is most often accented.

f) Accent often is placed on inflected endings, including the plural and past tense.

g) In most multisyllabic words ending in *-tion*, the primary accent falls on the syllable preceding *-tion*.

h) When there is a doubled consonant within a word, the accent usually falls on the syllable that ends with that consonant.

Statements b and f are untrue.

APPENDIX H

Glossary

Affix   A morpheme or meaningful part of a word attached before or after a root or base word to modify its meaning; a category that includes prefixes and suffixes.

Affricate   Consonant phoneme articulated as a stop before a fricative, such as /č/ or /ǰ/.

Agent   Thematic role of the noun in a sentence whose referent performs the action of the verb (*The girl threw the ball*).

Allophone   A predictable phonetic variant of a phoneme, such as nasalized vowels.

Allophonic variation   Systematic variability in production of phonemes; the fact that speech sounds "heard" as the same phoneme differ slightly in articulation depending on where they occur in word, for example the aspirated and unaspirated forms [pʰ] and [p].

Alphabetic   Pertaining to a writing system that uses a symbol for each speech sound of the language.

Alphabetic principle   The use of letters and letter combinations to represent phonemes in an orthography.

Alveolar   Consonant spoken with the tip of the tongue on the ridge behind the upper teeth, such as /t/.

Anaphora   Referential linking between pairs of words within or between sentences; the process of replacing a longer word or phrase with a shorter one, as with the use of a pronoun for a noun or a noun phrase.

Antonyms   Words considered to represent opposite meanings.

Articles   Determiners; words in a grammatical class of noun modifiers that are not adjectives, such as *the, a, an*.

Assimilated prefix   A prefix changed from its abstract form so that it matches the initial sound of the root to which it is attached, such as *at* in *attach* (*ad* + *tach* = *attach*).

Assimilation   Process by which the phonetic features of one phoneme influence or are spread to a neighboring phoneme; assimilation results in phonemes becoming similar.

Automaticity   Fluent performance without the conscious deployment of attention.

Auxiliary verbs   Helping verbs that co-occur with a main verb to denote tense, aspect, or modality (*I will have been gone*).

Back vowels   Vowels formed in the back of the mouth, such as /o/ or /u/.

Base word   A free morpheme, usually of Anglo-Saxon origin, to which affixes can be added.

Bilabial   Consonant formed with the lips together, such as /b/.

Blend   A consonant sequence before or after a vowel within a syllable, such as *cl, br,* or *st*; the written language equivalent of *consonant cluster*.

Bound morpheme   A morpheme, usually of Latin origin in English, that cannot stand alone but is used to form a family of words with related meanings. A bound root (such as *-fer*) has meaning only in combination with a prefix and/or a suffix.

Central linguistic processing   The mental activity of language encoding, comprehension, and recall that occurs independently of speech or hearing.

Closed sound   *See* Consonant.

Co-articulated   Spoken together so that separate segments are not easily detected.

Coda   The part of a syllable that comes after the nucleus or peak.

Combining form   A morpheme that occurs only in combination with other forms but may combine in various ways with other morphemes to create compounds or derivatives; many Greek-derived morphemes are combining forms.

Complementary antonyms   Opposites that do not overlap; the negation of one is the meaning of the other (*male–female*).

Complementary distribution   The relationship between two or more allophones such that each occurs in phonetic environments where the other(s) never do.

Complex syllables   Syllables that contain one or more consonant clusters.

Comprehension monitoring   The mental act of knowing when one does and does not understand what one is reading.

Conjunctions   Words such as *and, but,* and *or* that perform the grammatical function of joining sentences, phrases, words, or clauses.

Connotative meaning   The affective and experiential associations conjured up by a word.

Considerate text   Text written in such a way that takes into account the needs of the reader for structure, clarity, completeness, redundancy, and other clues to meaning.

Consonant   A phoneme that is not a vowel and is formed with obstruction of the flow of air with the teeth, lips, or tongue; also called a *closed sound* in some instructional programs; English has 40 or more consonants.

Consonant cluster   Adjacent consonants within a syllable, before or after a vowel sound; oral language equivalent of the term *consonant blend.*

Consonant digraph   Written letter combination that corresponds to one speech sound but is not represented by either letter alone, such as *th* or *ph.*

Content words   Nouns, verbs, adjectives, and adverbs; words that carry most of the meaning in a sentence.

Continuant   Speech sound that can be spoken uninterrupted until the speaker runs out of breath (/m/, /s/, /v/).

Co-referent   Noun phrases that refer to the same entity.

Countable nouns   Nouns that can be enumerated.

Decodable text   Text in which a large proportion of words (approximately 70%–80%) comprise sound–symbol relationships that have already been taught; used to provide practice with specific decoding skills and to form a bridge between learning phonics and applying phonics in independent reading of text.

Decoding   Ability to translate a word from print to speech, usually by employing knowledge of sound–symbol correspondences; also, the act of deciphering a new word by sounding it out.

Deixis   Reference that relies entirely on context, as in *here* and *there.*

Denotative meaning   Dictionary meaning, what a word refers to.

Derivational morpheme   Morphemes, added to roots or bases to form new words, that may or may not change the grammatical category of a word.

Descriptive grammar   A linguist's description of what speakers unconsciously learn about the rules of their language.

Diphthongs   Vowels that have a glide and may feel as though they have two parts, especially the vowels /æw/ as in *house* and /ɔj/ as in *oil*; some linguistics texts also classify all tense vowels as diphthongs.

Discourse   Linguistic units larger than the single sentence.

Distinctive features   Phonetic properties of phonemes that account for their contrast with other phonemes.

Entailment   A logical relationship between two sentences such that the truth or falsehood of the first sentence necessarily implies the truth or falsehood of the second sentence.

Expository text   Text that reports factual information and the relationships among ideas.

Free morpheme   A morpheme that can stand alone in word formation.

Fricatives   A class of speech sounds articulated with a hiss or friction.

Front vowel   Vowel spoken with the tongue positioned in the front of the mouth.

Function word   Belonging to the grammatical classes of words that are not content words, including conjunctions, articles, pronouns, prepositions, and auxiliaries; these are closed categories to which new words are seldom added.

Generalization   The act of applying a linguistic rule or pattern to a new word, phrase, or sentence; also, a pattern in the spelling system that generalizes to a substantial family of words.

Generative   In a grammar, the quality of rule structure that allows an infinite number of specific, novel expressions.

Glide   A consonant phoneme that glides immediately into a vowel; also called *semivowel*.

Glottal stop   When the vocal air stream is stopped completely by closing the opening between the vocal cords (the *glottis*).

Goal   The thematic role of the noun phrase toward whose referent the action of the verb is directed (*The actor strode toward the open stage*).

Gradable antonyms   Opposites having a relationship in which more of one is less than the other; the relationship exists on a continuum on which degrees of a quality can be specified (*brilliant–dull*).

Grammatical category   Traditionally called a *part of speech*; members of a category can be used only in certain specified ways within the structure of a sentence.

Grapheme   A letter or letter combination that spells a single phoneme; in English, a grapheme may be one, two, three, or four letters, such as *e, ei, igh,* or *eigh*.

Hierarchical structure   The arrangement of groupings and subgroupings of phrases within a sentence.

Hieroglyphics   Egyptian picture writing.

High   Vowel sounds formed by placing the tongue close to the roof of the mouth.

Homorganic nasal rule   Rule that a consonant that follows a nasal consonant will be produced in the same place of articulation as the nasal (*contact*).

Ideographic writing system   Writing system that uses stylized characters to denote whole concepts or words directly.

Idiom   An expression whose meaning may be unrelated to the meaning of its parts.

Inflection   A bound morpheme that combines with base words to indicate tense, number, mood, person, or gender; contrasts with *derivation* (*peaches, walking*).

Instrument   The thematic role of a noun phrase that refers to the means by which an action is performed.

Interdental   Consonant sound spoken with the tongue between the teeth.

Intonation   Pitch level of the voice; contour.

Labials   Consonant sounds articulated with the lips; includes bilabials and labiodentals.

Labiodental   Consonant sound articulated with the lower lip and upper teeth.

Lax   Short vowels produced with little tension in the vocal cords; contrasts with *tense*.

Lexical semantics   The study of meanings of words and their relationships.

Lexicon   The mental dictionary of a speaker; the part of linguistic memory that contains knowledge of words.

Linguistic context   The context provided by the language in which a word is embedded.

Liquid   Speech sound in which air is obstructed but not enough to cause friction.

Location   The thematic role of the noun phrase whose referent is the place where the action of the verb occurs.

Long   Term used by educators to denote a vowel that is spoken with tension in the vocal cords and that is often pronounced with relatively longer duration than lax vowels.

Low   Referring to the position of the tongue away from the roof of the mouth.

Marked   Referring to the member of a gradable antonym pair that is not used in formulating questions of degree (*low* is the marked member of *low/high;* for example, one asks, "How *high* is the deck?").

Metalinguistic   Pertaining to an acquired awareness of language structure and function that allows one to reflect on and consciously manipulate the language.

Mid   Spoken with the tongue midway between the roof of the mouth (high) and its lowest position away from the roof of the mouth.

Minimal pair   A pair of words that contrast only in one phoneme.

Morpheme   The smallest meaningful unit of language.

Morphology   The study of meaningful units of language and how they are combined in word formation.

Morphophonemic   Pertaining to rules or aspects of language that specify the pronunciation of morphemes; pertaining to a writing system that spells meaningful units (morphemes) instead of surface phonetic details in speech; a characteristic of English orthography.

Multisyllabic   Having more than one syllable.

Narrative text   Text, usually with the structure of a story, that tells about sequences of fictional or real events and is often contrasted with expository text.

Nasal (stop)   Spoken with the air stream directed through the nasal cavity.

Neutral (derivational) suffix   A suffix that does not change the base form or root to which it is added.

Noncountable nouns   Nouns that cannot be enumerated.

Nonneutral (derivational) suffix   A suffix that changes the pronunciation and/or spelling of the base word or root to which it is added.

Nonsystematic   Pertaining to variation in speech that is not predicted by rule, that is incidental or regional or individual.

Noun phrase (NP)   The syntactic category of expressions containing some form of noun and capable of functioning as the subject or object in a sentence.

Object   The noun phrase that follows a verb that depicts action performed on or to something (*Tom held the red pencil*).

Obstruents   Consonants that are produced with an obstruction of the air stream, including stops, fricatives, and affricates; contrasts with *sonorants*.

Onset   The part of a syllable before the vowel; some syllables do not have onsets.

Orthography   A writing system.

Palatal   Spoken with the tongue against the roof of the mouth behind the alveolar ridge.

Partially productive   A characteristic of morphemes that can be used for word formation only to a limited extent.

Peak   The part of the syllable, usually the vowel, that carries the most vocal energy; also called the *nucleus*.

Phone   A phonetic realization of a phoneme; the speech sound that is actually produced in spoken words.

Phoneme   A speech sound that combines with others in a language system to make words.

Phoneme awareness   The conscious awareness that words are made up of segments of our own speech that are represented with letters in an alphabetic orthography; also called *phonemic awareness*.

Phonemic awareness   *See* Phoneme awareness.

Phonetic alphabet   An alphabet in which each speech sound has its own unique symbol.

Phonetic variation   Variability in the way speakers of a language articulate the phonemes.

Phonetics   The study of linguistic speech sounds and how they are produced and perceived.

Phonics   The study of the relationships between letters and the sounds they represent; also used to describe reading instruction that teaches sound–symbol correspondences, such as "the phonics approach" or "phonic reading."

Phonological awareness   Metalinguistic awareness of all levels of the speech sound system, including word boundaries, stress patterns, syllables, onset–rime units, and phonemes; a more encompassing term than *phoneme awareness*.

Phonological processing   Perception, interpretation, recall, and production of language at the level of the speech sound system, including functions such as pronouncing words, remembering names and lists, identifying words and syllables, giving rhymes, detecting syllable stress, and segmenting and blending phonemes.

Phonological rules   A level of language structure; rules that embody what speakers know about the speech sounds in their language.

Phonology   The rule system within a language by which phonemes are sequenced and uttered to make words; also, the study of this rule system.

Phrasal grammatical category   A constituent of a tree diagram depicting sentence structure that is potentially larger than one word.

Phrase   A part of a sentence that is potentially larger than one word and that serves a grammatical function as a unit.

Pictograms   Visual or graphic symbols that directly depict their own meaning, such as the *no smoking* symbol common in hotels and restaurants.

Pitch   The tonal level of a vocal or nonvocal sound, determined by its sound frequencies.

Pragmatics   The system of rules and conventions for using language and related gestures in social contexts; the study of that rule system.

Predicate   One of two main constituents of a sentence, containing the verb.

Prefix   A morpheme that precedes a root or base word and that contributes to or modifies the meaning of a word; a common linguistic unit in Latin-based words.

Prepositions   A class of function words that occur first in a prepositional phrase.

Prereading   Pertaining to the stage of reading development before children understand the alphabetic principle.

Prescriptive grammar   The attempts of grammarians to define, legislate, or dictate proper use of language in a culture.

Pronouns   A class of function words that are used as substitutes for nouns or noun phrases.

R-controlled   Pertaining to a vowel immediately followed by the consonant /r/, such that its pronunciation is affected or even dominated by the /r/.

Reading fluency   Speed of reading; also, the ability to read text with sufficient speed to support comprehension.

Reference   The association of one entity in a noun phrase with another.

Referent   The entity referred to by a noun phrase.

Relational antonyms   Antonyms that describe a relationship between two people, such as *husband/wife, parent/child*.

Rime   A linguistic term for the part of a syllable that includes the vowel and what follows it; different from the language play activity of *rhyming*.

Root   A morpheme, usually of Latin origin in English, that cannot stand alone but that is used to form a family of words with related meanings.

Schwa   A nondistinct vowel found in unstressed syllables in English.

Semantic class   A group of words that are treated as members of a category.

Semantic features   A symbol system of pluses and minuses used to denote abstract qualities of noun meaning.

Semantic field   A group of words connected by meaning associations, such as all of the words that denote the quality of height.

Semantic properties   The component features of the meaning of a word.

Semantics   The study of word and phrase meanings.

Semivowel   Another term for a consonant glide that has vowel-like qualities.

Sentential semantics   The study of sentence meaning.

Short   Used by educators to denote a lax vowel.

Sight words   Words that are known as wholes, do not have to be sounded out to be recognized quickly, and are often taught and learned as "exception," "outlaw," or "nonphonetic" words.

Simple sentence   A sentence composed of a single noun phrase and a single verb phrase.

Simple syllables   Syllables that have no consonant blends or clusters.

Situational context   The context for comprehending language that is provided by the person who is speaking, the person who is listening, the objects or experiences that are being referred to, and other background information.

Sonorants   Speech sounds that are spoken with resonance and continuancy, including vowels, glides, liquids, and nasals; contrasts with *obstruents*.

Stop   Consonant speech sound that is articulated with a stop of the air stream.

Stressed   Accented syllable articulated with greater loudness, duration, or pitch.

Subject   The grammatical role of a noun phrase that appears directly below the *S* in a phrase structure diagram, one of two necessary parts of a sentence.

Subordinate category   A category that is subsumed by another or included within a superordinate category.

Suffix   A morpheme, added to a root or base word, that often changes the word's part of speech and that modifies its meaning.

Superordinate category   A category that subsumes others; the main or umbrella category under which others are included.

Suppletive   A verb form to which rules for adding inflections do not apply, such as *went, gone*, or *lay*.

Suprasegmental   Prosodic features such as tone, utterance length, and stress.

Surface   The visible or audible linguistic expression that may be the result of transformations applied to a deep or hidden linguistic form.

Syllabary   A writing system designed to represent syllable units with single symbols.

Syllabic   A phonetic feature present in the sounds that constitute the nucleus of syllables, including vowels, liquids, and nasals.

Syllabic consonant   Consonant that becomes the nucleus of a syllable; liquid and nasal consonants may be syllabic

Syllable   Unit of pronunciation that is organized around a vowel; it may or may not have consonants before or after the vowel.

Syllable boundary   Division between adjacent syllables, which is not always the same in speech as in print.

Synonym   A word that means the same or almost the same thing as another.

Syntax   The rule system governing sentence formation; the study of sentence structure.

System   A group of interrelated elements forming a complex whole; the functional relationship of those elements.

Systematic   Methodical, carried out using step-by-step procedures determined by the nature of the system being used or taught.

Tense   Linguistic term for a long vowel, spoken with tension in the vocal cords.

Theme   The thematic role of the noun phrase whose referent undergoes the action of a verb.

Transformation   An operation that converts the constituents of a sentence structure into a different sentence structure by adding, deleting, or rearranging those constituents.

Transitive property   The property of verbs that must be followed by a direct object.

Truth conditions   The circumstances that must be known to determine whether a sentence is true.

Underlying   The aspects of linguistic rule systems that are invisible or that lie below the surface of an utterance.

Universals   Properties that are found in all human languages.

Unsegmented   Pertaining to a word that has not been broken down into its constituent syllables, onsets and rimes, or phonemes.

Unstressed   Unaccented syllable.

Unvoiced   Spoken with no vocal resonance; also called *voiceless.*

Velar   Speech sound articulated with the tongue on the ridge behind the teeth.

Verb phrase (VP)   The syntactic category of a phrase that contains the verb and that can function as the predicate of a sentence.

Voiced   A speech sound articulated with vibrating vocal cords.

Voiceless   *See* Unvoiced.

Vowel   An open phoneme that is the nucleus of every syllable and is classified by tongue position and height, such as high/low or front/mid/back; English has 15 vowel phonemes.

Vowel team   A vowel grapheme or spelling that uses two or more letters for a single speech sound.

Index

*Page numbers followed by "f" or "t" indicate figures
or tables, respectively; those followed by "n" indicate endnotes.*

Notes

Notes

Notes

Notes

Notes

Notes

Notes

Notes

Notes

Notes

Notes

Notes

Additional strategies to teach reading from literacy experts—including Louisa Moats!

Multisensory Teaching of Basic Language Skills
Edited by Judith R. Birsh, Ed.D

"This is the first text on multisensory teaching that brings together information on research, theory, and clinical experience . . . . It should be in the hands of everyone currently practicing." —<u>Dyslexia Discourse</u>

Discover how to reach students—no matter what their learning style—with these exciting instructional techniques! Comprehensive and practical, this guide reveals how and why multisensory teaching methods work in any classroom. Backed by research and clinical experience with children and adults with learning disabilities, the authors put theory into practice as they show specific teaching approaches to promote

- phonological awareness
- alphabet skills
- spelling and grammar
- reading accuracy and fluency
- reading comprehension
- handwriting and composition
- organization and study skills
- communication with parents

Field-tested instructional materials and activities are also included, along with observation and assessment models. This guide to multisensory instruction is critical reading for every pre- and in-service educator.

Stock Number: 3491 Price: $59.95
1999 • 608 pages • 7 x 10 • hardcover • ISBN 1-55766-349-1

___ Yes! I want ___ copy(ies) of Multisensory Teaching for $59.95 each

Name:_____

Address: _____
(Orders cannot be shipped to P.O. boxes.)

City/State/ZIP:_____

Daytime phone:_____

E-mail address (optional):_____
You'll receive special web site discount offers and our FREE e-mail newsletter! Your e-mail address will not be shared with any other party.

___ Check enclosed (Payable to Brookes Publishing Co.)

___ Purchase Order attached (Please bill my institution.)

___ Please charge my   ___ American Express   ___ MasterCard   ___ Visa

Card No.: _____ Exp. date: ___/___/___

Signature (Required on all credit card orders):_____

Copy this form and mail it to Brookes Publishing Co., P.O. Box 10624, Baltimore, MD 21285-0624;
FAX 410-337-8539; call toll-free (8 A.M.–5 P.M. ET) 1-800-638-3775 or 1-410-337-9580 (outside the U.S.);
or order online at **www.brookespublishing.com**

Within Continental U.S. Shipping Rates for UPS Ground delivery* If your product total (before tax) is: $0.00 to $49.99 add $5.00 $50.00 to $399.99 add 10% of product total $400.00 and over add 8% of product total *For rush orders please call 1-800-638-3775 For international orders please call 1-410-337-9580	*Prices subject to change without notice and may be higher outside the U.S.*		
		Product Total	$_____
		Shipping Rate (see chart)	$_____
		Maryland Orders add 5% sales tax (to product total only)	$_____
		Grand Total U.S.	$_____

Your source code is: BA27

If you are not completely satisfied, you may return books and videotapes within 30 days for a full credit of the purchase price. Items must be returned in resalable condition.

6549